Praise for

"In a funny, surprising, and straightforward voice, Noa Tishby rolls the entire history of Israel into a blunt and insightful read. The perfect anti-textbook for anyone who slept through class, this is not your Bubbie's history book."

—Bill Maher, host of *Real Time with Bill Maher*

"Noa Tishby writes with wit and authority. This is a fascinating—and very moving—book that should be read by anyone for whom Israel is a mystery."

—Aaron Sorkin, award-winning screenwriter of *The West Wing* and *The Social Network*

"With passion, humor, and deep intimacy, Noa Tishby reveals the real Israel that continually eludes even many so-called experts. Refreshingly straightforward, Tishby manages to be 'simple' but not simplistic. She knows that real love requires honesty, and so she confronts Israel in its sometimes maddening complexity."

—Yossi Klein Halevi, senior fellow of the Shalom Hartman Institute in Jerusalem and author of the *New York Times* bestseller *Letters to My Palestinian Neighbor*

"In this book Noa does what she does best, rising to the challenge of expressing a rooted, spirited, and often personal defense of her homeland when so many others have shied away. Good people like Noa do not remain silent when all else around them is failing. They speak up. Now that we have her toolkit, so must we."

—Maajid Nawaz, author of *Radical* and coauthor of *Islam and the Future of Tolerance*

"Noa Tishby's contemporary examination of Israel's past, present, and future is the book we've been waiting for. With insight, intelligence, levity, and humor, she reintroduces us to a place we thought we knew so well. I found myself educated, inspired, and ultimately moved to tears as she reclaims this complicated state in the name of its daughters and fights to restore its reputation for the next generation."

—Sarah Treem, writer, director, Golden Globe winner, and creator of *The Affair*

"Noa Tishby bravely provides a guide to understanding Israel through the personal story of her family. More than anything, this is a hopeful book that calls for a peaceful tomorrow through a courageous look at the past."

—Gideon Raff, creator of *Prisoners of War* and *The Spy* and Emmy-winning screenwriter and executive producer of *Homeland*

"Noa Tishby is whip-smart, charming, funny, frank, and fearless. So is her book. Here is the real story of Israel told by a natural storyteller. Touching and captivating."

— Rabbi David Wolpe, author of *David: The Divided Heart*

"Everything to do with this subject is controversial, but Noa Tishby doesn't shy away. In fact, she leans into it with conviction (and good writing), making the book an engaging and provocative invitation to debate."

—Rodrigo Garcia, screenwriter and director

"Heartfelt, funny, and genuine—for anyone confused by the furious debates about Israel, time spent with Noa Tishby's book feels less like a college class than like drinks with a smart and passionate friend."

—Matti Friedman, *New York Times* op-ed contributor and author of *Spies of No Country: Secret Lives at the Birth of Israel*

"Noa Tishby's book is a powerful antidote to the widespread misunderstanding and willful misrepresentation that often obscures the truth about Israel. Much like the book itself, Noa is a fearless truth teller in an age of fashionable lies."

—Congressman Ritchie Torres (D, NY15)

"A timely and significant work, Tishby's *Israel* is essential reading for Arabs, Jews, Americans, and the rest of the world. As an Arab reader, I am a son of that region, and yet reading the book I learned a lot about my birthplace and saw the other side of the paradox that was invisible to me. This book is supported by hard facts—not for the purpose of argument or debate but, rather, to build bridges between the Jewish and Arab worlds. The result is a beautiful and inspiring human journey that allowed me to learn more about my birthplace, my precious Jewish neighbors, and our homeland."

—Mosab Hassan Yousef, bestselling author of *Son of Hamas* and star of the documentary *The Green Prince*

"Having lived in Jerusalem for two years, I can assure the outsider that it is not possible to understand the modern Jewish state without an insider to guide you. Noa Tishby has written this book from that perspective to update our understanding of Israel for the twenty-first century. This is an important book by an essential voice working to find the hidden order within the *balagan* (Hebrew for chaos) that is the common linchpin of the world's 3.8 billion Abrahamic adherents."

—Eric Weinstein, mathematician, managing director of Thiel Capital, and host of *The Portal*

"Tishby tells her small country's enormous story with wit and passion. Israel shouldn't be the only book a reader opens about the Middle East, but it's an excellent place to start."

—*New York Journal of Books*

"An energetic and intimate popular history of a fraught land . . . the author's candid viewpoint offers good food for thought."

—*Kirkus Reviews*

"Brisk and informative."

—*Publishers Weekly*

"This is a book well worth the read for anyone who cares about, or needs a crash course on, the Jewish state."

—*Hadassah Magazine*

"Noa Tishby provides a unique and remarkable perspective on Israel. An insightful writer and powerful woman, she creates a lasting image of the country's entrepreneurial spirit and contributions across the world."

—Ray Kurzweil, inventor, author, and futurist

"A must-read."

—Ben Shapiro, #1 *New York Times* bestselling author of *The Right Side of History* and *How to Destroy America in Three Easy Steps*

ISRAEL

A SIMPLE GUIDE TO THE MOST MISUNDERSTOOD COUNTRY ON EARTH

NOA TISHBY

FREE PRESS

New York London Toronto Sydney New Delhi

Free Press
An Imprint of Simon & Schuster, Inc.
1230 Avenue of the Americas
New York, NY 10020

First Free Press trade paperback edition September 2022

FREE PRESS and colophon are trademarks of Simon & Schuster, Inc.

For information about special discounts for bulk purchases, please contact Simon & Schuster Special Sales at 1-866-506-1949 or business@simonandschuster.com.

The Simon & Schuster Speakers Bureau can bring authors to your live event. For more information or to book an event, contact the Simon & Schuster Speakers Bureau at 1-866-248-3049 or visit our website at www.simonspeakers.com.

Printed and bound by CPI Group (UK) Ltd, Croydon CR0 4YY

10 9 8

The Library of Congress has cataloged the hardcover edition as follows:

Names: Tishby, Noa, 1977– author.
Title: Israel : a simple guide to the most misunderstood country on earth / Noa Tishby.
Description: New York : Free Press, 2021. | Includes bibliographical references and index.
Identifiers: LCCN 2020045327 (print) | LCCN 2020045328 (ebook) | ISBN 9781982144937 (hardcover) | ISBN 9781982144944 (paperback) | ISBN 9781982144951 (ebook)
Subjects: LCSH: Tishby, Noa, 1977– | Israel—History.
Classification: LCC DS117 .T57 2021 (print) | LCC DS117 (ebook) | DDC 956.94—dc23
LC record available at https://lccn.loc.gov/2020045327
LC ebook record available at https://lccn.loc.gov/2020045328

ISBN 978-1-9821-4493-7
ISBN 978-1-9821-4494-4 (pbk)
ISBN 978-1-9821-4495-1 (ebook)

To Ari

CONTENTS

Approximate Borders of United Israeli Kingdom of King David and King Saul
Aram Damascus
(Modern-day Syria)
Mediterranean Sea
ISRAEL
Philistines
Dead Sea
Moab
Amalek

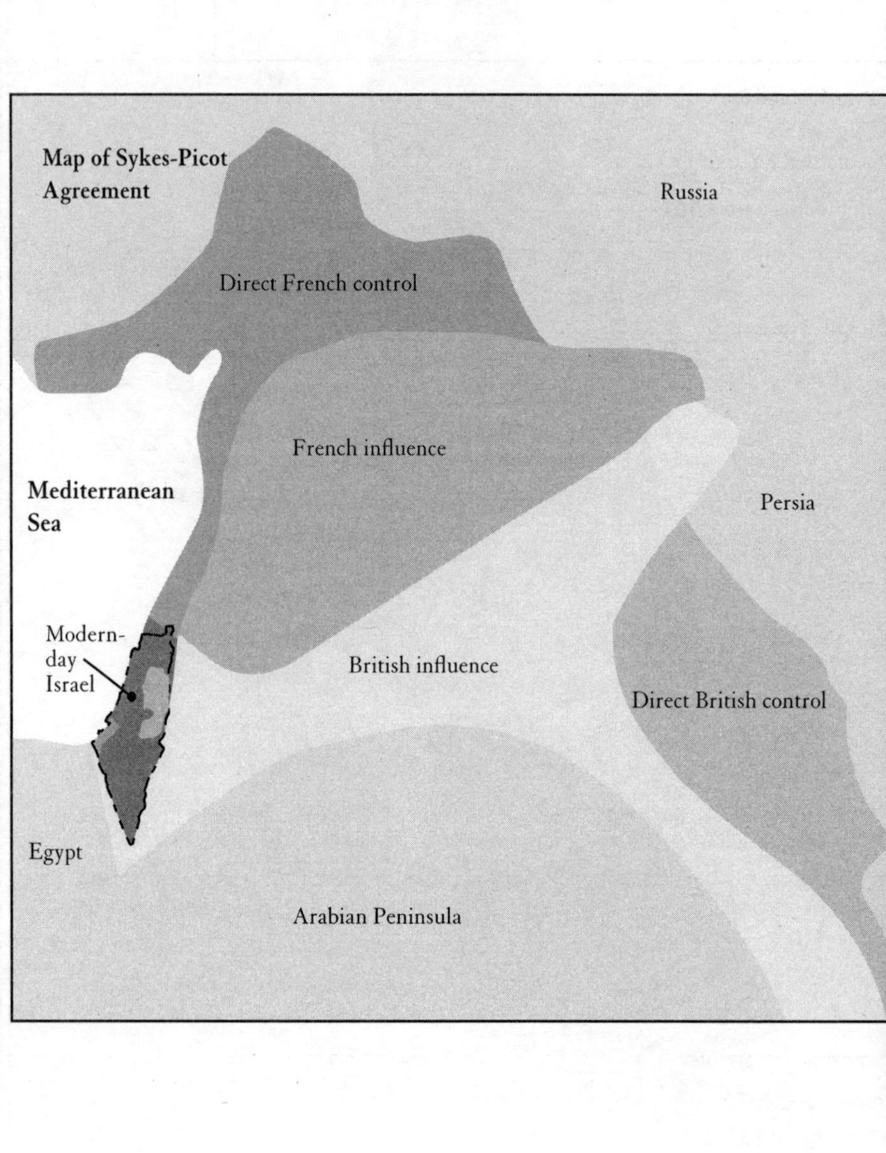
Map of Sykes-Picot
Agreement
Russia
Direct French control
French influence
Mediterranean
Sea
Persia
Modern-
day
Israel
British influence
Direct British control
Egypt
Arabian Peninsula

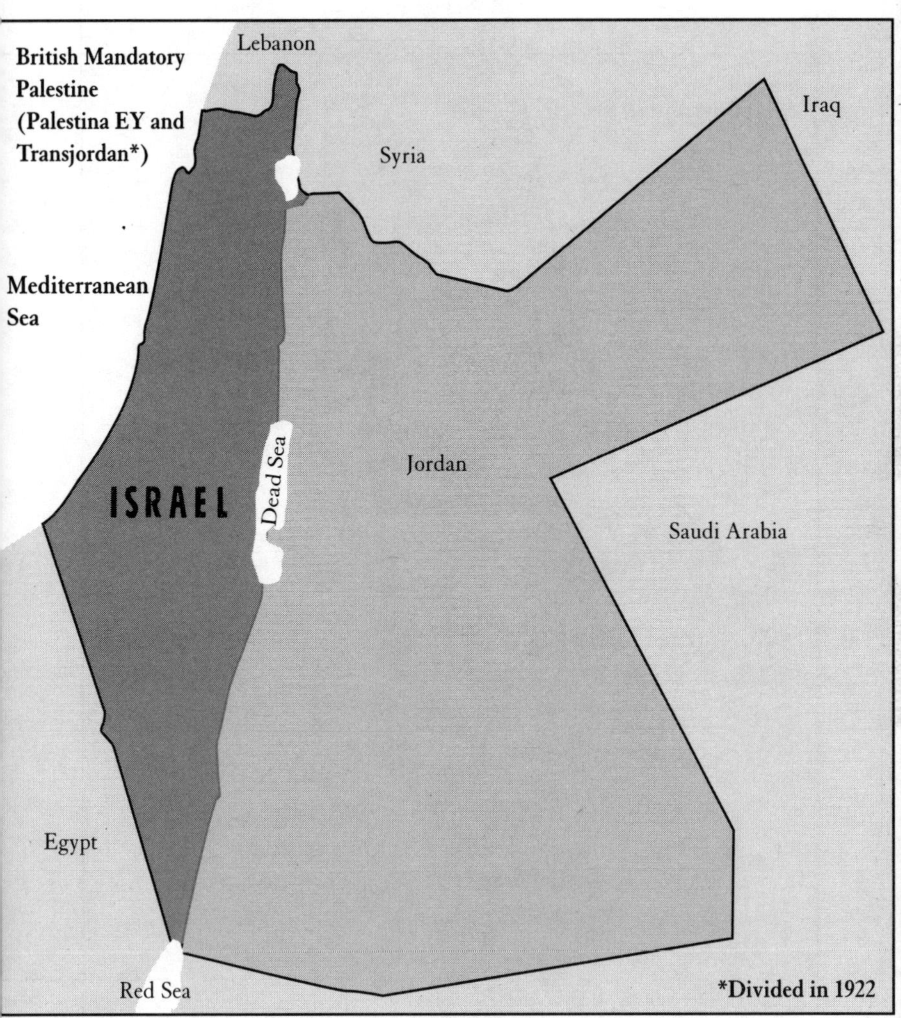

British Mandatory Palestine (Palestina EY and Transjordan*)
Lebanon
Syria
Iraq
Mediterranean Sea
Dead Sea
ISRAEL
Jordan
Saudi Arabia
Egypt
Red Sea
*Divided in 1922

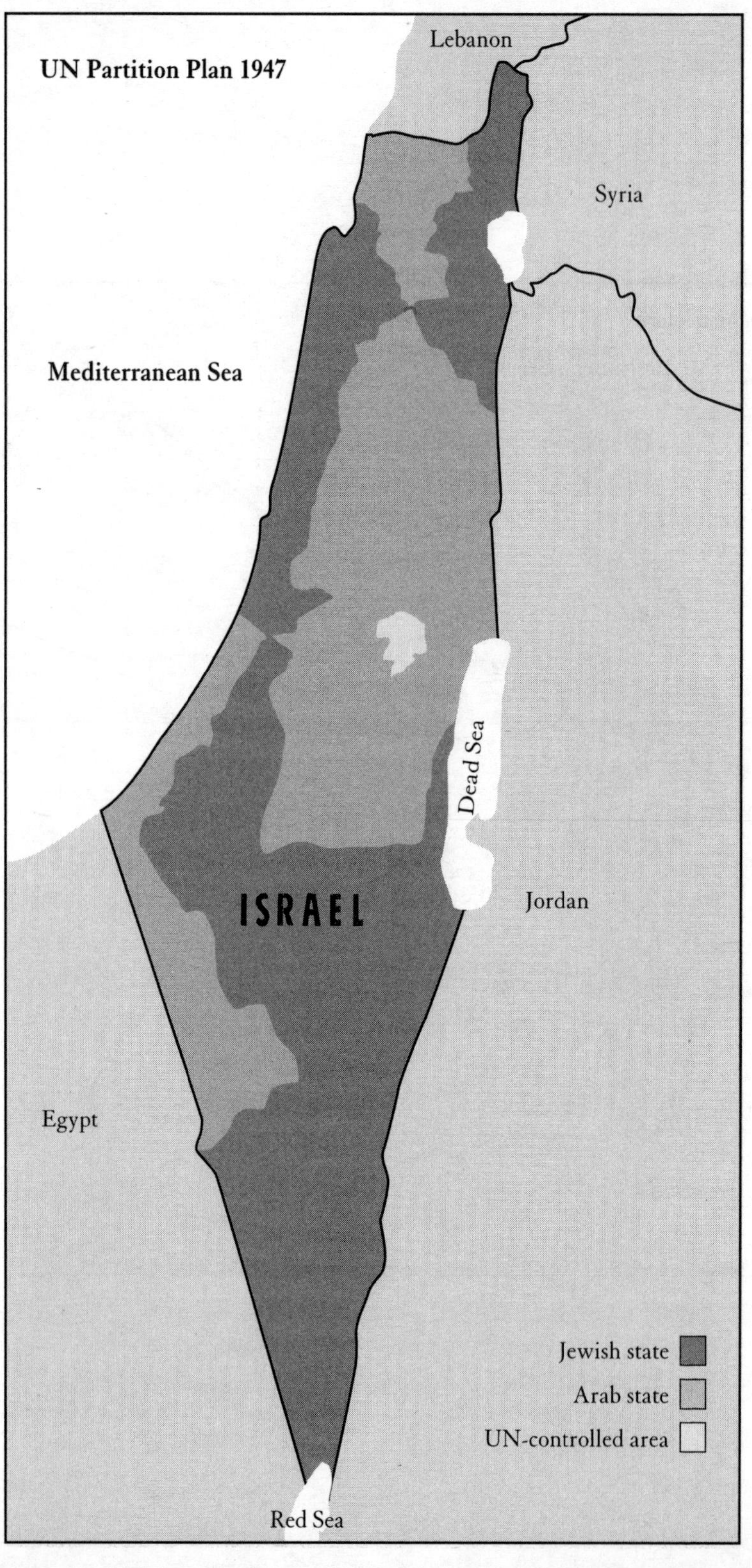
UN Partition Plan 1947
Lebanon
Syria
Mediterranean Sea
Dead Sea
ISRAEL
Jordan
Egypt
Red Sea
Jewish state
Arab state
UN-controlled area

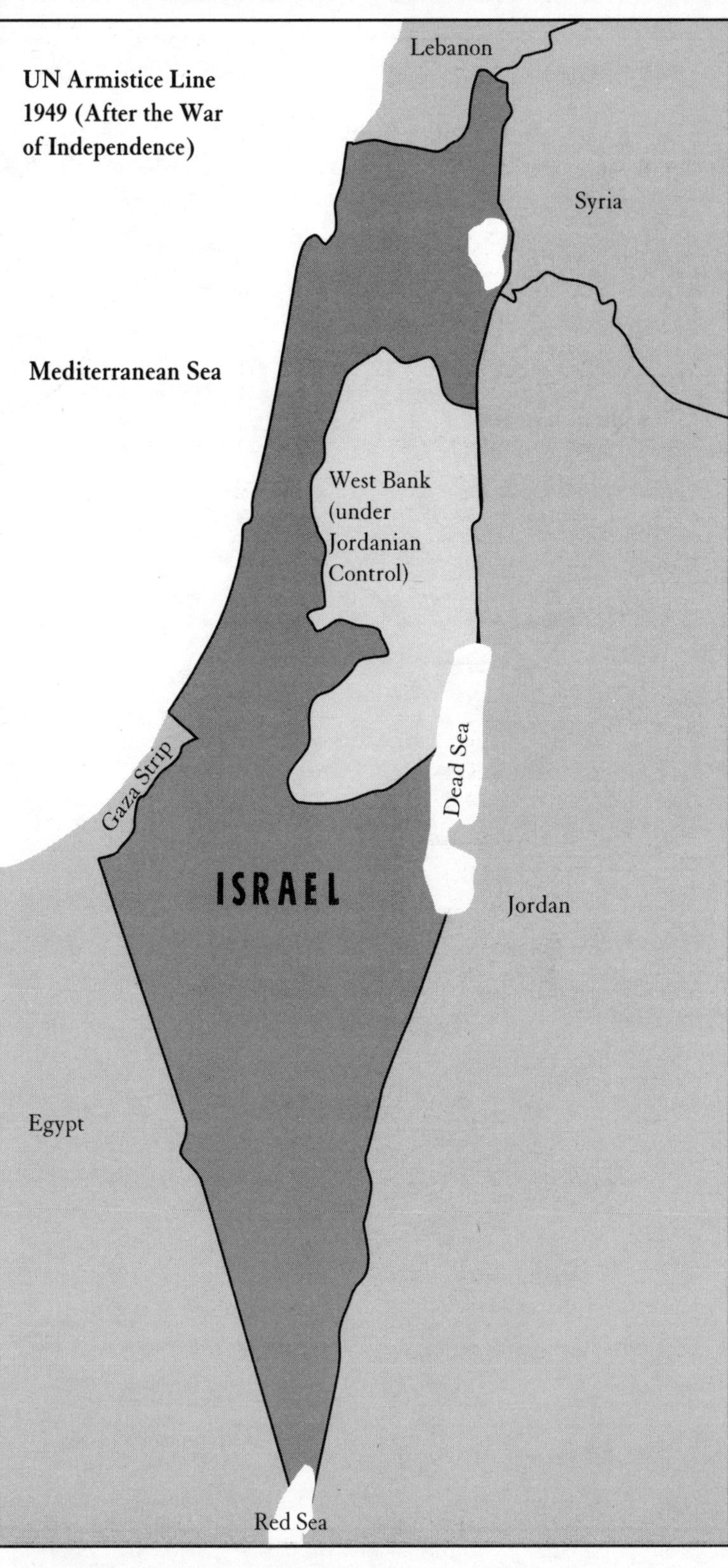
UN Armistice Line
1949 (After the War
of Independence)
Lebanon
Syria
Mediterranean Sea
West Bank
(under
Jordanian
Control)
Gaza Strip
Dead Sea
ISRAEL
Jordan
Egypt
Red Sea

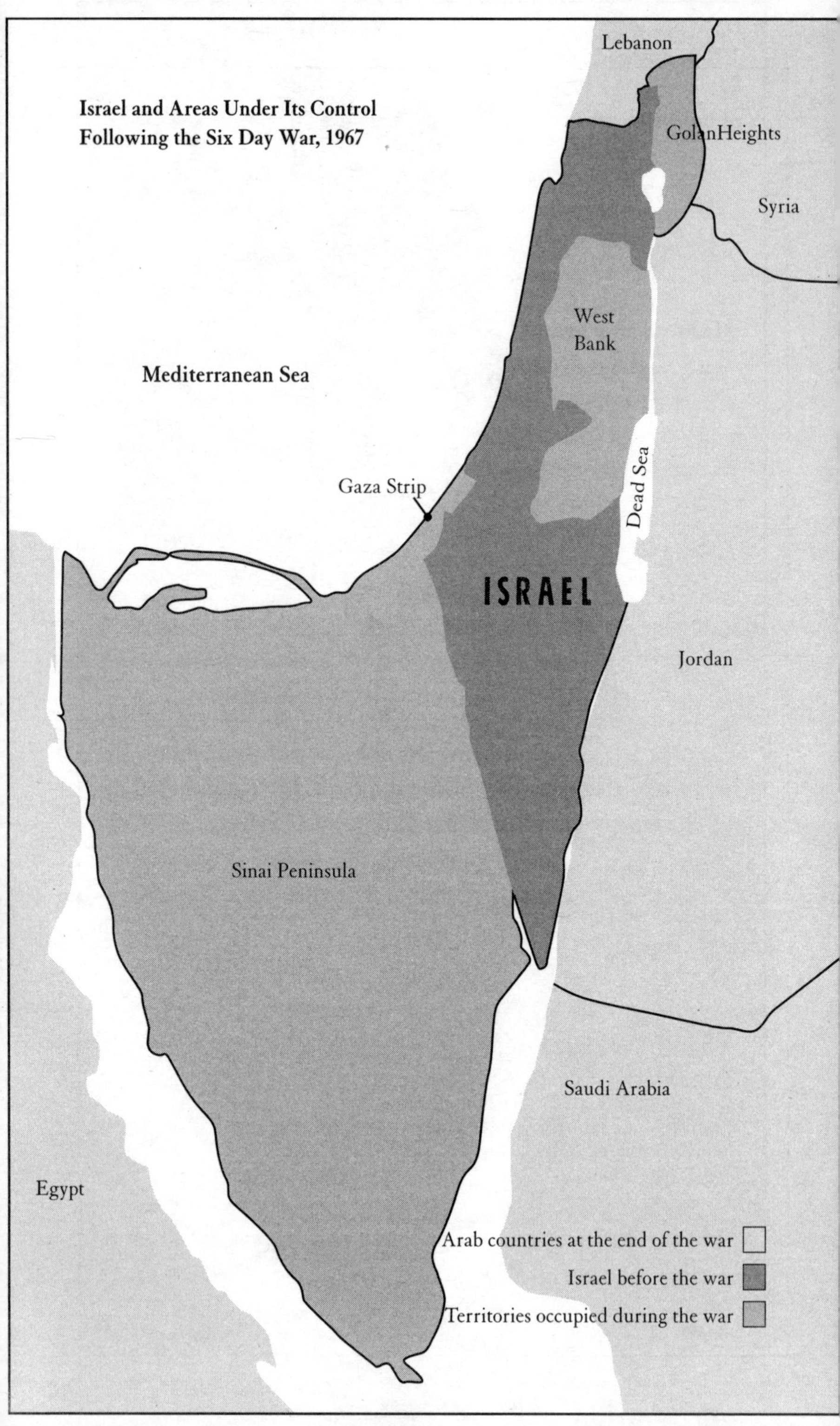

Israel and Areas Under Its Control
Following the Six Day War, 1967
Lebanon
GolanHeights
Syria
West
Bank
Mediterranean Sea
Dead Sea
Gaza Strip
ISRAEL
Jordan
Sinai Peninsula
Saudi Arabia
Egypt
Arab countries at the end of the war
Israel before the war
Territories occupied during the war

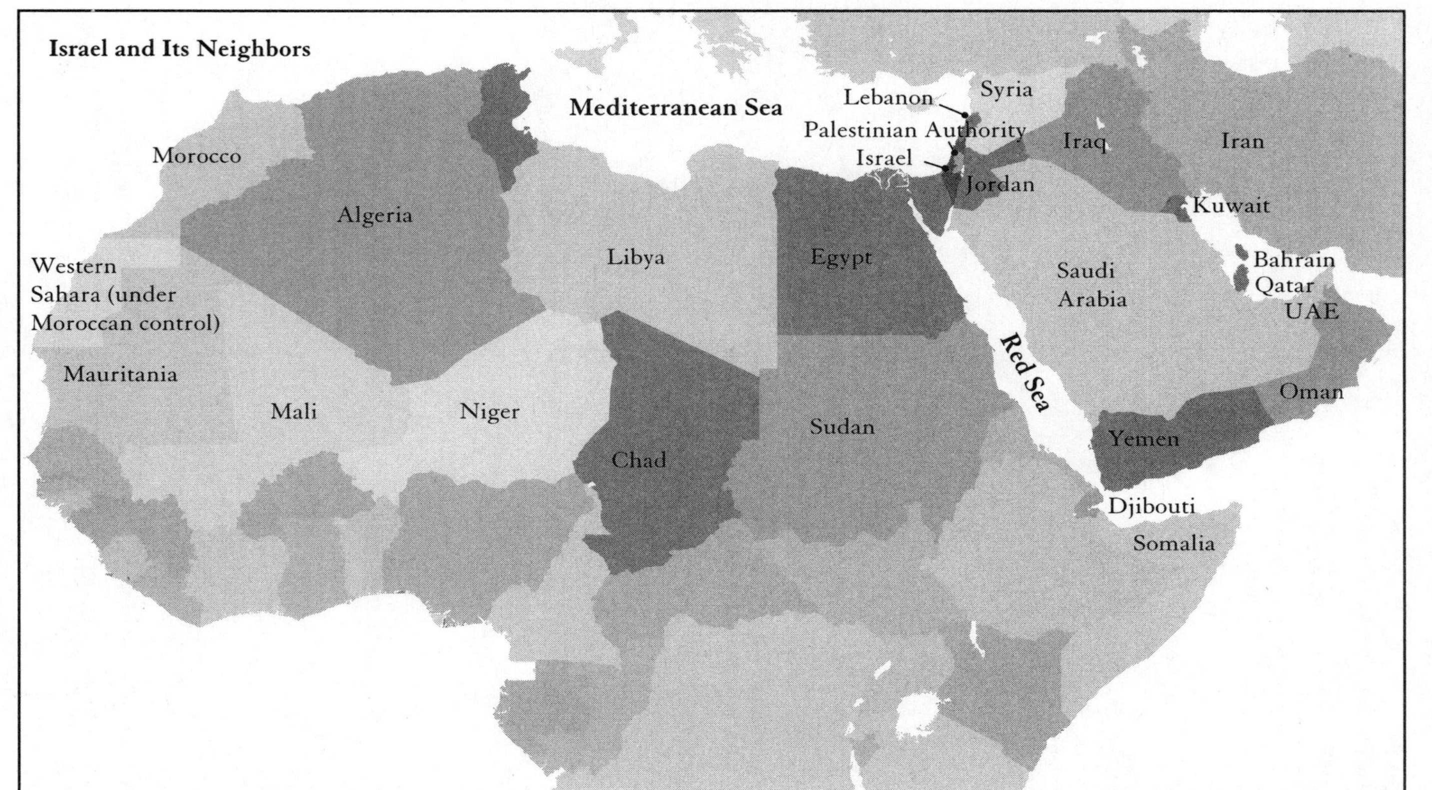
Israel and Its Neighbors
Mediterranean Sea
Morocco
Algeria
Western
Sahara (under
Moroccan control)
Mauritania
Mali
Niger
Libya
Chad
Egypt
Sudan
Lebanon
Syria
Palestinian Authority
Israel
Jordan
Iraq
Iran
Kuwait
Saudi
Arabia
Bahrain
Qatar
UAE
Oman
Red Sea
Yemen
Djibouti
Somalia

PART I

DREAM

CHAPTER ONE

A BRIEF HISTORY OF ME

AND WHY YOU CAN TRUST ME WITH THIS STORY

WITH GREAT POWER COMES GREAT . . . YOU KNOW THE REST

It takes a second for a person to realize that their life has changed forever. As I was standing there, a nineteen-year-old soldier in the Israeli military, with my back against the wall, nervous and sweaty, it dawned on me that this was it. My life would never be the same.

The evening had actually started out fairly chill. It was my younger sister's twelfth birthday, and my dad, stepbrother, and I were taking her and her friends ice skating and to get some McDonald's at the mall. I wasn't on alert. A mall didn't sound like something threatening or problematic. It was just my sister's birthday—and it would change my life.

But before we move forward, let's take a step back. My name is Noa Tishby, and I was born in Israel. I was raised in the suburbs of Tel Aviv, in a middle-class, politically active family that can trace its lineage through the creation of the state. My grandmother was one of the founders of the first kibbutz (a collective farm; more on this later) in Israel, my great-grandfather was the founder of the Ministry of Industry and Trade, and my grandfather was Israel's first ambassador to West African countries and served as a member of the Israeli delegation to the United Nations.

Needless to say, this left a strain of intrepid curiosity in my DNA. Growing up, I accompanied my parents to various protests and demonstrations, and we had ministers and ambassadors over for dinner several times a month. Politics was all around me, which is why it was somewhat surprising that I decided to go into the entertainment industry.

I started having the urge to act as a child. Like, a really young child. I used to see kids on TV and I just *knew* that was what I wanted to do. No one from my family was in the industry, and my mom, being the ninja that she is, neither knew nor cared much about it (a fact that remains true to this day). Supportive yet flummoxed, she said what any normal mom would say: "When you grow up, you can do whatever you want." So I waited until I was all grown up, a wizened twelve years of age, and started taking myself to places in Tel Aviv where I heard that casting directors roamed the land. I found my first crappy agent, who sent me on the bus to auditions. I didn't ask my parents; I just did it.

Around the age of thirteen, I started booking national commercials and TV appearances, which, ultimately, led to my parents' discovery of my extracurricular activities. I enrolled in my first drama class, and it was love at first sight. I got hooked.

I got a drama scholarship from the Tel Aviv Museum of Art and spent most of high school participating in school plays and musicals. Upon graduation, I did what (nearly) everyone in the country does: I joined the Israeli Defense Forces (IDF). National service was, and still is, mandatory for most Israelis; and since, at the time, soldiers in the IDF were not allowed to work outside of the service, I put my career on hold. But that didn't mean I gave up on my dream. Instead of buckling down on my push-ups, I auditioned for the military's performance corps—the entertainment troops. Funny as it may sound, the troops are extremely selective. Their audition process is the theatrical equivalent of Krav Maga. Seriously. It took several grueling months for the military to decide that instead of putting me into a Nikita-type position, or alternatively, making me serve coffee to a random commander, they could use my singing skills. I was in!

I might not have been the most feared secret agent, but I was a valued member of *The IDF Circus Show* (don't ask, but there were no elephants involved). Every day, we drove from one military base to another, and every night we performed sketch comedy and covered hit songs. Basically, a nightly USO tour. The novelty wore off pretty quick, but the view from the back of the bus was priceless. From the Golan Heights to Hebron to the Gaza Strip, I saw how people lived and how the military worked. The army was indeed a true melting pot, and I got to see places and meet people I wouldn't have had the chance to meet otherwise. It was also where I was introduced to the magical method of "threading," or plucking your eyebrows with just a single thread. It, like the service itself, changed my life forever.

Toward the end of my service, I received a call from my agent about a couple of job prospects. The first was incredible. I was offered the part of Rizzo in a new stage production of *Grease*, directed by the biggest director in the country and starring the biggest names of that time. Just so we are clear, I was obsessed with *Grease*. Obsessed. I knew it by heart, I *loved* the role of Rizzo, and I was beside myself with excitement. The second offer was to audition for a pilot for a new TV show. The casting director was looking for a sixteen-year-old ingenue, and at just over nineteen I made perfect sense.

I went to the audition and waited outside with all the other teenagers. They didn't give us texts—or, as we call them, "sides"—to memorize in advance; they just handed us a piece of paper on the spot to do a "cold read." I scanned that text, and man, it was crap. It was the most clichéd phone conversation between a teenage girl and her mom, and it wasn't to this little brat's liking. When they called my name, I walked into the room, sat down, and asked the director if I could improvise. He was a bit shocked, but he said yes, so I threw the text on the floor and improvised a call, miming holding a phone to my ear and everything. When I finished, the director looked at the monitor, then looked back at me. "Can you smile for us, please?" I did. He looked at the monitor again, looked back at me, and said: "I have a role for you, but it's not this one." I didn't get the role of the innocent teenage girl. I got the role of the main villain. The main love interest. The main bitch.

With both of these offers on the table, I went to my commander to beg for a break. I told him about the musical and the pilot and asked if, maybe, I could start my career while completing my service like a good soldier girl. He didn't even pause to think about it. The musical was a no. Performing *Grease* onstage every night would take me away from performing for the soldiers every night. But that little TV show? Fine. It was only a pilot. He told me to go film it and come back. And so I did. That career move was one of the biggest turning points of my life.

Grease came and went without leaving any lasting impression on anyone. However, that little pilot turned out to be the dictionary definition of an overnight sensation. The show, *Ramat Aviv Gimmel*—named after one of the most affluent neighborhoods in Tel Aviv—modeled itself after American prime-time soaps of the era, *Melrose Place* and the like. It took place in a fashion company, and I played the new hotshot designer brought in to revamp the brand, who, naturally, had an affair with the head of the company and subsequently got entangled in a series of delightful catfights with the CEO's older and superchic evil wife. It was silly, over-the-top, and the Israeli audience devoured it. The show became a massive hit.

Ignorant of this all, I was still in the bubble of active military service. My fellow soldiers ribbed me about playing an older vixen on that TV show, but other than that, it was all business as usual. Until that fateful day at the McDonald's.

This is how my journey began, back in the nineties, my back against the wall, my father and stepbrother dragging me away from a pile of kids screaming out my character's name (Daphne, if you're wondering) and begging for an autograph in those simple pre-selfie days.

AN AMERICAN DREAM

By the time I turned twenty-two years old, I was a full-on veteran of the Israeli entertainment industry. I booked the role of Anita in the Habima National Theater's production of *West Side Story* (a huge upgrade from *Grease*!) and put out a number one R&B album in English with my boyfriend (the first time in Israel a local artist sang in English!), all while shooting the number one show in the country. My days started at a 5 a.m. on the set of *Ramat Aviv Gimmel* and ended around 12 a.m. after my nightly performance of "A Boy Like That." I didn't sleep much, and I loved every minute of it. I was even offered a gig hosting the Israeli equivalent of *The Tonight Show* for the summer, and I considered taking it—until I had a not-so-chance meeting at a restaurant in Tel Aviv.

It was a sticky July day when I received an invitation for me and a guest to attend a dinner party hosted by the Israeli mega producer Arnon Milchan. My head spun as I envisioned Arnon seeing me, talking to me, and saying unequivocally, "I will make you the next Julia Roberts." He did produce *Pretty Woman*, and that seemed like proof enough that this would be my long-awaited ticket to LA.

I'd actually been dreaming of America since I was a preteen (it wasn't just a Hollywood thing). My first fantasy of the country came in second grade, when I was stricken by a plague of lice. I mean*, a lot* of lice. So many lice that my pillow sometimes seemed like it was moving all on its own. No matter what my parents did, we couldn't get rid of them, and the only clever idea my father came up with was to give me a buzz cut. A BUZZ CUT! At the age of eight it was pretty dramatic, so, yes, you could say I was fully traumatized. I went to school in a hoodie and dreamed of the day I could flaunt my horse mane of a ponytail again. It took me months to get used to my new gender-fluid look (before it was a thing), and in the meantime, I planned my big escape—I would grow my hair and move to a new school in America, where the kids would never know of my lice-ridden past and where I would speak English with a full-on American accent.

It had taken a little over a decade, but my fantasy was finally coming true, and I was ready—American accent and all. I went to Arnon Milchan's event with my plus one—my dad, naturally—and when we arrived, I positioned our party of two at our own little table. A few minutes passed before Arnon came over to say hello, and just like that, I started speaking to him in English. He picked up the cue and, after a short conversation with me and my dad, invited us to a meeting the following day.

At that meeting, Arnon informed me that, short of handing me roles, he would try to help me out, and that I must move to Los Angeles. He said the following line, which stayed with me for years: "If you make wine, you need to live in France. If you make watches, you need to live in Switzerland. And if you are in show business, you need to live in Los Angeles."

DING.

I heard him. Loud and clear.

Four months later, I resigned from *Ramat Aviv Gimmel*, stopped recording my second album, dropped out of hosting *The Tonight Show*, left the role of Anita to my understudy, left my apartment and my boyfriend of three years, packed two suitcases, and got on a plane to Los Angeles. Clearly, I was a little cray.

Now let me just state what is by now pretty obvious to all of you—I did not end up becoming Gal Gadot. Not even close. My career in the US had some amazing breakthroughs, like signing a six-record deal with a major record label, and some epic fails, like having that label fold when the music industry crumbled at the turn of the millennium. I did work consistently, booked a few roles here and there, and got a lot of fans in the industry, but I also did *not* book many roles and got frustratingly close to even more of them. I regularly became a strong second choice for major parts, which left me with, well, basically nothing.

I was always an entrepreneurial person, even as a kid. When I was in high school and didn't get accepted to a teen singing group, I started a competing one on my own. We put on a rock musical about the life of King David that became a cult phenomenon and went on to have a ten-year run. I needed to be creative and involved, and as such, I grew intensely frustrated with the LA waiting game, along with the general expectation that, as a young woman, I should sit prettily and quietly until my number came up, or didn't. So I started looking for projects to create and produce. I read in an Israeli newspaper about a new Israeli TV show that was making waves in the country. It was called *Be Tipul*, and it was about a therapist who, for half an hour, simply sat in a room with other actors and had a therapy session. Talking heads. "What a brilliant concept," I thought. And this was how I found my first format.

A format? you may ask. Let me explain. In television lingo, content is divided into two main fields, scripted and non-scripted. Scripted shows are every drama and sitcom you know, and non-scripted shows are reality shows, game shows, etc. Shows that literally do not have a script. Traditionally, the non-scripted format has been easier to "adapt" to international audiences, which is why pretty much every country on earth has their own version of *American Idol*. In the scripted world, however, it's a bit trickier. Scripts need to be translated, rewritten, and culturally adapted to each new territory. A year or so prior I'd had a role on a sitcom for NBC that was based on a British show called *Coupling*. This is not a brag, but proof that even though scripted adaptations weren't done much at the time, I knew it *could* be done. And I knew that *Be Tipul* could be the first show from Israel to do it.

I organized a meeting with the creator, and I told him straight up that I was going to sell his show to HBO. He seemed puzzled. At the time, this was a completely bonkers idea. Not only had no one ever done this before with an Israeli television show, no one had ever even *thought* of doing it.

I ended up selling *In Treatment* to HBO. I coproduced the show with Mark Wahlberg and Stephen Levinson, and we filmed 155 episodes that ran for three seasons, got nominated for twelve Emmy and Golden Globe awards, won a Peabody Award, and got renewed for a fourth season in 2020. This paved the way for Israel to become a TV format powerhouse; and, for a second, Israel became the country that sold the highest number of TV formats to the US, even more than the UK.

From a struggling actress waiting her turn, I became a struggling actress *and* a producer to be reckoned with. Apparently these two things are not mutually exclusive.

A TURKISH NON-DELIGHT

I was opening up major channels of communication between Israel and America, but still a lot of people seemed to not know where, or even what, Israel *was* exactly. The realization that Israel had a massive PR problem came up as soon as I started coming to the US and speaking to, well, people. I realized that what was common knowledge to me was total news to almost everyone. Just because I knew about Christopher Columbus, the Declaration of Independence, and the Emancipation Proclamation didn't mean that anyone knew Israel's history, its background, and the dangers it dealt with on a daily basis. It didn't mean that anyone knew who Israelis *were*. I was shocked. I mean, Israel was such a hot button issue for so many people around the world, surely if people have such strong opinions about a country, they'll be somewhat familiar with at least some basic facts, right? My gosh, was I wrong.

I encountered misinformation in all forms, even from the most well-intentioned and properly educated people. One day, while hanging with my old crew of young actors, writers, and directors, a successful up-and-comer you all know who would go on to win many awards, an Oscar among them, sidled up to me.

"So, you're from Israel!" she twanged.

"Yes, I am," I replied.

"Well, I was just wondering, how do your parents feel about you?"

I looked at her, confused. "I'm pretty sure they're proud of me," I said. "Why, is there something I should know about?"

She blinked, head cocked to the side, and continued. "I was just wondering how they feel about you being, you know, modern and all, without all the headgear," she said, making circular hand movements surrounding her face and head, in what can only be explained as the charades description of a hijab.

To set the record straight: while rocking a hair covering can be a choice ranging from tradition to modesty to self-expression, hijabs are mainly worn by Muslim women in the presence of men outside their family. While I love me a stylish accessory as much as the next woman, my experience with headgear is limited to a sunny day or Burning Man (for more on that, see chapter three).

Stories like this repeated themselves in hundreds of variations for years to come. Over and over, I would find myself telling the story of Israel. Explaining that we are not, in fact, Afghanistan. Explaining how the country came to be, how the borders came to be, drawing hundreds of maps of the region on hundreds of napkins at various dinner parties. I had to explain how freaking modern Israel is and what exactly the difference is between a kibbutz and a settlement (big difference, just so we're clear).

I realized people didn't know some basic facts, like that Israel is the *only* country in the Middle East that has been an uninterrupted democracy since its founding in 1948, after the United Nations granted the Jews a state following the horrors of the Holocaust. The Arabs were also granted a state at the time, but they chose to refuse it and start a war. I heard people call Israel a colonialist state, which is absurd, as it is a refugee state that was *decolonized* from British rule. I heard some people call Israel an apartheid state, which is also absurd when you know that the third largest political party in Israel is an Arab party. I realized some people see the *entire* problem in the Middle East as an Israeli-Palestinian conflict—a David-and-Goliath story that pits an army-less people (the Palestinians) against one of the most technologically advanced militaries in the world (Israel). It's easy to cheer for the underdog, but this dynamic is categorically not the case. The conflict is not between the Palestinian and Israeli people but rather between the *entire Arab world and Israel.* Twenty-one Arab countries, population approximately 423 million, and one Jewish state, population approximately 9 million. In that matchup, who is the David and who is the Goliath? I realized that people were disproportionality fascinated by Israel, that almost everyone had an opinion, but that a lot of people simply didn't know what they were talking about. I found myself explaining this and more to people, and I became a source of information and clarification on the topic for my community.

However, what followed in the years to come is what qualifies me to write this book. After all, no one wants to read a historical and somewhat political book about one of the most contentious countries on the planet from a random actress-slash-producer, no matter how lovely she may be.

It all came to a head one night in 2010. It was about 11 p.m., and I was sitting in front of my computer, browsing this new and exciting platform called Twitter, when I realized that Israel was trending. In the Turkish language: "*Israil.*" I knew enough about international relations to understand that this was probably not a good thing. And it wasn't. The headlines were aggressive: "Israeli military kills nine Turkish peace activists trying to deliver aid to Gaza." The internet was ablaze with outraged posts and shared posts. Now, remember this was 2010: social media was just starting to take shape. We were still naively participating in what we thought was a fun, authentic, and transparent form of connection and communication, not a virtual monster that would take over our lives and hack our brains (to paraphrase my fellow countryman, the mega-bestseller Yuval Noah Harari). But still, the news didn't feel right. I'd served in the army, and this just wasn't something we would do.

I dug around, and—no surprise—the facts were completely at odds with the story that was going viral. The Turkish flotilla comprised six ships and nearly seven hundred passengers. While some were probably well-intentioned activists, at least forty were hard-core Islamists with ties to terrorism who were sailing from Turkey to Gaza with the intent of breaking the blockade on the Gaza Strip that had been imposed by Israel and Egypt (yes, *and* Egypt). The blockade was the result of terrorist activities by Hamas, which included shooting rockets into Israel and a general desire to wipe the country off the map (as stated in the Hamas charter; we'll get to that, too). The Israelis first tried to make a deal with the Turks, suggesting the ships anchor in an Israeli port where the goods would be checked and brought into Gaza by land, but the Turks refused. Israel then tried to make the ship stop, and only after being ignored did operatives from Israel's navy board the vessel. As the commandos descended from a helicopter, they faced "organized and violent resistance,"[1] including attacks with iron rods.

When a protestor grabbed a weapon from one of the commandos, the soldiers opened fire. Ten[2] Turkish citizens were indeed killed, which was a regrettable loss of life, but it's critical to note that at least some of these men had come prepared to fight, and a fight they got.

It took a few days for videos of the attack to come out, and they validated Israel's version of events. But by then, public opinion and the internet-verse had already decided that Israel, just like that, out of the blue one fine morning, killed nine peace activists who were chilling on the deck of The Love Boat.

I found myself glued to my computer screen for the next few days, picking Twitter wars with various trolls and realizing: "Jerusalem, we have a problem." Israel got bad enough PR in old-school media, but a tsunami of awful was about to hit online, where lies, misinformation, and "facts" become "reality" in a blink. The IDF and the Israeli government were still operating in the stone age, under some form of "We are verifying facts before putting them out there, so please be patient, this could take a few days." But in this new online world, it was no longer a matter of days; it was a matter of seconds. For the first time, I feared for the future of my country. Israel's PR problems were about to turn into an existential threat.

It became my personal mission to put myself out there online to try to get to the truth. As I tweeted up a storm and drove myself crazy, a few like-minded people messaged me. We all rallied around the same thought: someone had to take on social media, and since the Israeli government wasn't paying enough attention at the time, it needed to be us. In 2011, our incredibly self-motivated group formed Act for Israel, the first online advocacy and rapid response organization dedicated to truth spreading and pre-bots troll fighting. It was like heading into the Wild West with an iPhone and a MacBook Pro.

This was when my advocacy became not just this thing I did at dinner parties but a true calling. I started working with pro-Israel organizations around the US, with NGOs, and unofficially with the Israeli government. We created tweets and posts, working to push out positive news and debunk falsehoods when we saw them. Act for Israel also created presentations to explain to people in positions of power, in the Israeli government and in other big organizations, how this new world worked. We leaned on data, like the fact that 87 percent of people under the age of thirty got their news from Facebook. At the time, this sort of thing was a complete and total shock to anyone we met with.

We spread the gospel of this changing online reality, sending bloggers to Israel, collecting data on tweets and posts, and meeting with NGO, government, and Israel Defense Forces officials, such as the IDF spokesman, Brigadier General Yoav (Poli) Mordechai. As I briefed him on this electronic intifada, a *second* flotilla from Turkey was on its way to Gaza, and we followed it closely as I walked him through our presentation.

Poli later told me that as soon as I walked out of his office, he called in his team and instructed them to completely overhaul how the Israel Defense Forces used social media. Based on our presentation and the meeting I had with him, the IDF fully revamped their online strategy and became active on social media. And regardless of our presentation, that second flotilla ended quickly and quietly and, thankfully, with no life lost.

This is when advocacy and political activism became a major part of my life, my work, and my identity. But it took another viral event for the Israeli public to get behind me. And as usual, it was out of my control.

AN UNOFFICIAL AMBASSADOR

It was Sunday, November 18, 2012, and I was in bed in Los Angeles, bawling. I had hit a career high, heading a new joint venture between one of Israel's largest networks, Reshet, and ITV Studios USA while simultaneously producing a new sitcom for CBS that was created by an Israeli writer. That morning, I'd woken up to a scathing email from my otherwise lovely writer. There was a misunderstanding about my role as his producer. When I didn't do something he was expecting me to do, he got upset, and since he was such a brilliant writer, he sent me a sharp and snappy email that simply tore me to shreds. It basically said I was a horrible person and a horrible producer and would amount to nothing, and since he was so smart and talented, I fully believed him. That email killed me, and so I planned to spend the rest of the day in bed crying my eyes out.

I was still in bed with my Labrador, Tuli, when my friend Tracy showed up at my doorstep. In the midst of my personal battle, I'd totally forgotten our battle plan for the day. Israel was in the middle of yet another war with Hamas, dramatically named Operation Pillar of Defense. Israel had begun the operation in response to the ongoing attacks by Hamas on Israeli soldiers and civilian towns in the south of the country. Something needed to be done. Using a precision drone, the IDF took out Ahmed al-Jabari, the senior leader of the military wing of Hamas. Since Mr. Jabari was not a puppy trainer, I was okay with that. But there was an international media outcry, and Israel was again portrayed as the big bad wolf.

Tracy and I had planned on going to a demonstration organized by the Israeli American Council, but needless to say, I did not want to go. Puffy-eyed, I told her to go without me. She refused. I moped, she coaxed, and after another handful of tissues, I covered my face in heavy makeup and a huge pair of sunglasses, and we headed out to the Israeli consulate building in Westwood, Los Angeles.

The demonstration was business as usual. A few hundred pro-Israel demonstrators stood on one side of the road, and a few hundred anti-Israel demonstrators stood on the other. (Note that whenever there is an Israeli event or gathering, there is an anti-Israel protest in close vicinity.) I carried a sign that read "Free Gaza from Hamas," because even though I am pro-Israel, I am also pro-Palestinian, just anti-Hamas, a terrorist organization which aims to annihilate Israel, and which uses international aid money to build attack tunnels instead of schools and hospitals.

People on both sides of the street were passionately expressing their First Amendment rights when one of the organizers recognized me.

"We're so glad you are here!" he said, running up to us. "Would you like to say something?"

I wasn't sure. "Like what?"

"I don't know, whatever you want," he said, and dragged me to a microphone.

I don't remember exactly what happened next. All I remember is that I took the microphone, stood on a small box, and started speaking from my heart. I said all that I knew to be true. That Israel wanted peace, that Hamas was terrorizing both the Israelis *and* the Palestinians. I spoke authentically and from my experience.

I went to sleep that night without a second thought, but the following morning, I was woken early by the sounds of incoming calls and text messages. I don't want to sound too dramatic, so I won't say that I had a million missed calls, texts, tweets, and likes from everyone I knew and every media and news outlet in Israel, but it sure felt that way. Apparently, while I was sleeping, a producer by the name of Sharon Mor had done what was not that common at the time. She filmed my speech and posted it. And it blew up in Israel.

I'd been a known entity in Israel for a while now, but this was the first time my fellow Israelis saw my advocacy in action. I was suddenly dubbed "The Ambassador" in the Israeli media, and it was only then that I realized I had somehow naturally followed the footsteps of my grandfather Hanan Yavor, the *actual* ambassador in the family. My grandfather paved the way to Israel's international relationships with Africa. He was the first Israeli ambassador to Ghana, Nigeria, and

Liberia (and a nonresident ambassador to Barbados!), and a member of the Israeli delegation to the United Nations. He was a committed, idealistic, and highly respected diplomat. I will get into his extraordinary life in the final chapter of this book, but for now I'll just say that at that moment I realized, that unbeknownst to me, my DNA had kicked into action. I couldn't help myself anymore, I had to get involved.

But it wasn't always like that. When I had just moved to America, I was completely disconnected from anything Israel. Until one sushi dinner that changed everything.

RECONNECTED

It was a sunny September morning, a few months after I moved to Los Angeles. The phone rang at my boyfriend's Hollywood Hills house, and my dad was on the line. "Happy holidays!" he cheered. "How are you celebrating tonight?" I sat up, coffee at hand, and frowned. "What holiday is it?" I asked him. "It's Rosh Hashanah! *Happy New Year!*" my family hollered at me from the other side of the world. My heart sank. I got off the phone, walked out to the expansive balcony, and stared at the pool and at the Hollywood sign, which was hovering above me, judgingly. I'd been in LA for a few months, finding my footing in a new town, making new friends, and trying to invent a new career for myself, and I had zero idea that the Jewish new year was that night. Since I was raised secular, I didn't even bother to keep track of any of this. However, hearing my family on the other line, celebrating this *thing* together, made me want to cry. And the feeling surprised me. I walked up to my boyfriend and told him that it was a holiday and I would like us to do something special.

That night, my Australian boyfriend, another friend, and I ended up in Sushi Katsu-Ya on Ventura Boulevard. As we raised our glasses, my boyfriend turned to me and asked: "So, what *is* the Jewish new year?" I blanked. I didn't know what to say. "Oh well" he said, and shrugged. *"Happy Rosh Hashanah!"* And he downed his sake. I'd never felt lonelier or more disconnected in my life.

I was obviously missing my family—there is no surprise there—but it was more than that. That night in Katsu-Ya, I realized that, in identifying myself as a liberal globalist, I might have skipped the part of identifying *myself* first. I was shocked that I couldn't describe what on earth Rosh Hashanah was. I always thought of myself as an *Israeli*, but what did that even mean if I wasn't living in Israel or didn't know what to say to my friends when they asked me a simple question about my background?

That little incident proved to be monumental in my life. It pushed me to explore, for the first time, what it meant to be "an Israeli," what it meant to be Jewish, and to see it all from an outsider's perspective that wouldn't have been possible had I still been living in Israel. Living outside of the country allowed me to re-explore everything I thought I knew, and everything I realized I didn't know, like what the F#@K Rosh Hashanah was and—more importantly—why I should care.

When I was still living in Israel, I prided myself on my secularism. I wanted nothing to do with religion, so I tried to dismiss my Jewishness in its entirety. Or at least, that's what I thought.

Remember the youth group I was a part of as a teen, and the hit rock musical we performed around the country? We were a bunch of secular kids; we looked like, acted like, dressed like, and listened to the exact same music kids our age did anywhere from London to Los Angeles. Yet the topic of our raunchy, controversial, sexy AF show was—David. The king. From the Old Testament. Yaron Kafkafi, who wrote the brilliant piece, did a deep dive into the story, and he swept us kids along with him. I was a sassy seventeen-year-old, prancing around Tel Aviv in a tight miniskirt and a (very) low-cut shirt, carrying a freaking Bible in my bag. And of course I was able to read that Bible in my bag, since it was written in my mother's tongue. In fact, many of the musical's lyrics were quotes straight out of the old book, so we performed them in the same place the story happened and in its original language. The show became a cult phenomenon, with hundreds of kids our age and younger knowing every single one of those ancient words by heart. It was the Israeli version of *The Rocky Horror Picture Show*—and we were all singing the Bible. I was and still am obsessed with the story of David, not as a religious text, but as a modern tale I can learn from *today*.

And this, I later learned, is a very Jew-y thing to do. To keep the old traditions and adapt them to modern times. An ancient text can be the most modern, and the holiest and most pious is also sometimes the most provocative and gutsy. An ancient story, which was kept for generations, can get a new life and, as such, new relevancy. I carried around that five-thousand-year-old text in my best-of-the-nineties bag without, for a second, thinking there was anything weird about it. It seemed totally normal, until that night at Katsu-Ya.

When I stepped outside of my bubble I embarked on a journey that enabled me to see the beauty of it all. I found the built-in liberalism in Judaism and in Zionism. I learned to admire the highly Jew-y culture of debate and dissent. I found amazing stuff, like how the Jewish holidays are connected to, for example, the moon (I mean, *who knew that??*), and I saw how it all had shaped me as a person, consciously and subconsciously. I also realized that a super-driven, secular, and slightly flamboyant seventeen-year-old carrying a Bible in her bag was, indeed, a little bit weird. In the most wonderful of ways.

That dinner catapulted me on a journey that got me to this book. I started researching Israel, its history, the history of the conflict, the spiritual aspects of Judaism. I started to analyze Israel more objectively and understand how it's portrayed around the world. I held Israel accountable for its mistakes and celebrated its accomplishments. And when I was able to articulate for myself the severe misunderstandings about Israel and how fragile she still is, I jumped in to speak up.

I needed to speak up because change can only come after the acknowledgment of reality. How can we aim to make change in the Middle East if we don't know how we got here? If you don't know where to start a journey, you can't get anywhere. This is a very simple concept, actually. Imagine you go online trying to book a flight, but you don't put in your departure location. It would be somewhat of a challenge to get anywhere. In the same way, if you want to create a future, you have to know where you're at, otherwise you'll just keep doing the same thing, over and over again.

If we want to create a new possibility for the future of the Middle East (or anywhere, really), we can't create it on top of hidden agendas, by political maneuvering, or without knowing at least some of the *actual history*.

This is why I wanted to write this book. Not because the story has never been told, but because it has never been told *this way*. To know where you're going, you have to know where you came from. And that's what happened that night in Katsu-Ya. I took ownership of where I came from.

This is not a history book per se. It is more of a her-story book. Her story and mine.

So let's start from the beginning, or at least the beginning of written times as we know them.

CHAPTER TWO

A BRIEF HISTORY OF THE LAND OF ISRAEL

THE WATER YOU SWIM IN

Caesarea is one of the most beautiful places in Israel. Built on the shores of the Mediterranean Sea, it is an ancient town originally established around the first century BC. It is now a gorgeous money haven where prime ministers and Russian businessmen build their massive mansions.

The town, located about a forty-five-minute drive north of Tel Aviv, turned into a tiny local port around 31 BC. It remained relatively humble until it was conquered by Herod the Great, who completely transformed it per his megalomaniac ways. Herod the Great, a locally born Edomite slash Jewish hustler, had climbed the political ladder faster than an acrobat in Cirque du Soleil. His father, Antipater, had been made a chief minister of Judea by Julius Caesar, who controlled Judea along with just about the rest of the world, and Antipater introduced his boy to all the right people. Herod was able to get a job as representative of the Romans to the province of Galilee and, after fleeing due to family infighting and pleading his case with Rome, was installed as king of Judea by the Roman Senate, overthrowing the Hasmonean dynasty, which had been in place since 140 BC.

Ambitious and powerful, Herod quickly killed off all threats to his power (including three of his sons, his brother-in-law, and his Hasmonean wife) and started building massive structures all over the country, naming them after himself and his Roman benefactors (as evidenced by the name Caesarea, for Caesar). The Herodian dynasty lasted from 47 BC to almost AD 100, but the structural legacy has persisted to this day.

It was spring 2008, and I was driving north from Tel Aviv to Caesarea to check out a wedding venue for my pending nuptials with my lovely fiancé Osher, who is now my lovely ex-husband. We were in the car with Yaron, my first drama teacher, who wrote the musical *David* from chapter one and who also happens to be an amateur historian and tour guide. At some point, Osher, who is from Australia, looked out the window and yelped, "What is *that*?" Yaron and I looked in the direction Osher was pointing and then turned our heads back to the road. "Oh that?" I said. "That's nothing. Just another Herodian aqueduct. We have a million of them."

It was only when I saw the shock on Osher's face that it occurred to me that this was not "nothing" at all. Osher, my worldly, very successful, well-traveled companion, was blown away. Yaron and I had taken this two-thousand-plus-year-old structure for granted. It was the water we swam in. It wasn't until Osher pointed it out that we even saw its uniqueness.

Israel sits on so much freaking history and archaeology, it's unfathomable. An archeologist friend told me once that being an archeologist in Israel is completely different than being one anywhere else in the world. He told me that for most digs, you start from the highest point available—in Hebrew we call it the *tel*—which is usually where the ruler used to live. This is where the best, most impressive, and most resilient structures were built, and therefore the ones most likely to survive. But when you dig in Jerusalem, for example, you just dig wherever you can, and you're bound to find something old and priceless buried underground.

Which makes renovations a nightmare. That same friend who drove us to Caesarea, Yaron, was renovating his apartment in the northern part of Tel Aviv. It wasn't a big renovation at all; in fact, all he needed to do was close off an already existing balcony on the ground floor. Even for that minor thing, Yaron had to go through a bureaucratic nightmare and get written consent from the Israeli Antiquity Authority. Anytime you build anything new in Israel, a crew of Indiana Jones extras is enlisted to make sure that nothing historically precious accidentally gets destroyed.

The reason for this is, of course, thousands of years of civilizations that lived, loved, and built on that land, making it a haven for archaeologists and history buffs from all over the world. This highly researched and documented history of the land cannot be separated from the future of the land, or from any political debate we are currently having about the State of Israel.

Which brings us to the following episode of *Sesame Street*: "Back to Basics."

BACK TO BASICS

In order to have any legitimate discussion about Israel, you need to know a few basic facts.

The first fact is that the State of Israel is approximately 8,019 square miles. Just for reference, the state of New Jersey is 8,723 square miles. So, as countries go, Israel isn't a big one. It takes about six hours to drive from north to south and about an hour from east to west. That's it.

This pint-sized strip of land sits on the shores of the Mediterranean Sea, south of Syria and Lebanon, west of Jordan, and north of Egypt. It's surrounded by twenty-one[1] mostly Arab countries and Iran, which is part Arab and mostly Persian. One could say it's a rough neighborhood. Protests during the Arab Spring in the early 2010s brought a glimmer of hope for change, but after the people of the region demanded democracy and freedom, they instead got, for the most part, more extremists and failed states. The region is unstable, to say the least.

While some of Israel's neighbors are rich in natural resources, there is nothing in the ground in Israel. No natural treasures at all. No diamonds, gold, or oil. This changed to some extent with the discovery of natural gas off Israel's shores in the last two decades, but in terms of natural resources, this new discovery is pretty much it. Israel is actually located in the *driest* part of what is called the Fertile Crescent and is highly dependent on rain for its drinking water, but since it's hot most of the year, water is scarce. Water conservation is a big deal in Israel. All Israelis grew up with national ad campaigns pleading with us to conserve water. This mentality is so embedded in my psyche that I can't handle it when I see or hear a faucet running. This, too, saw a recent change, with the launch of water desalination. The project was successful, and alleviated some of the country's water concerns, but not my already built-in aversion to the sound of running faucets.

In short, there is nothing particularly special about the natural location, yet for some reason Israel is the physical origin of two monotheistic religions (Judaism and Christianity) and the third holiest place to the third monotheistic religion (Islam) as practiced today. God only knows why. Literally.

Perhaps some of Israel's relevance is tied to its geographic centrality in the region. Smack between Europe, Asia, and Africa, it became a major crossroads for the developing worlds. It was used as a party-stop for trade and migration, and some of the oldest findings of agriculture, ceremonies, burials, and fire from the Neanderthals onward can be found in the ground and in caves around the country.

That's all well and good, but what *exactly* is "Israel"? Wasn't the country only established in 1948? Yes and no. The first time the borders of what would later become the ancient Kingdom of Israel are described in writing is when the land of Canaan is mentioned in the Old Testament as follows:

> וַיְהִי גְּבוּל הַכְּנַעֲנִי מִצִּידֹן בֹּאֲכָה גְרָרָה עַד־עַזָּה בֹּאֲכָה סְדֹמָה וַעֲמֹרָה וְאַדְמָה
> וּצְבֹיִם עַד־לָשַׁע

This line describes borders ranging from approximately modern-day Lebanon in the north, to the beach in the west, to Jordan in the east, to the Negev desert in the south. This was super early—most biblical scholars date it to about 1500 BC—and the land was said to have been populated with tribes of old nations practicing early stages of organized communities, agriculture, and city and society building.

According to biblical texts and the scholars who study them, it was sometime during the thirteenth century BC that the Hebrews came in and divided the land into areas governed by the twelve Jewish tribes, who started to form one Jewish nation. Sometime around 1030 BC to 928 BC the country became a sovereign Jewish kingdom, referred to in the Scriptures as the United Israelite Monarchy. This is when, according to the Old Testament, the twelve traveling tribes of Israel united in order to establish one cool kingdom. They also wanted to become more like other nations of the era and demanded that kings replace their judges, who had previously acted as their local organic leaders. This led to the reign of King David. That same one I became obsessed with as a drama school rat teen. The Bible then tells us that David's wife gave birth to the future king Solomon, who went on to build the First Temple in Jerusalem in what scholars assess is around 930–970 BC.

Before I continue, however, let me take a beat here and clear something up. I don't define myself as a religious person at all. I am a spiritual person, in the sense that I am humbly aware of the fact that we humans are just a blip in the face of a greater power, whatever you want to call it. God or the Universe or Mother Earth. I do not know if the Bible, Old Testament, New Testament, or any other holy text is *real* or not, so I will respect them and will never argue for or against any of them. So why bring up religious texts at all? Because the claim that Israel is the home of the Jewish people has a lot to do with these holy books, and what is written in them is very much still present in our political debate every single day. So of course I'll mention them, especially when I can also point to *many* archeological findings and other sources of written history that corroborate this time line. Yet another written historical corroboration of the Jewish people's connection to Jerusalem and Israel can be found in none other than . . . the Quran itself. Contrary to recent political attempts to say otherwise, it is indeed true, and everyone is welcome to check this out. (Among other verses see Quran: *Surah Bani Isra'il* verses 17:2,[2] *Surah of Jonah* verse 93,[3] and *Surah al-Ahraf (of the Barrier)* verse 137.[4])

But let's get back to modern world. Scientists have been able to carbon-date structures and artifacts back tens of thousands of years, before humanity even started using the written word. An Egyptian inscription—the Merneptah Stele,[5] dated to approximately 1200 BC—mentions a campaign in which the Egyptian ruler defeated "Israel." Archaeologists have found an abundance of remains and artifacts in Jerusalem associated with the First Temple, including a twenty-six-hundred-year-old seal (called a bulla) with a name written on it in

Hebrew, "Natan-Melech, Eved Ha'Melech," a tooth-breaking name that appears in the Second Book of Kings.

In that book, there are many outrageous descriptions of drama, with inner struggles, wars, sex, and blood. But while I can't verify who, exactly, slept with whom, I can verify that a Jewish state did exist as the United Israelite Monarchy approximately three thousand years ago, before it split into two separate Jewish states, Israel and Judea. All these ancient and dramatic events happened on the exact same land where Israel is located today. I don't believe this because of religious credo but because of archaeology, science, and history.

This isn't about God, so let's keep her out of it. I'm sure she's way busy, anyway.

A QUICK HISTORICAL RUNDOWN OF A HAND-SWAPPED LAND

Like most kingdoms, that first Jewish kingdom came to an end. Around 722 BC, the Kingdom of Israel was conquered by the Assyrian Empire. The Jewish Kingdom of Judea survived for another 136 years, until the Babylonian king Nebuchadnezzar attacked around 587–586 BC, destroying that First Temple built by Solomon in Jerusalem and exiling the Jews to neighboring countries. This was the first of two Jewish exiles and diasporas.

Next came the Persian Empire (which lasted from approximately 539–332 BC). Cyrus the Great, the first king of the Persian Empire, was actually pretty groovy, and in 538 BC, he published the Cyrus Decree allowing all exiled nations of the region to go back to their homelands and reestablish their faiths, traditions, and rituals. The Cyrus Decree is mentioned in the Bible, in the book of Ezra (Chapter 1, verses 1–4). The actual Cyrus Cylinder with that Cyrus Decree, as more or less described in the Book of Ezra, was found in modern-day Iraq in 1879 and is now on display in London.

Cyrus was not a Jew lover in particular, but he was a pragmatist and preferred to allow all nations to go back to their old lands than have his empire self-implode. Smart move, if you want to avoid rebelliousness. This led to what is sometimes referred to as the first Zion Return—the Jews' return to their homeland and the building of the Second Temple in Jerusalem.

After the Persians came the Greeks. In 332 BC, Alexander the Great of Macedon (or of ancient Greece, if you ask a Greek) didn't just take over Israel, he pretty much took over the whole region from Greece through the Middle East to Mesopotamia, Persia, and all the way down to India. In today's terminology, Alexander the Great would be described as a globalist. He was a huge proponent of cultures merging, which is why his conquest of Israel started what's known as the Hellenistic period (approximately 332 to 63 BC). Instead of killing all the Jews, the Greeks allowed the Jews to live their religious lives freely, practice Judaism, and assimilate as they saw fit.

Antiochus III (Antiochus the Great) followed and continued allowing the Jews to resettle and practice Judaism, going so far as to acknowledge them as loyal and important citizens of his realm.

That was not the case with his son Antiochus IV Epiphanes, an eccentric character who used to visit local public bathhouses and was known as the Mad One. Antiochus was not into the Jews practicing their Judaism and in 167 BC outlawed Jewishness altogether and forced the Jews to worship Zeus. This Zeus-pushing did not go down particularly well with the Jews, and in 167 BC a rebellion erupted, led at first by Mattathias and later by a brave man called Judah the Maccabee of the house of the Hasmoneans. As the story goes, Judah the Maccabee retook the Jewish Temple, which had been defiled by the Greeks, and after cleaning it out, he found only one single canister of oil. He used the oil to light the seven-pronged temple lamp, also known as a menorah, and low and behold, the oil lasted for eight days. (Happy Hanukkah, everyone!)

The Jewish dynasty of the Hasmoneans ruled Israel from around 167 to 37 BC, reestablishing the Jewish state and national sovereignty. For the first time in a few hundred years, the Jews self-governed once again, didn't have to pay taxes to an outside ruler, and were free to practice Judaism in Israel.

That Jewish party ended like most parties in the region, with the invasion of the mighty Romans around 63 BC. In approximately the year AD 66 the Jews had had enough with the Romans and started a highly ambitious rebellion, which did not end well. In AD 70 Roman Emperor Vespasian tired of the rebellious Jews and sent his son Titus to Judea to crush the uprising. Titus orchestrated a long and horrific siege on Jerusalem. After months of fighting, the city fell, Titus broke through the walls, destroyed Jerusalem, and burned the Second Temple. He killed or exiled almost every Jew living in the area, causing diaspora number two. A small number of Jews remained in the land for generations after; however, as a collective this diaspora would last until 1882. We'll get to that later.

The Roman Empire ruled the land from around 63 BC to 324 AD and is responsible for some of the most astonishing architectural structures, which, like much of the city of Rome itself, are still standing in all their glory. This is when Herod the Great ruled and built, among other cities, the above-mentioned Caesarea, as well as the series of aqueducts my ex-husband admired. He also built the stunning fortress of Masada, a multilevel palace located on a mountain in the middle of bum-F nowhere in the Judean desert, where you can still find the remains of glorious colorful floor mosaics and some sophisticated ancient floor-heated saunas and spas. This was also the site of yet another failed Jewish rebellion and an eerie mass suicide, according to historian Josephus Flavius.

It's around this time that a poor and enlightened Jewish man from Nazareth started roaming the land, preaching peace, love, humility, and forgiveness. He was indeed ahead of his time.

After the Romans came the Byzantine period (approximately AD 324–638), wherein Emperor Constantine converted the entire Roman Empire to Christianity and his mom, Helena, built the Church of the Holy Sepulcher in Jerusalem. Constantine and his successor, Justinian the First, also did not vibe with the Jews being Jewish and tried to force mass conversions. The Jews at the time suffered greatly, but since I am here and still a Jew, I must assume that the Romans' long game did not work out too well.

Around the year AD 638, six years after the death of the Prophet Muhammad ﷺ, his heirs Abu-Bakar and Omar ibn al-Khattab started their conquests west and invaded the land. These waves of Muslim conquests created the Muslim Empire, or the Caliphate, from AD 638 to 1099. During this time, the rulers, or the caliphs, divided their land into regions, and called the southern side of Israel from about Jaffa down "the region of Philistine," based on the Roman regional names Palaestina Prima and Palaestina Secunda.

After years of living under oppressive Byzantine rulers, the Jewish population was hoping to be better treated by the coming Caliphate. While the Muslim leaders didn't slaughter the Jews or force them to convert, they did relegate Jews and Christians to second-class citizens, referred to as dhimmis, which literally means "protected persons." These dhimmis were allowed to self-govern, but they faced various social restrictions (like they couldn't ride camels or horses), judicial limitations (they couldn't testify in court against Muslims), zoning laws (their houses had to be lower than their neighbors'), and taxes. At a time when much of the ancient world was so freaking violent, walking your horse or paying a high tax was not that bad for conquered people, but still, it wasn't pleasant.

Next came the Crusaders, who controlled the land from 1099 to 1260. True to their name and reputation, they slaughtered any non-Christian who stood in their way, took over the land, and renamed Jerusalem "The Kingdom of Jerusalem." Unlike the Muslims, they forced the local population to convert or, you know, die. They suffered a brief loss to An-Nasir Salah ad-Din Yusuf, better known as Saladin, when he conquered Jerusalem in 1187, only to rise again under the British-French prince, Crusader, and warrior Richard the Lionheart in 1191.

Seventy years later came the Mamluks, a nation of mixed-origin slaves from the Balkans, Georgia, Egypt, Turkey, and many other places that don't exist today. The Mamluks converted to Islam and controlled the land from around 1260 until 1517.

In 1517, the place was invaded by the Turkish Sultan Salim, who made it a part of the Ottoman Empire, where it remained until 1917, after the First World War, when the Brits took over the empire-building game. The British Mandate of Palestine initially spanned from the borders of the modern state of Israel all the way east, including the Emirates of East Jordan, to the borders of the French Mandate of Syria and Iraq in the northeast and the Hejaz desert (present day Saudi Arabia) in the south. In 1921 the British Mandate divided the land at the Jordan River, and Transjordan (later Jordan) was created. The British Mandate borders then closely resembled Israel's borders today, and it was called "Palestina EY," the Hebrew initials for the land of Israel. The country was under British law, ruled by a high commissioner reporting to the secretary of state for the colonies in the British government.

That British Mandate wound down after World War II, when on November 29, 1947, fresh out of the Holocaust, the United Nations granted the Jews their land back and allowed for the establishment of modern-day Israel.[6]

Which brings us to 1948, the reestablishment of the modern state of Israel.

INDIGENOUSNESS

Phew! We just went through over twenty-five hundred years of history at rapid speed. That wasn't too bad, I hope? The importance of having this historical recap stems from another argument I have heard many times: indigenous rights. This topic is highly important and needs to be addressed; however, it is misunderstood or manipulated in the context of Israel. There is no doubt, whether you are a follower of any religious text or a humanist, that Israel is the ancestral land of the Jewish people. There are simply too many opposing facts for anyone to disclaim this, so any attempt to do so should be highly questionable. This is a crucial point to keep in mind when having a discussion regarding the region, so I wanted to make sure this point was crystal clear.

Unfortunately, many supporters of indigenous peoples' rights across the world promote an anti-Israel agenda. But the only people who can date their inhabitance of the land back twenty-five hundred years and more are the Jews (and, perhaps, the Canaanites, may they rest in peace). Regardless of your politics, and no matter how you feel about everything to follow, hard evidence supports the fact that the Jewish people are indigenous to the land of Israel.

This may be a tough fact to swallow, but it is a fact nonetheless, so just take a deep breath and down a shot of tequila, if you must. Ready? Here goes. Over the course of recorded history, the land of Israel was a lot of things, but it was never a sovereign Palestine. There was never a state called Palestine, not there, not anywhere else on the planet. This doesn't mean there shouldn't *be* a Palestine, but as of now, there just hasn't been. There has only ever been one sovereign state on that particular land, and the only indigenous people to ever actually rule that sovereign state are the Jews.

(To recap: before the modern-day establishment of the State of Israel, the land passed from the Kingdom of Israel to the Persians, the Greeks, the House of Hasmoneans [Hello, Hanukkah!], the Romans, the Byzantines, the Muslims, the Crusaders, the Mamluks, the Ottomans, and the Brits.)

You would simply be factually incorrect to say that the land was ever an exclusively Palestinian state. In fact, no other nation that has controlled this land, excluding the Turks, the Jews, and the Brits (and possibly the Romans and the Greeks—depending on how you define things), is even around! All of them are gone—or ancient history!

This point is particularly important in the recent debate, since so many people like to say stuff like "Israel has to give that land back!" To them I would like to say: "Give it back to whom, exactly? The Mamluks?"

CHAPTER THREE

A BRIEF HISTORY OF THE MIDDLE EAST IN THE LAST CENTURY

AND WHAT A MESS IT WAS BEFORE ISRAEL EVEN GOT THERE

BURN, BABY, BURN

A couple of years ago I decided to go to Burning Man for the first time. If you haven't been or seen the pictures, here's the general vibe: Burning Man is an annual event held at a specifically erected town called Black Rock City in Northern Nevada, on a dried-up lakebed called the Playa. Once a year for a week, some eighty thousand or so people practice new ways of society building, artistic creation, self-expression, and other radical social experiments. They survive together, through scorching hot days and freezing cold nights, persisting through whiteout sandstorms and celebrating on expanses of white, fine, talcum powder–like sand that, in a certain light, looks just like the surface of the moon.

While this may sound idyllic or romantic to some people, to me it sounded terrifying. First, because I am not a natural born "Burner." I am more of a geek than a party girl, and the thought of not showering for a week makes me want to grab a tub of Lysol and run a double load of laundry. Second, I didn't know what to wear.

Burning Man is as much about the costumes as it is about societal experimentation, and dressing up is yet another form of radical self-expression. And it shows. The outfits at Burning Man are jaw-dropping. Think *Mad Max* meets *Moulin Rouge*, and you get the picture.[1]

But still, something pulled me toward it, and before I knew it I'd registered. In preparation, I spent hours in thrift stores, researched ideas online, and spoke to my actual Burner friends. Still, I couldn't zero in on what I wanted to wear—or, rather, who I wanted to *be*—in Burning Man.

After days of anxiously trying to coordinate my costumes with the quicksilver Playa weather, something clicked, and I realized that Northern Nevada was nothing more than a desert. It's where I'm from. It's what I know! I looked at my sequins and tulle, and I asked myself just one question: "What would Lawrence do?"

Thomas Edward Lawrence, better known as Lawrence of Arabia, was born in 1888 in Tremadog, Wales. From a very young age, Lawrence knew he was different. He was smart and observant and already interested in archaeology at age fifteen. After graduating from the University of Oxford with a degree in history (with a focus on Crusader castles), he traveled around the Middle East on archaeological excavations.

A Brit, Lawrence was used to chilly temperatures, yet he was able to handle the desert heat, which often reached well above 110 degrees. How? you may ask. Because he had an extraordinary command of appropriate fashion choices. Yes, I'm talking about those dramatic, long, white robes and statement-piece gold crowns. Lawrence learned from the Bedouins that in order to maintain a cool body temperature in the blazing heat, he needed to *cover up*, not *strip down*.

Now, why am I telling you about Lawrence at all? Well, I believe that in order to understand anything about the Middle East as we know it today, one may not need detailed insight into the Mamluks, but one does need to have a good grip on World War I, regional colonialism, and the treaties and fallout thereafter—a trifecta that some people call the original sin.

In this chapter, we'll head back to the early 1900s, where we'll follow my hero T. E. Lawrence—a legendary archaeologist, writer, historian, diplomat, cartographer, fashion icon, and brilliant military strategist—who led the Arab Revolt in World War I, which played a major role in the victory of the Triple Entente (Britain, France, and Russia) and forever changed the course of Middle Eastern history.

THE MAKING OF A WAR, THE MAKING OF A HERO

After graduating from Oxford University in 1911, Lawrence got a job at the British Museum, on an archaeological expedition to the northern Syrian site of Carchemish, which was under Ottoman control. As only one of two Westerners on the site, he didn't simply dig into the ground but also into the traditions, lives, and culture of the locals. He became fluent in Arabic and would often visit his fellow workers in their homes, learning the nuances of Arab life and unknowingly preparing himself for his extraordinary future.

Lawrence loved the Middle East so much that he would stay in Syria even after the digs closed for the summer and his archaeology boss and mentor Leonard Woolley returned to England. Having immersed himself in the lives of the locals, he became something of a local himself, and ultimately a trusted arbitrator of tribal disputes and an expert in Kurdish relations.

During this period of time, Lawrence met Salim Ahmed, known as Dahoum, a fourteen-year-old water boy who turned into his closest companion. Together, the two traveled all over the region and all the way to Oxford and back.

Lawrence was still digging in Carchemish when the "British Museum" recruited him for a new job: a mission dedicated to "tracing Moses and the Jews through Sinai" to search the Negev desert for a mythical land referred to in the Bible as the Wilderness of Zion. I use quotation marks because while the British Museum did indeed recruit Lawrence, under the Palestine Exploration Fund, they were under orders from the British military. These guys couldn't have cared less about the Bible. What they cared about was getting their hands on updated maps of the region.

At the time, the entire Middle East was divided between colonial Europe and the Ottoman Empire. Egypt and Sudan were under British control; Algeria, Morocco, and Tunisia were French; Libya was Italian; and all the land from Turkey to Syria to way down south of Yemen was Ottoman. Some of the region was free—aka "under European influence" rather than direct rule—but these areas weren't states as we know them today but rather conglomerates of local Arab tribes.

Every controlling power was watching its back, and by 1914, as tensions were ratcheting up to World War I, it wasn't clear who would side with whom. Great Britain, France, and Russia were on one team, and Austria-Hungary and Germany were on another. No one knew if the Ottomans would take a knee or suit up. It was a time of great uncertainty. And as the major powers hunkered down to prepare for the war to end all wars, the British military recruited a small, elite team to map out the Negev desert.

Huh??? Why, on the brink of a world war, did the Brits care so much about this chunk of empty land? Three words: the Suez Canal. This shy little waterway might not look like much, but it was the single body of water that directly connected the Mediterranean Sea to the Red Sea. Meaning it was the single thing that connected the

East to the West. Meaning it was the single thing that connected the British Empire to its most important colony—India. This thumbnail of water held the key to the British economy. Which is why Lawrence was recruited to map out all the surrounding land, in case the Ottomans teamed up with Austria-Hungary and Germany and staged a ground attack.

Lawrence turned in his brilliant maps, and not a minute too soon. By August of that year, the Ottomans had secretly chosen Germany's side, and by October they had officially joined in the war, and Lawrence joined the British Army.

World War I started by a terrible accident. Due to colonial disputes in exotic lands and centuries-old somewhat ego-driven grievances, Europe was entangled in a web of interlocking allegiances and arguments that were knottier than my hair after an interval class at the gym. The match that would light this powder keg was struck on the 28th of June 1914 when Gavrilo Princip, a young Serb, shot and killed Austro-Hungarian heir Archduke Franz Ferdinand. Serbia and Austria moved to declare war on each other, and in a series of miserable moves, the rest of Europe followed.

With the fighting in full swing, the British Army stationed Lawrence in their new Arab Intelligence Unit in Cairo. There he met the Amir of Mecca's son, Prince Faisal, and the two men developed an unlikely friendship. Faisal's tribesmen were already trying to rebel against the Turks, mounting ill-fated attacks on the Ottoman Army. These Arab tribesmen were fierce and keen warriors; however, they were painfully disorganized and poorly disciplined. Though they were in no way, shape, or form a military, Lawrence saw the potential in these fearless men and took it upon himself to unite the people to a common cause.

Imagine, if you would, this five-foot-five-inch blond-haired, blue-eyed, highly educated, and somewhat eccentric British man. Now imagine him throwing on a white Arab robe, jumping on a camel, and disappearing into the desert for weeks at a time. Lawrence didn't ask for orders from the British Army. He didn't even ask for permission, nor did he inform his commander, General Allenby, of his military plans. His philosophy was very Silicon Valley: innovate first, apologize later.

Lawrence wasn't a white savior. He used his love and knowledge of Arab culture, language, and traditions to inspire thousands of dispersed tribes to fight together as one unit alongside their king, Faisal, against the Turks. He noted his men's strengths and weaknesses and trained the fighters in a new regional military technique: guerilla warfare. He led attacks on the Turkish railroad system, which was carrying supplies and food from Damascus to Medina, and then ordered his fighters to retreat to the mountains. He got to know the desert terrain so well, he led his men to the shores of the Red Sea and executed a stunning attack on the all-important tiny town of Aqaba. Instead of attacking the city from the water, which is what the Turkish military was expecting, he led a ragtag group of fifty-five hundred camel-riding tribesmen through thousands of miles of the Nafud mountainous desert, which was considered impassible, and attacked and conquered Aqaba from the other side—the desert side. Only after taking over Aqaba and then traveling throughout the Sinai Peninsula did Lawrence contact the British military to say: "By the way, I got you one of the most important points in the region. You're welcome." Those images of Lawrence charging ahead on his camel, followed by thousands of Arab tribesmen, swords drawn, his white robe flapping behind him in the desert wind, are legendary.[2]

The tribes put their lives on the line to follow Lawrence and Faisal, and Lawrence returned the honor. In exchange for revolting against the Turks, all the Arabs asked for was—what else?—independence. The British government agreed (the Hussain-McMahon Correspondence), only to go behind everyone's back and negotiate a secret agreement with the French to divide the whole Middle East between themselves (the Sykes-Picot Agreement), with a vague promise to Russia for "some" influence over Egypt once the war was won, before they made a third commitment to the Jews, just to keep it interesting.

This third commitment came about in 1917, a month before Great Britain captured Jerusalem from the Ottoman Army. On November 2, 1917, the Brits issued the Balfour Declaration, promising to reestablish an independent "national home for the Jewish people" in the backwater former Ottoman province of Palestine.

That war and its fallout, with the conflicting agreements, agendas, and drawings of new borders, sums up the mess the region was experiencing years before Israel was even around.

SOWING THE SEEDS OF UGH

The following year, on November 11, 1918, World War I ended in a victory for the Allies! And a victory for the Arabs! And a victory for the Jews! Until the secret dealings between the English and the French (aka the Sykes-Picot Agreement) came to light.

Lawrence was livid. He had been living with the Arabs for nearly a decade and had worked tirelessly to help them achieve their political ambitions. He was invited to be an advisor to the British delegation at the postwar Paris Peace Conference, but he really attended in order to be an escort and translator for his friend and cofighter Prince Faisal.

The two men were walking around the gardens of Versailles in traditional Arab robes and headgear, causing quite a stir. The Europeans looked down their noses and accused Lawrence of having conflicting agendas, officially working for the British government but really working for the Arabs. And they were right. Lawrence helped Faisal write a speech lobbying for Arab independence, translated it to English, and, on the fly, translated it to French as well.

In a mind-blowing twist, Faisal sought not only Arab independence, but also *Jewish independence*—thanks, in part, to his good pal Lawrence. T.E. was a rare breed at the time. He was both sympathetic to the Arab desire for independence and a passionate supporter of the Jews returning to their homeland. During his time in the Middle East, he'd met many Jews who had bought land from local Arabs, Turks, or Christians, and he loved what he saw. He appreciated their new agricultural villages and in a letter from 1909 wrote: "The sooner the Jews farm it all the better: Their colonies are bright spots in a desert."[3]

And he didn't just write about it; he acted on it as well. Lawrence worked to connect the Jews and Arabs and worked as a facilitator and a translator in several meetings between Prince Faisal and the leader of the Zionist movement (and later, Israel's first president), Dr. Chaim Weizmann. Those meetings went superbly well. The two men hit it off, and on January 3, 1919, the parties signed a historic agreement acknowledging that both peoples should have sovereignty: the Arabs in the Hejaz and Syria, and the Jews in their ancestral land of Israel.

On March 1, 1919, while attending the Paris Peace Conference, Amir Faisal wrote Dr. Weizmann the following:

> We Arabs, especially the educated among us, look with the deepest sympathy on the Zionist movement. . . . We are working together for a reformed and revived Near East, and our two movements complete one another. . . . The Jewish movement . . . is national, and not imperialist: our movement is national and not imperialist, and there is room in Syria for us both. Indeed I think that neither can be a real success without the other. . . . I look forward, and my people with me look forward to a future in which we will help you and you will help us, so that the countries in which we are mutually interested may once again take their place in the community of the civilized peoples of the world."[4]

This, I remind you, is a letter from the most prominent Arab leader of the time to one of the most important Jewish leaders of the time. Lawrence understood that the Jews belonged to the land, and so did Faisal. Lawrence also understood that the West should give the Arabs self-determination, and he was right about that, too. Unfortunately, the European powers did not agree, and no number of letters, agreements, or speeches convinced them otherwise.

By the end of the Paris Peace Conference, Faisal may have left with a nice cup of tea and a thank-you for fighting on behalf of the Crown, but he certainly did not get any independence for his people. Instead, the Allied forces divided up the former Ottoman Empire into new and invented states based on colonial interests rather than natural borders, tribal affiliation, family connections, or a desire for self-determination. A gentlemanly move, indeed. The Al Saud family got Saudi Arabia (no one knew there was *that* much oil there at the time). France got Syria. The British created "Transjordan" because it was near the Jordan River and they couldn't be bothered to come up with a better name. They also turned a tiny sliver of the region—including parts of the former Kingdom of Israel and the Ottoman province of Palestine—into the British Mandate of Palestina EY, with a promise to the League of Nations (the precursor of the UN) to sometime in the future "secure the establishment of the Jewish national home."[5]

The pre-nationalistic, prewar Middle East was not divided into counties or borders as we understand them today. It was an ancient web of tribal affiliations, religions, and ethnic groups that operated in a huge open region, controlled mostly by the Ottomans. The British and French made up a bunch of countries in the region with the Sykes-Picot Agreement, but it's not like they *ignored* prewar borders, because there were relatively few borders to ignore. Most of the region had been part of the Ottoman Empire or was overseen by another colonial power. Any other borders that did exist before the war may have been loosely defined by a mountain range or a lake, but loyalty was mostly to a family clan, to a Hamula. While borders didn't exist as we know them today, the constellations of families and tribes that did exist were critically important, and each had its own set of allegiances and disputes with other families and tribes, and they were, of course, all ignored. So now just imagine the Brits and French walking into a room carrying a piece of paper with a freshly inked agreement, announcing to a group of Kurds and Sunni and Shiite Arabs: "Congratulations, you are all now Iraq!"

As you can see, Arabs and Jews alike were lied to and seriously screwed by the Sykes-Picot Agreement. The Jews didn't get Israel, the Arabs didn't get anything, and the whole region became a complete disaster—a disaster caused by colonial forces meeting a desert land occupied by villages, little towns, bigger towns, and many camel-riding, tent-dwelling nomadic tribes with loyalty to their ancient traditions.

At this point you might be thinking: Where was America?

THE FIRST KARDASHIAN

It was April 6, 1917, when US president Woodrow Wilson reluctantly declared war on Germany, and the United States entered World War I. The president did not want to get involved, and he held firm for a couple of years; however, Germany's attempt to help Mexico gain lost lands from the Mexican-American War, and German attacks on ships headed to and from the US in the Atlantic Ocean, forced Wilson to join in on the side of the Allies. The problem was, US public opinion was still on the fence about committing to a potentially costly and devastating war in a land far, far away. Wilson knew that in order to convince the American people, he needed to tell a good story. To achieve this goal, the government enlisted a super-talented young journalist by the name of Lowell Thomas to go to the front line and find stories that would "drum up Americans' enthusiasm for the war and for their new allies,"[6] a questionable journalistic method, but one that was not unheard-of at the time (or today, really).

So off Thomas went. He first traveled to France, then to Italy, but found nothing inspiring in the grim quagmire of the European trenches. Shortly after the British captured Jerusalem, Thomas arrived to check it out. On one most auspicious morning, as he was walking down the streets of the Old City, Thomas saw a "blue-eyed, fair-haired fellow wandering about the bazaars wearing the curved sword of a prince."[7]

Always the storyteller, Thomas understood immediately that he had stumbled upon someone extraordinary. That little man, Lawrence, was introduced to him by Jerusalem governor Sir Ronald Storrs as "the uncrowned king of Arabia."[8]

The title stuck. Thomas had his photographer Harry Chase immediately take pictures of Lawrence on Storrs's office balcony in Jerusalem, and shortly after, a film crew went to capture Lawrence in action.

Thomas spent only about a month with Lawrence in the desert; however, he took hundreds of pictures and filmed hours upon hours of reel. When he came back to the US after the war, Thomas edited the footage into the most cutting-edge live-stage multimedia show, called *With Lawrence in Arabia*. The show was one of the first narrated documentaries ever produced. Thomas himself stood onstage and presented the story as the footage played on a screen behind him, perfectly timed to an original *Arabian Nights*–style score. *With Lawrence in Arabia* opened in New York but soon crossed the pond to London, playing everywhere from Madison Square Garden to Covent Garden and Albert Hall. The show became a massive hit, eventually playing to over three million people worldwide. The footage is breathtaking, even by today's standards, and it received rave reviews at the time. As *Lloyd's Weekly* wrote: "During the lifetime of the present generation there has been nothing in London so completely engrossing as this."[9]

The images of the small-in-size, huge-in-charisma, blond-haired, blue-eyed Lawrence, in his gold crown and flaring white robe, charging ahead on his camel to lead thousands through the vast vistas of the Arabian desert, set the world on fire. T. E. Lawrence, now known worldwide as Lawrence of Arabia, was the first person in the world to become an international superstar in his lifetime, based on *himself*. He became the world's first real-life star, the first . . . reality star. The first Kardashian.

Lawrence had a love-hate relationship with his fame, and by most accounts wasn't too Kris Jenner-y about the whole thing. Lowell Thomas, however, claimed that Lawrence "had a genius for backing into the limelight."[10] Either way: what a rock star. Lawrence died in a motorcycle accident at forty-six years of age. His funeral was attended by the giants of history, including Winston Churchill, who said he was "one of the greatest beings alive in this time."

A hundred years later, I went to Burning Man.

As soon as it dawned on me that the Playa was nothing more than the Hejaz desert, I knew exactly not just what I wanted to wear but who I wanted to be. While everyone else pranced around practically naked, I ditched my feathers and wrapped myself in long, white cotton cloths—body, face, and all—and on top of my head I placed a hand-made golden rope inspired by the Arab rope crown, the agal. As one of the only covered-up girls in the entire festival, I got a lot of attention, and when asked about my costume, I shared my obsession with Lawrence of Arabia. Soon I got my Playa name: Noa of Arabia. I've kept it ever since.

In a final tribute to Lawrence, I will close this chapter with his own words. In an article he wrote in September 1920 titled "The Changing East," Lawrence says:

"The Jewish experiment is in another class. It is a conscious effort, on the part of the least European people in Europe, to make head against the drift of the ages, and return once more to the Orient *from which they came* [author's emphasis]."[11]

Lawrence knew that the Jews came from that land. They weren't colonialist invaders. They were idealistic, entrepreneurial—and they had no other choice.

They were being pushed out of the Old World and they had to rebuild their new-old country, or else.

My grandparents and great-grandparents were among them.

CHAPTER FOUR

A BRIEF HISTORY OF ZIONISM

AND WHY IT STILL MATTERS

I COME FROM A STRONG STOCK

On a warm July night in 1918, in a small town called Yekaterinburg, about 1,111 miles east of Moscow, Russia, in the basement of a grand and otherwise lovely house, the last tsar of Russia Nicholas II; his wife, Tsarina Alexandra; their four daughters; and their sickly young son were shot from close range by a bunch of Bolsheviks. My grandmother told me that story as a child. How the last of the Romanov girls were covered in concealed diamonds that were sewn into their undergarments, a chilling testament to both their wealth and the futile hope they held all the way up to the bitter end to be freed from their captors. Those diamonds caused the final scene to become particularly gruesome. The girls were basically wearing gold-, diamond-, emerald-, and pearl-encrusted life vests, which made the Bolsheviks' bullets bounce off of their bodies and fly onto the walls, and so the men had to shoot them over and over and over again. My grandmother was an eleven-year-old child in Russia when that bloodbath occurred.

In a nutshell, the Romanov dynasty ruled Russia with an iron fist for a little over three hundred years, and as opposed to, for example, the British royal family, they did not get smart and pivot with the changing currents of history. Thus, instead of building an empire, becoming a colonial superpower, and then understanding when to politely withdraw, the dynasty ended in that basement, in a scene worthy of a Tarantino remake. And so began the reign of the Bolsheviks.

The Bolsheviks had a fabulous idea, catastrophically executed. They were Marxists who preached a classless society where power was shared by all the people, everyone was equal, each citizen was nothing but a common worker working for the greater good of the nation and dedicated to simple manual labor, with no personal ambitions whatsoever. They believed, at least at the beginning, that they were creating a utopia that would take over the world. Coming out of hundreds of years of harsh monarchy, it seemed magical to the people, including my young grandmother. As she wrote in her diary:

> There is much uproar among us young adults, the proud citizens of tomorrow, citizens of a free land. A land which we must build anew, from the ground up, a land where the possibilities for personal growth are so vast! The spring of us youth on the backdrop of the spring of this huge land, which have broken away from the chains of slavery.

To translate her prematurely mature prose into less dramatic language, she was really excited. Here was this people's revolution, the promise of cosmopolitan socialism, where *everyone* was equal, and each comrade was to contribute equally to build this great equal society, Mother Russia. Well, that all sounded great—unless, of course, you were a Jew.

My beloved grandmother Fania Artzi, or as I called her *safta* Fania (Hebrew for Grandmother Fania), was born to the Tomashov family, in Bobruisk, which was at the time a part of "White" Russia and is now Belarus. The town was small, about seventy thousand people, and about 70 percent of the population was Jewish. The Jewish children of Bobruisk, like many Russian people, were drunk with socialistic idealism. Everyone believed in the revolution and rushed to the Komsomol, the youth division of the Communist Party, to be a part of this brave new world. But it wasn't long before my grandmother and her friends realized that the revolution was not meant for them. When the Belarusian students asked to learn the Belarusian language, they were granted that wish. However, when a young Jewish boy from her school asked to be taught the Hebrew language, he was branded a counterrevolutionist and was exiled to Siberia. Those Bolsheviks did not mess around.

My grandmother described that event, that kid being sent to Siberia, as a turning point. Why, she and her friends wondered, was this supposedly "free" republic trying to break down the Jews? Antisemitism had been a systemic hot ticket in Russia for generations, but they all believed that the revolution had finally raised the flag of equality. However, that flag quickly came down. My grandmother and her buddies started looking for a place where it was safe to be Jewish *and* live by the ideals of equality and simplicity.

In 1924 my grandmother got her hands on a pamphlet called *Hahalootz*, or *The Pioneer*. The pioneer movement was created a few years prior by a Jewish-Russian idealist named Joseph Trumpeldor. Trumpeldor, a decorated Russian military war hero and former POW in Japan, was describing exactly what my grandmother was looking for: a new movement to rebuild the old homeland based on communal ideas, shared living, shared ownership of all personal possessions, and self-sufficiency. And a safe place for the Jews, where they can finally be liberated. This was the ticket! A movement that allowed her to be Jewish *and* a socialist! She promptly set her sights on becoming a pioneer.

There was only one problem. She was fifteen years old. The movement did not accept anyone under the age of eighteen, so my entrepreneurial grandmother decided to do the rational thing and start an offshoot of that group called the Young Pioneer. This was a dangerous move. In Bolshevik Russia, being a part of any self-identifying group was a one-way ticket to a permanent holiday in the Siberian wilderness. In order to join that secretive group and start the young offshoot, my safta had to go through grueling tests and examinations to prove to the older members she was not a "provocateur," a spy working for the Bolsheviks. In her diaries my grandmother describes a film noir–esque scene in which her "audition" was to take place:

> I remember the day the test was to be taken, in which the negotiations for joining were executed. It was a dark and stormy night, white and wintery. Winds and snow were falling outside as the door opened and comrade D.S. called me in. Despite having prepared myself for that meeting for a while, I walked behind him as my heart pulsed fiercely, my body tensed towards that conversation, which will determine the rest of my life. He did not speak much, only presented two questions, which set my heart at a storm only matched by the fierce storm raging outside in all her vicious glory. The two questions were: A. How do I imagine the building of the country? Will it be built by money and intellectual currency, meaning will we be the managers and the simple workers will be the Arabs? Or by simple labor of the Jews themselves? And B. Am I willing to personally abandon the continuation of my high education and the "career" expected of me, and come to Israel to be a simple worker in any manual labor which will be required of me?

My fifteen-year-old grandmother passed the test, and the Young Pioneer was created, in total secrecy.[1] It was a small group of five to six kids from her school who would get together on dark nights and go to the forests near the town to educate themselves and share their vision for rebuilding their ancestral land. They had other trusted friends guard those meetings, protecting them from "the evil eye of the Russian detectives." They scoured the black market for banned European writers such as Pinsker and Borochov, and took upon themselves the task of studying the reemerging Hebrew language. The language they spoke at home was, naturally, Russian. Hebrew was being revived for a daily use, after being somewhat dormant and used for two millennia only by biblical scholars and during religious rituals. Those kids joined the effort to revive their language, study it, modernize it, and use it exclusively. They would meet at night, read, learn, practice sports. They also taught themselves how to grow vegetables, philosophizing and formulating their dreams of the new land hunched over a bed of onions.

In 1924, when safta Fania was seventeen years old, a provocateur was discovered among their group. He gave the authorities a list of the names of the group's participants, and the Bolshevik police searched all members' homes; all but a few were exiled to labor camps in Siberia. My grandmother survived the search, and she tells the following story:

> I was the one entrusted with keeping communications with the neighboring towns. I would get letters and pass the information on to our group. One day I got a letter. It was known that when we get a letter, we must read it and destroy it immediately, however for some reason I wanted to show the letter to my friends so I kept it at home. That letter was with me when the GPU [the "State Political Directorate," or the intelligence service and secret police of the Russian Soviet Federation So-

cialist Republic] came in for the search. It was wintertime and a snowstorm was raging outside. The windows in Russia were double-sided, one could not open them, and the restrooms were placed outside the house. What could I have done when I had the letter right there with me? If I rip it, they will find the pieces, the double windows cannot be opened and the toilets are outside so I can't throw it away. If they find the letter, I will get sent to Siberia immediately and without a trial. The year was 1924 and we have been trained on how to act in a case like that. The instruction was to eat the letter. I can still taste the paper in my mouth. They turned the house upside down, turned the beds inside out, looked everywhere and couldn't find the letter. That Nathan told them I was in charge of communications and would have letters at home but when they couldn't find them, they had to let me go. They said: "We will come again and we will find you." I didn't wait any longer and I ran away.

Shortly after, my safta's family left Russia penniless and embarked on a boat, infested with rodents and thieves, from Odessa to the promised land.

What they discovered there was nothing short of a disaster. My grandmother arrived in Jaffa in 1925. Their ship docked far from shore, and they were brought to land by small boats with lots of noise and grand confusion. As they entered the old city, they were immediately met with an Arab funeral and a Jewish "Adloyada" (Purim carnival celebration). The small and ancient Jaffa was a mess—it was crumbling, dirty, and dangerous. Built into a harsh and barren landscape, the rest of the country did not look any better, and her challenges did not stop. It was a far cry from the idealistic dream she and her friends had weaved in the woods outside Bobruisk.

But what exactly was that idealistic spell my grandmother came under as a teen that caused her to risk her life? What was this malarkey that was suddenly swelling through Europe and the rest of the world, magically sweeping young Jews off their feet? It was called *Zionism*, and it would eventually reach a Malcolm Gladwell–level of tipping point.

GOOD IDEAS ARE ALWAYS CRAZY, UNTIL THEY'RE NOT

There has been a lot of chatter about Zionism recently and even more talk about anti-Zionism. Often, one or the other is used as an argument for or against US, Israeli, or US-Israeli policies. After thousands of conversations with highly educated people, I have come to realize that most don't know what this word actually means, or when and why it came to be. That's what we're here for!

In light of the rise in antisemitism in the United Kingdom at the time of the Labor Party's five-year leadership under Jeremy Corbyn, Jonathan Freedland wrote a piece in the *Guardian* titled: "Jews Are the Canary in the Coalmine." This expression dates back to the early 1900s, when coal miners would take canaries down into the tunnels with them as real-life carbon monoxide detectors. If the gas levels killed the canaries, the miners had early warning to abandon the tunnels ASAP. Freedland wrote:

"When a society turns on its Jews it is usually a sign of a wider ill-health. Hasn't history shown us that racism never stays confined to mere 'pockets.' Once the virus is inside, it does not rest until it has infected the entire body."[2]

As I mentioned before, antisemitism did not begin with the Bolshevik Revolution and the birth of my grandmother in 1907. In Russia, antisemitism had been on the rise since 1791, when Catherine the Great, intending to finish the job her predecessor Empress Elizabeth started, created the Pale of Settlement, forcing all the Jews in the Russian Empire to live in segregated areas along the empire's border. She continued by removing citizenship from Jews, enforcing double taxation and other discriminatory laws, and spreading propaganda that Jews were the ultimate evil in that oh-so-benevolent regime.

Things went south from one heir to the next and reached horrific proportions when, in 1827, Catherine's grandson Nicholas I (fondly known at the time as the Russian Haman) enacted a mandatory draft, conscripting Jewish kids as young as twelve for up to twenty-five years of service. Yes, those numbers are correct: twelve years old and twenty-five years of service. The horror this created in Jewish communities is unfathomable. But the worst was still to come. There were organized pogroms and murders starting from around 1821 that intensified ("The Storms in the South") until the 1881 assassination of Tsar Alexander II, when the government gladly used this murder as an excuse to suppress human rights and target "agents or foreign influence," aka Jews.

In 1903 all that hatred exploded with one of the first pieces of viral fake news, called *The Protocols of the Elders of Zion*. This document, created by the tsar's secret police force,[3] made the fantastical claim that the Jews were part of a global conspiracy to take over the world. At the time, there were about 10.6 million Jews in the world compared to a population of 1.6 billion. In other words, Jews were .6 percent of the global population, and they were highly restricted, discriminated against, and persecuted. How would a global takeover even work? This document was so fake, I can't believe I have to write about it today, but it's still held up by conspiracy theorists worldwide! Even Henry Ford, famous American industrialist known for creating the game-changing Ford assembly line, used *The Protocols of the Elders of Zion* as the basis for a series of articles he published starting May 22, 1920 (and continuing for years!), called "The International Jew: The World's Problem," in his newspaper, the *Dearborn Independent*.[4] So there we are. At the turn of the century, *The Protocols of the Elders of*

Zion became an instant bestseller, leading to the massacre and exile of hundreds of thousands of Jews.

The Jewish population needed a lifeboat. Cue the Zionist movement.

The Zionist movement emerged against the backdrop of a general intellectual awakening that was sweeping over Europe. The Age of Enlightenment in the 1700s and the Spring of Nations in the mid-1800s saw democratic and liberal revolutions and unrest in almost every country. Citizens everywhere demanded more power to the people. They also started giving more weight to science and logic rather than religious or monarchal creed. All these revolutions inspired a Jewish Enlightenment as well, in which Jewish scholars and philosophers promoted secularism, liberalism, and general, not only biblical, education.

At the time, Zionism seemed crazy revolutionary, but the Jews had been talking about reestablishing their homeland for two millennia. Each year on Passover, as we read the Haggadah, we tell, yet again, the story of the Jewish exodus from Egypt and complete the saga by saying: "Next year in Jerusalem." This had been going on for many centuries, so the epigenetic memory of the homeland has always been potent, to say the least. But it was more of a theoretical concept, a dream. The thought of *actually* returning to Israel, to reestablish an *actual* country, became a necessity with the rising tides of antisemitism. It originally started with dudes like Rabbi Alkalai of Serbia, who wrote a detailed plan to rebuild the Jewish homeland in Israel back in 1843. Moshe Hess's 1862 book *Rome and Jerusalem* also advocates for the reestablishment of a Jewish state that would be agriculturally based in order to "redeem the soil." The thought of a Jewish refuge emerged even in the United States, when in 1825 Mordecai Manuel Noah, an American Jew from Philadelphia, came up with the idea of carving a land in the budding USA to serve as a Jewish state, home for the Jews. He bought land in Grand Island, New York, and named that imaginary Jewish refuge of his "Ararat." Gulp. That idea clearly did not catch on, and Noah later conceded that the Jews should just, you know, go back to where they belong: Israel.

This, my friends, is the origin of Zionism. The necessity for Jewish safety and self-determination in their ancestral home, a movement of Jewish liberation. Not that complicated.

The word *Zionism* comes from one of the seventy biblical words used to describe Jerusalem—Zion. In fact, Jerusalem is the city's first name; Zion is her second. She has sixty-eight other names, but we don't need to get into all of them now. The term *Zionism* was coined by writer and journalist Nathan Birnbaum in 1890 and was cemented into history in 1896 by Theodor Herzl, the mad scientist behind the invention of the modern State of Israel, the man who turned this crazy idea into reality.

Theodor Benjamin Ze'ev Herzl was born in 1860 to a liberal and successful German-speaking family in Budapest, Hungary. Theo's family took part in the Jewish Enlightenment, and as such he was given a proper secular education and was an avid reader, with a special affinity for Goethe and Shakespeare.

Theo wasn't so hot on his Jewishness at first, and was way more interested in assimilating into European culture. He completed his doctorate in law and worked as a lawyer for a short period of time before giving up his profession in order to devote himself to his true passion: writing. He wrote a few plays, some of which actually became successful, but this is not what would send him on a foray into the pages of history.

Into his young adulthood, Herzl considered himself a "cultural Jew." He pooh-poohed the spiritual underpinnings of Jewishness and the connection to peoplehood, and believed that through education and immersion one could shake off inherited Jewish characteristics. He believed, like so many throughout history mistakenly believed, that if Jews could assimilate enough, antisemitism would cease to exist.

His move to Paris radically changed his opinion. He joined a Viennese newspaper as the Paris correspondent and, shortly after arriving in France, caught wind of a political scandal called the Dreyfus Affair. Alfred Dreyfus was a French artillery officer of Jewish descent who, in 1894, was falsely accused of spying for the Germans. Even after evidence of his innocence came to light, he was continually harassed by the French military. Dreyfus was put on trial, which caused a massive stir and became an in-your-face example of the insidiousness of Europe's antisemitism.

As part of the press, Theo was present in the courtroom when the guilty verdict was handed down and was a firsthand witness to the humiliating public ceremony in which Dreyfus's regalia were stripped away. "On 5 January 1895 Dreyfus was publicly disgraced at a ceremony of degradation staged in the courtyard of the Ecole militaire. In front of a crowd screaming 'Death to Judas, death to the Jew.' "[5]

No one knows if the trial itself *caused* Theo to rethink his position, but around the same time, he had a realization: while *he* wanted to shake off his Jewishness, the world was never going to let him do that. He realized that assimilation did not eliminate hatred and that antisemitism was not going away anytime soon. So Herzl did a one-eighty and decided that not only should the Jews stay Jewish, but they should also go back to their ancestral homeland and reestablish their own state. At least, if they ever wanted to be safe again.

My friend Gidi Grinstein says that Judaism can be viewed through four pillars: religion, peoplehood, *tikkun olam*, and nationhood. Religion and faith are personal and are observed differently by different individuals. Peoplehood can be described as shared legacy, history, family, and educational traditions, which link many generations. *Tikkun olam* is the Jewish command to strive to make the world a better place. And nationhood is the modern manifestation of a basic human need: a connection to a land and the need for self-determination and self-governance. The manifestation of nationhood is the longing for the homeland of the Jews for two thousand years of exile and the passion to create the modern-day State of Israel. (Much like the Jews' nationhood, the Palestinian people also have that urge and that need for self-governance, and many Zionists hope to see that happen. Fear not, we'll get to that later.) Not every Jew practices or identifies with all four pillars, but I think they are a great prism to use when thinking about one's Jewishness. Herzl clearly took on the nationhood part of his Jewishness and ran with it.

It's hard to emphasize just how radical this concept was. Think about it. We are talking nineteenth century. Jews were spread out all over the world, congregated in small ghetto-ish neighborhoods (or shtetls), ebbing and flowing from one oppression and/or discrimination to the next. Throughout two thousand years of exile and persecution, they kept repeating: "Next year in Jerusalem." But who *really* believed this? Not too many people, that's for sure. The idea seemed so far-fetched that initially the majority of Jews around the world dismissed it. Luckily, Theo was a great writer. He understood that in order to move humans into action, and re-create a nation, one must "influence the masses by speaking to their imagination, with great symbols. . . . Nations are effected by flags, decorations, songs."

These were the words he wrote in 1895 to the Baron Hirsch, a German Jewish philanthropist, when he asked the baron for funding for this mad plan of his. The visit did not go well, but Herzl already knew what to do. He knew that if he couldn't appeal to logic, he would have to appeal to the heart. And he understood that people of all races, religions, and ethnicities are moved by stories. Good stories. Inspiring stories. And he was, after all, a brilliant storyteller.

In 1896, thirty-six-year-old Theo wrote one of his most important pieces, one that would propel a revolution. It was a short pamphlet called *The Jewish State*, and in it he described—you guessed it—the Jewish state. In clear, quick, and simple language, Herzl laid out his vision for a modern solution to what he called "the Jewish

Question." He began with the words "The idea which I have developed in this pamphlet is a very old one: it is the restoration of the Jewish State."

His premise was none other than the one outlined above: we had sovereignty before, so we should probably have it again. Why? To survive. As he writes:

> The world resounds with outcries against the Jews, and these outcries have awakened the slumbering idea. . . . No one can deny the gravity of the situation of the Jews. Wherever they live in perceptible numbers, they are more or less persecuted. Their equality before the law, granted by statute, has become practically a dead letter. They are debarred from filling even moderately high positions, either in the army, or in any public or private capacity. And attempts are made to thrust them out of business also: "No dealing with Jews!"[6]

His final point: "Let the sovereignty be granted us over a portion of the globe large enough to satisfy the rightful requirements of a nation; the rest we shall manage for ourselves."

In simple words, Herzl was asking for international recognition for a Jewish state.

That little pamphlet, much like other consequential pieces of art or literature, was shredded to pieces by almost all critics at the time. Political circles displayed hostility, reviewers laughed at it, respectable papers refused to cover it, and the ones that did called it everything from silly to mad to desperate. It also caused fear in some religious circles. The most receptive audience turned out to be the Russian Jewry, which is how that revolutionary idea made its way to my grandmother in the years to come.

But despite the initial chilly reception, Theo didn't give up. Crazy fox that he was, he organized an event called the First Zionist Congress, which took place on August 29, 1897, in Basel, Switzerland. Herzl gathered representatives of Jewish communities from all over the world for the first time, and 208 delegates from 16 countries showed up to discuss their collective future. Herzl believed that the Zionist movement should be public, proud, vocal, and supported by the global community. The delegates gave speeches, created group discussions, congratulated themselves, and did it all in tailcoats, no less. Herzl insisted on everyone wearing tails in order to signal to themselves and the rest of the world that this was indeed a celebratory event, and a respectable one, too!

But when it came to what Zionism actually *was*—its political structures and goals for the future—no one could agree. There were different thought processes and agendas, and participants fought passionately on how to execute this completely insane idea (as the joke goes, every Jewish community has at least two synagogues: the one you attend, and the one you won't step foot in). Some thought Zionism meant immediate migration to Israel, while others thought it meant fighting for civil rights for Jews wherever they resided. Some thought Zionism should be based on socialism and working the land, while others thought it should be anchored around religion or capitalism. They were, after all, a bunch of Jews, so they kept on arguing, all the way to . . . now.

Beyond the internal debate, the Zionists faced threats from a number of powerful entities, among them the Russian tsar, the pope, and the Turkish sultan. This whole concept of rebuilding a Jewish nation-state was, at the time, so insane, the world powers were concerned about possible internal implications. The participants knew there were spies in the audience, and they made sure their desire for a state did not come across as a rebellion against any country. They made a concerted effort to clarify that all Zionists would fully cooperate and collaborate "according to the laws of various countries" they were operating in.

After three days, the delegates agreed to the following main points of Zionism:

- Building a home for the Jewish people in the land of Israel, based on equality and social justice
- Encouraging *aliyah* (or migration) to Israel and connecting the diaspora
- Reviving the Hebrew language
- Solidarity against antisemitism

The delegates were super-moved by their shared vision. As the congress came to its closing, the audience cheered and cried for over an hour.

A few days after Theo's return to Vienna he wrote in his diary the following prophetic words: "In Basel, I founded the Jewish State. If I said this out loud today, I would be greeted by universal laughter. In five years perhaps, and certainly in fifty years, everyone will perceive it."[7] (Exactly fifty years later, *almost to the day*, and sadly after Herzl's passing, the baby United Nations voted for the establishment of a Jewish state in the land of Israel.)

In 1902, Theo wrote his first novel, *Altneuland*, or, in English, *An Old/New Land*, to lay out in more detail that pipe dream of his for a Jewish state. In the book, Theo pulls from his liberal and universal upbringing to describe a utopian state based on liberal values, cooperation, collaboration, and full equal rights for men and women from all races, religions, and ethnicities. He describes an economic middle ground that incorporates capitalism to make sure the country doesn't fall into oppressive socialism. He advocates for free education, separation of church and state, maternity pay, overtime pay, and environmentalism. The main principle of this fictional society is tolerance, and its slogan is "Man, you are my brother." Remember, this was 1902, not 1967! I think it's safe to say that John Lennon would have loved the man.

Altneuland opens with the zinger "If you wish it, it will not be just a dream," and ends with the one-two punch "A dream and an action are not as different as people tend to think, for all of human actions are initiated into completion from a dream. And if you shall not will all that I have written into reality, a dream it is and a dream it shall remain."[8]

This was the beginning of the whole shebang. The spark that started the end of two thousand years in the diaspora. Zionism.

Theo's personal life was not as rosy. He suffered from ill physical health, and his wife and children struggled with severe mental health issues, accompanied with outbursts of violence and frequent hospitalizations. He did not let any of this stop him. For the rest of his life, he traveled through Europe and the Middle East looking for political allies and support from world leaders such as the German kaiser, the Russian tsar, and the Turkish sultan, to no avail. Theo never managed to get the international community behind him, and despite never stopping to push for that dream he spoke of, he didn't get to see it come to life.

It would take a massive event, a worldwide catastrophe that would wipe out 3 percent of the world population and almost half of the Jewish population, for the political atmosphere to change and allow for the Jews to reestablish a home.

It would take a Holocaust.

WHY ZIONISM? WHY STILL?

I grew up knowing I was a Zionist. I didn't know exactly what the word meant, but I knew that I was one. My whole family was Zionist. Both my parents were born in Israel before it was declared a state, but my grandparents and great-grandparents came to Israel because they were Zionists. Each of them took part in building the country, and as a result, they were the ones who survived. The rest of my family, who stayed behind in Europe, perished when the Nazis implemented "the final solution" to exterminate the Jews. Zionism saved my grandparents' lives, and it allowed me to be born.

Growing up in Israel, I was extremely naïve. I thought Zionism was pretty self-evident, and I had no idea that *anti*-Zionism had actually become a thing. I didn't even realize that antisemitism was still a thing! I seriously thought that the atrocities of World War II had settled both arguments. My first reality check came on an overnight ferry ride from Athens to the exotic Greek island of Ios.

Greece is about a two-hour flight from Tel Aviv, and when I was a teen, the Greek islands were our Tijuana or Panama City Beach. Our Florida destination. I was seventeen years old, and my BFF Yaeli and I took a morning flight to Athens and from there a cheap and very slow ferry to Ios, which at the time was party central. (Imagine Spring Break Euro-style, with a lot of drunken Italians.) It was a hot August night, and I was approached by a very tall and very handsome young man. We started chatting and found a cozy corner on the dark deck to get to know each other better, and maybe even do what teens do at that age. It soon came up that I was from Israel and hot dude came from Germany. He paused uncomfortably, for what seemed like a very long time, and a cold and indecipherable look appeared on his face. Assuming this probably had something to do with our nations' joint pasts, I decided to ease things up by saying something to the effect of "Well, all *that* happened a long time ago. Our countries made amends and are great allies now. We should learn from the past and move forward, and make sure it never happens again."

Hot dude looked me straight in the eye and, under the most romantic of Mediterranean moons, while peacefully sailing toward paradise island, said the following, which I remember verbatim, as I have repeated this story ad nauseam throughout the years: "Well, we actually don't know if it *really* happened. There are a lot of books that say that it didn't." To be clear, the "it" he was talking about was the Holocaust. But that wasn't all! As my jaw dropped open, he continued, "And even if it did happen, your country took all the money we gave you and used it for your wars."

I felt like someone had spilled a bucket of ice water on my head. In total shock, I excused myself and went back to Yaeli to tell her that the hot dude wasn't getting anywhere near lucky tonight, and also—*did she know that there were people who actually thought that way?? And cute ones, too???*

This story is not at all a representation of the German people at large, who have gone above and beyond to learn from their past. But it is to show that as an Israeli Jew, I took for granted the notion that everyone knew about the Holocaust, *believed it happened*, and understood why Israel came and needs to be. I thought Zionism was a highly self-explanatory concept, and I was shocked to discover the misunderstanding and misinformation about it and about Israel in general.

So back to the central question: What is Zionism? It's pretty simple, actually. Zionism is about the Jews, like any other nation, being allowed to self-govern in their tiny piece of ancestral land. They are allowed to have a state! Zionism is a merging of liberal values and cultural Jewishness, in simple words: it is a national liberation movement. Zionism was *never* about having an *exclusively* Jewish state. Never was and never will be, and we will get to that soon as well. The main idea behind the Zionist movement was a "return to history." Revive an ancient land with the mission to *constantly improve*, and, true to its mission, Zionism is indeed constantly transforming.

Gidi Grinstein also described Zionism to me not as a set thing but as a verb, something that is still in action. It is after all a movement, and as such, always on the go. Much like the Jewish tradition that answers a question with a question and encourages humans, regardless of religion, to debate each other and philosophize from dusk till dawn, Zionism is still here to learn, to debate within itself, and to transform.

Identifying yourself as a Zionist doesn't mean that you'll be supporting each and every action of the Israeli government with eyes wide shut. In true rabbinical tradition and those liberal values it was founded upon, Zionism in and of itself has been debated from day one and will continue to be debated while aiming to perfect its society. As such, the Jews have a constant responsibility to make sure our vision of that state continues to stay true to that core Jewish value of making the world a better place. This is what the founding fathers of Israel intended, and—what can I say?—when it comes to this topic, I am an originalist.

My beloved safta Fania caught the Zionist bug. In a small town in White Russia, while the snowstorms were raging outside her door, she risked her fifteen-year-old life to see her dream come true. She understood that if she wanted to be safe, she should take charge of her own destiny and make a move. After two thousand years, a dormant ancient dream was suddenly waking up. Zionism intoxicated youth from Europe to the Arab world to the United Sates. It was a crazy idea, and as always, great ideas are crazy. Until they are not.

Safta Fania and the rest of my family's elders made the move to fulfill that ancient dream, and for that I am eternally grateful.

So how on earth did these dreamers actually get this done? How did they build that state? And what happened to a young Russian girl when she arrived in this new/old land? Apparently, there was a lot of hardship, excitement, death, life, peace, love, idealism.

I thank the Lord she wrote it all down.

CHAPTER FIVE

CHASING THAT DREAM

THE DAWN OF HIPPIE CHIC

The first trip I took with Ross, who would later become the father of our son, Ari, was to New York City. As we were sitting one evening on the balcony of our room at the Thompson hotel, taking in the Lower East Side skyline view, I started telling him about my childhood and about my grandmother. "You know what a kibbutz is, right?"

"Sure," said the Southern man. "It's a neighborhood."

I looked at him and sighed. "This is going to take a lot of work."

In 1910 a small crew of two women and ten men settled on land (bought by the Jewish National Fund in 1900) located by the south bank of the Sea of Galilee and invented a totally new way of living: a kibbutz. They called this new thing of theirs Kvutzat Degania, which was later changed to Kibbutz Degania. The word *kibbutz* comes from the Hebrew word *kvutza*, or group. Degania comes from the Hebrew word *dagan*, or grain, which was what they were about to start growing.

These young and crazy pioneers realized that they couldn't survive on their own and so they invented a new structure of communal group living. They decided that in order to overcome the harsh environment, they should become one unit. The idea was that an individual is not as strong as a community, and therefore the community should be put before the individual to provide for all the individual's needs. Together, they started working the land living by the social idea of mutual guarantee—one for all and all for one—based on the Marxist slogan "From each according to his ability, to each according to his needs." Huzzah!

The structure worked such that there was no personal property whatsoever; everyone owned everything equally and worked for everyone else's well-being and the community's needs. They lived together, ate together, and got paid the exact same amount, no matter what job they had. You could run the place or cook the meals, and you'd still get paid the same. Each morning all members would get up, go to the dining hall, and take a look at the day's work schedule. One day you'd be working the fields, the next you'd be milking a cow. They took off their traditional wool coats, put on khaki shorts, and went out to plow the fields so they could grow some food—or else there'd be no dinner.

The kibbutz was, initially, an agricultural community jointly led by kids who had no idea how to farm. This was, after all, a group of teenagers and young adults who'd lived in small ghettos across Europe, following traditional religious rules, facing discrimination, avoiding persecution, and freezing their butts off in temperatures cold AF. They came to a country that was mostly barren (we'll get to that) and infested with diseases such as, but not limited to, malaria, typhus, and cholera. The minimal training they got in Zionist youth groups, deep in the darkness of European forests, hiding from the Communists' evil eye while working the fertile Belarussian soil, was nothing like the super-dry or super-swampy land they encountered upon their arrival. (Yep, the land was both. It didn't rain much and it was boiling hot in summer, and there were a million mosquito-infested swamps everywhere.) The kibbutzim (along with other agricultural communities called moshavot) became one of the foundations on which Israel was created. Even though they were actually a small part of the establishment of the country, only 8 percent of the general population, the kibbutzim made a huge impact both on the ethos of the country to be and its industry. They paved the way for the basic economic system under which Israel still operates today—capitalist yet also a light social democracy. Like Warren Buffett spiced with a dash of Bernie Sanders.

The kibbutzim also paved the path for Herzl's vision of gender equality. In the Zionist movement, women got equal voting rights to men by the Second Zionist Congress in 1898; however, in the early days of the kibbutz, the men were certain that they would be able to transfer the Old World misogynistic way of living to the New World and leave the gals to cooking, cleaning, and childcare. Not so fast. As my safta Fania wrote:

> The kibbutz, in its lion's share, is the fruit of the efforts of the women, fighting for their freedom. The kitchen in Degania is unorganized, because us, the women of Degania, refuse to give up any other working field of the collective. In order to get in the kitchen—I need to give something up which is more dear to my heart. And what is better for the collective? An organized kitchen or the women's rightful place as an equal part of the collective?

The young pioneering Wonder Women knew that they were equal pillars in the creation of the country, so they presented the men with an ultimatum: we are either totally equal or we are out. It worked. A year after the establishment of Degania, the women were granted equal rights to men, including, of course, the right to vote. The year was 1911. Just for reference, the United States granted women the right to vote in 1920, Switzerland in 1971, and Saudi Arabian women got to vote for the first time in 2015.[1]

The fiscal structure of the kibbutz also allowed for women's financial liberation, or at least equality, which was not available anywhere in the world at the time. The women were paid exactly the same amount as their bosses or their husbands, and as such, they had unique freedoms, especially in those days when most women were not an integral part of the world's workforce.

Another revolutionary contribution women made to the kibbutz was communal childcare. The kibbutz regarded "work" as a value in and of itself, and therefore there was no real possibility for a woman to choose to be a stay-at-home mom or a homemaker. The women realized that in order for them to be treated as equals, they needed help raising their kids. So they created the concept of joint upbringing; it does, after all, take a village. From birth to the end of the school years, the kibbutz kids were raised together by a nurse or a teacher, away from their parents, whom they would only see once a day for a few hours in the afternoon. They slept together in "kids' rooms," ate together, and went to school together.

Future contemplation and research into the ramifications of this child-raising method and its long-term effects vary. Anecdotally, I can tell you that some former kibbutz members I know loved every minute of it, and others report traumatic experiences and emotional scars, including issues with attachment and long-term relationships. Some mothers have shared with me the trauma of parting from their babies, and we're pretty clear today: this is not for everyone. Regardless of the personal sacrifice and the hindsight conclusions, as a means to build a utopia in a harsh land, it worked, and it provided the mothers with the support system they needed in order to fully participate. When communal child-rearing stopped serving a necessary function, it became optional and then eventually faded away.

Israel, right from her inception, became a greenhouse for a new breed of super powerful women. When you realize this, you're suddenly not surprised that Israel's prime minister Golda Meir was only the world's third female prime minister (the first was Sirimavo Bandaranaike in Ceylon, now Sri Lanka, and the second was India's Indira Gandhi). It also suddenly makes sense that when DC Comics were searching the planet to find the cinematic embodiment of Wonder Woman, they choose an Israeli Amazon, the one and only Gal Gadot.[2]

Despite the fact that the kibbutzim were all about hippie-dippy communal living, they understood that they were but little islands in a capitalistic society. Their ethos survived, however, and it is now happily making a comeback.

Equality, sustainability, community, love, and rock 'n' roll way before Woodstock or avocado toast.

BABY NOA AT THE BANKS OF THE SEA OF GALILEE

It gets super-hot in the Jordan Valley in August. It's a very different kind of hot. Not humid like Miami or dry like Los Angeles. It's a heavy, thick heat that sticks to your skin like a spray-on glue, adding a thin film of oil to it. An adult might find this heat sensual and sexy, but as a child that heat meant summer was here and freedom was near.

I was about seven or eight years old when my mother would drop me off to spend half my summer with my safta Fania in Degania. The old road number 767 was a winding one. My mom and I would be in the car together, spiraling left to right between the mountains and then down below sea level. I leaned forward, back before there were backseat seatbelts, and we played a game: who could spot the Sea of Galilee first. That view of the large blue-green lake, nestled calmly between the mountains, was majestic.

Like Israel's national poet Rachel, an earlier member of Degania wrote in one of her many love letters to the Sea of Galilee: "Oh my Kineret. . . . Were you real, or did I just dream you?"

We'd make a right at the Sea of Galilee and cross the narrow bridge over the Jordan River and over the tiny dam. To my left was the lake, and behind it the Golan Heights, massive, green, and fertile. After we entered the gates of Degania, we parked the car and walked up an unpaved dirt road. On the left was my grandmother's "home," or, as they called it, her "room," one of the first ones to be built. It was nothing but a tiny, plain-looking cube structure with a small bedroom inside to your left, a living room next to it, and a shower on the right adjacent to a small kitchenette. Kibbutz members did not have full kitchens at home, because they had a joint dining hall, which was a two-minute walk across that dirt road.

I said goodbye to my mother, and away she drove, leaving me to happily fend for myself. Those were the days when a helicopter was just a flying machine and not a parenting style. My cousin Shira and I woke up whenever we thought appropriate, and my grandmother, already out working on her garden or setting up a reading class, paid us no mind as we left her small apartment and walked barefoot to the outskirts of the kibbutz where the Jordan River met the Sea of Galilee.

Shira and I walked the short distance to the mouth of the Jordan River and spent the day playing in the deep, dark green waters. There was a small, picturesque blue fishing boat tied to a mooring, and, under the shade of the eucalyptus tree, I daydreamed that one day I would bring my boyfriend to that most romantic of places. After spending the day in the water, my cousin and I walked back home in the hot sunset, wet, tanned, and exhausted.

Barefoot, we'd walk to the dining hall and grab a tray. We scooped up food from fresh, locally grown, fully farm-to-table buffets, years before the concept moved to Brooklyn. Hard-boiled or scrambled eggs from the chicken coop, homemade cottage cheese, homemade simple dark bread, homemade everything. On Fridays they served a clear chicken broth and homemade challah, which still may be my favorite food in the whole wide world. After dinner we'd rinse, then repeat the next day. As a kid, Degania was my favorite place on earth. It was pure magic.

Only later in life did I realize that even the kibbutz had it faults. There was freedom and fun and acceptance, but only to a certain point. Once I hit puberty and started developing an affinity for capitalistic things like fashion, shopping, and—God forbid—*Sweet Valley High*, I felt a whiff of communal judgment. But as a child, Degania was the manifestation of perfection, and it helped shape the person I became: an idealistic, hardworking hippie, notwithstanding the high heels.

The kibbutz is not for everyone, but it was a genius Israeli invention created to solve one big problem: how to start a country.

HER STORY

My grandmother landed on the shores of Jaffa in 1925. She and her parents and siblings took a ship from Odessa in hellish conditions. They got robbed, and were starving, resorting to eating dry crackers they would first soak in hot water to remove the worms. After landing in Jaffa, they were taken to what was described to them as a "new city being built," but was actually one house in the middle of nowhere in what would become the northern town of Afula. Calling it a house is a tall order, as that place had no floors or windows, just cement walls and a ceiling, and they were thrown out there all alone. Welcome to the Holy Land.

On the first night they ate bread, horseradish dipped in olive oil, and salt. In her diaries, my safta Fania mentions that she refused to try a tomato, as she had never seen one in Russia. They had no money, and so her mother started baking bread to support the family. The children would wake up in the middle of the night to make the dough, then go back to sleep to let it rise, and wake up again to the sound of the passing night train, and put it in the tiny oven, which was heated with olive waste. They got a donkey with two tin cans on each side, and safta Fania's father would travel the neighboring villages to sell the bread out of them. That was it.

"Life was harsh but we were happy," she writes.

All my grandmother dreamed of was to go live on a kibbutz so she could work the land, and she soon left her parents and four siblings and started to roam the countryside, looking for a place to fulfill that dream. She traveled from one little commune to the next, joining first the "Gidro Unit,"[3] where they paved "soling roads" on Mount Carmel out of tightened crushed stones that they broke by hand. Not surprising to anyone who knew her, she was a mighty rock cracker and would make a full cube of gravel per day, receiving 30 mils for her labor, which she naturally gave to her unit immediately.

From there she joined one of the most exciting places I have ever heard of: the Women's Farm. The farm consisted of a group of women who wanted to prove they did not need men. She actually writes that they were a part of the "Liberated Women." A reminder, we are talking about 1926! They were given a bunch of tents to sleep in, a cow, and a female guide named Zabin to teach them how to grow vegetables—and off they went to the wilderness somewhere east of Haifa, pitched a tent, and got to work. "We would dance until dawn, then go to work; it was glorious."

They ate golden apples, soup they made out of the vegetables they grew, and rice that they cooked with tomatoes, which she had learned to love by then. On one stormy night, a massive wind blew their tents away, and the girls were left soaked in water and exposed to the elements. Safta Fania describes them, completely drenched, in the dark, laughing their hearts out.

After a couple of years of living in tents and doing hard physical work, my grandma started to wonder when she was going to settle down and find her permanent home. One day she retired to her tent and did not want to come out. She was contemplating her future, the future of her fellow pioneers, and their never-ending challenges. She described what we would now call depression, but the term was only coined by Sigmund Freud ten years prior, in 1917, and had not traveled to that region yet.

She was lying in her tent, sad and broken, when a strange, short, stocky, shaggy-haired, and mustached man walked into their camp. He asked the kids about their experiences and well-being and was told that a girl from Bobruisk was having a hard time at a tent nearby. The man walked into the tent to find my grandmother lying in her cot.

"Who are you?" she asked.

"Doesn't matter," he said back. "All you need to know is that I am also a Jew from Bobruisk, and I would like to speak with you. That should be enough."

He sat on her cot and they had a conversation that would pull my grandmother straight out of her depression. She later found out that that man was Berl Katznelson, one of the founders of the Labor Party, a journalist, and a renowned thinker and leader of the Zionist movement. I wish I knew what they spoke about, but all she writes in her diary is that she came out of that conversation "as if [she] grew a pair of wings."

Her next life-changing moment came when, at one evening gathering, she found out that the first kibbutz in Israel, Degania, was looking to add four new members. This was a new opportunity, as the members of Degania believed their kibbutz should stay a small and intimate group and that any new member would disrupt their harmony. But times were hard, and Degania members were forced to take on more working hands. They needed one person for the banana field, one for the orange grove, one for the dairy farm, and one for the vegetable garden. My grandmother, the aspiring farmer, volunteered for the vegetable garden, and she became one of the first new members of the first kibbutz in Israel.

"And this is how I made it to Degania. I arrived without shoes and without any clothes. . . . I came to the Jordan Valley, I saw the Kineret [Sea of Galilee], I saw the view, and I said to myself: this is the place. This is where I will be buried."

The year was 1930, she was twenty-three years old.

Safta Fania had found her home. She moved to Degania, and a year later met her husband, Joel, and had their three children, Mira, Aki, and Roni, while continuing to work the fields as she had always dreamed. In her diaries she writes:

> We were lucky at the time. The kids were very well taken care of. They would come to us washed, cleaned, organized, and fed; all we had to do was play with them. I did not need to concern myself with any of this; the teachers and caregivers took care of everything. It was obvious, after all, as I was working out in the field, I had no time to take care of children. It wasn't hard. The children were healthy and strong and I had no problems with them.

As a mom, reading this horrifies me. How could you give your child away, from birth to young adulthood, to be fully raised by someone else, no matter how loving that someone else was? The thought of ten, twenty, thirty toddlers sleeping in one big room, crying out for their moms at night, makes my heart ache. However, the times were different, and their needs called for extreme measures. It was the moms of the kibbutz, after all, who had proudly created this concept.

My grandmother ditched her dresses, cut her hair short, and rejected makeup, jewelry, and high heels. She took fully to communal living and hard labor with an almost religious vigor. This sounds extreme, I know, but apparently it wasn't all work and no play after all. I heard a lot of whispers throughout the years about the grand ol' times those pioneers had, back in the day, in those sweltering tents, dripping with youth and ideology, stuck by choice in the middle of the night in the middle of nowhere. In her diaries, my grandmother speaks freely about "all those affairs" they had, not at all referring only to her husband's affairs. She mentions it as a matter of fact, with no self-judgment or guilt, in a true polyamorous manner. My dad used to smile and say something to the effect of "They really loved what we all don't hate." And my mother tells me there were three older men who lived next door to them at her kibbutz who took particularly good care of her when she was growing up: picking her up for playtime, taking an intense interest in her friends and schoolwork. She said it took her years to put two and two together, but she later realized that all three men most likely thought there was a chance she might be their daughter. (I am super-supportive of my grandmother celebrating her sexuality; however, my mom, Yael, does look very much like my grandfather Hanan, so I think that debate has been long settled.)

As was the case in many countries around the world, socialism was a lovely ideal, but horrific to scale. In order to survive in a capitalist world, a lot of kibbutzim turned to various industries throughout the years, and some actually became pretty well off. Privatization of lands, division of property, and pay for your actual work caught on and became a norm. And of course, kids went back to their parents' homes, thank the good Lord.

While this was progress for some people, safta Fania dreaded the onslaught of capitalism and laments in her diary: "I remembered when they opened up the store in the kibbutz and the members were willing to partake, I took it very badly. Even the kibbutz succumbed to *Machering*.* . . . It was a traumatic experience for me. How did we go back to these diaspora professions? . . . For me going to the kibbutz was to rebel against all of this."

And rebel she did, staying true to her socialist ideals even as the world changed around her. My own ninja of a mother was raised on the same ideals. She still dons a pixie cut, has never pierced her ears, and wears makeup only when I physically force her down to put some color on her cheeks—or, as she calls it, "*Ugh, you and your war paint*." You can't take the kibbutz out of my mom. She rides horses, swims, dives, specializes in ballistic missiles, and is generally a badass. Truth be told, I am not unlike her. I just do it with some lip gloss.

MEANWHILE, IN THE CITIES

Idealistic emigrants from the Old World weren't only aspiring socialists living in the kibbutzim. Many moved to villages, which were called "moshavot," like Petach Tikva (established 1878), Rishon Le'Zion, Zichron Ya'akov, and Rosh Pina (established 1882), or cities like Tel Aviv (established 1909) and Jerusalem, and put themselves to great use. One of these immigrants was my great-grandfather, Nachum.

Nachum Tisch was born in 1885 in the city of Yanov in the Grodno region of Russia, now Belarus. In 1905 he enrolled in a university in Germany to study electrical engineering, and then transferred to the University of Lausanne, Switzerland, where he became active in the exiled Russian socialist movement that was working to topple the tsar back in Russia. The sneaky eye of the tsarist regime was active all over Europe, and a provocateur gave Nachum's name to the authorities. When he

* From the word *Macher*, which is an ironic way to describe a fixer, an influential person, a mover and shaker. A *Macher*!

came back to visit his family in Russia in 1907, he was arrested and, since he was a Zionist, was sent to Siberia for fifteen years of hard labor imprisonment. After only six years in the Russian prison, he was released, escaped to Belgium, and from there to London, where he completed a degree in engineering. In 1920, based on his professional expertise and the fact that he spoke seven languages, Nachum was invited to join an international delegation as a British diplomat to discuss the setting of borders between Germany and Denmark in Schleswig-Holstein. He turned down this offer and took another one in its place.

My great-grandfather had been approached by the Zionist organization in London to start and head the Office of Industry and Trade in the Yishuv, the name given to all the pre-state Zionist groups who were building Israel at the time. He accepted without hesitation and in 1922 emigrated to Jerusalem, which, since the mid-1800s, had a Jewish majority once again.[4] Nachum Hebraized his last name from Tisch to Tishby (according to family legend, the name was given to him by his friend, Israel's national poet Haim Nahman Bialik) and became the first secretary for trade and industry in the office of the Jewish Agency. In 1925 he married Zila Wein, and they had two boys, Saul and Alexander Tishby, my grandfather. Alexander would marry my glamorous grandmother Dina, and they would also have two boys in Jerusalem, Rafael and my father, Daniel Tishby. My dad loved his grandmother and used to tell me and my sisters about her, fondly calling her "my grandmother Zila, the Cossack"—a not-so-subtle reference to her, well, stockiness. My sisters, Iris, Tom, and I joke that we got our somewhat curvy and sturdy physiques from safta Zila, bless her heart.

I've followed my great-grandfather's path through his archived writings and learned that he was a bulldozer. As opposed to my grandmother Fania, the idealistic socialist who was passionate about working the land and wanted nothing to do with money, my great-grandfather was an idealistic capitalist. He was convinced, and would tell anyone who would listen, that there would be no proper

Jewish state without a proper Jewish industry. He worked incredibly hard and became a huge part of the development of the local economy, literally creating something out of nothing. In 1925, Czechoslovakian Zionist businessman Otto Ables visited the Yishuv and ended his visit at my grandfather's office in Jerusalem. He wrote a book about his visit, aptly called *A Visit to Eretz Israel*. The final chapter of the book is titled, "Jerusalem Is the Washington of Israel," and it ends with an extensive description of my great-grandfather's vision for the future of the country.[5]

My great-grandfather's goals were assisting, supporting, and expanding local manufacturing and developing Israeli exports, with a focus on the textile, fishing, and stone industries. He supported the building of local ceramics factories for roofing, and helped create the recently revamped classic Israeli fashion house Ata (one of my favorites). He advocated for every industry, from silk to the creation of local beer breweries, which now seems very hipstery of him. He was also the one who brought the diamond industry to Israel.

My great-grandfather was also a huge proponent of members of the Yishuv not just making but intentionally *buying* local goods in order to grow the markets. My father told me his grandfather was the one who coined the phrase every Israeli knows, *Totzeret Ha'aretz*, which is a cool way to say "Israeli Made," but I can't find evidence for this anywhere. I did find evidence of him pushing for exactly that, and there are many stories of him fighting tooth and nail with the representatives of the British Mandate, as they did not believe the Jews in the Yishuv could ever create a sustainable local industry. All to say, I like to think that he did come up with that phrase, and let's not ruin a good story.

Nachum also argued for the importance of settling the deserted southern Bay of Akaba. To the east of the bay was the tiny village of Aqaba,[6] and Nachum argued that the Yishuv should establish not just a town on the other side of the bay but also a port. The place was too hot and too far off the beaten path, so the leaders of the Yishuv were not that into it.

Despite the powers that be, Nachum took the initiative to go south on his own and scout the area. He continued to call for a port in the bay (and in Netanya!) while commenting on the beauty of the underwater world before knowing that diving in the Red Sea would become a powerful industry on its own. It would take years, until the city of Eilat was established in 1949, for his ideas to come alive.

In the process, it seems like my great-grandfather butted heads with a lot of people, sending angry letters to officials all over the world, among them Chaim Weizmann, complaining that other letters were being ignored or his ideas not taken seriously enough. I found his correspondence with the leaders of the Zionist movement, both on the left and on the right of the political spectrum. He corresponded with the leftist Zionist leader who was soon to be Israel's first prime minister, David Ben-Gurion, and with Ze'ev Jabotinsky, the leader of the Revisionist Zionist movement (Jabotinsky's revisionist ideas are the basis of ideology for the right-wing Likud Party). Clearly my great-grandfather did not take any political sides, and it seemed to have cost him later in life when the state was created. Nachum was not an official party member, and I believe this may be why he did not get to head the office he created when it became an official arm of the new country. The foundations he created, however, are the foundations for Israel's industry and its ethos to this day.

My father wasn't a big talker, and he told us nothing about his side of the family except for his Grandma Zila, and almost everything I got for this book is from remaining family members and archived material. But having such a passionate and entrepreneurial capitalist as an ancestor does explain my own entrepreneurial tendencies (Hi, HBO!) and my affinity for the fun stuff in life, including but not limited to the occasional, albeit restrained, shopping trips. I graduated from *Sweet Valley High* a while ago, so we're good on that front.

REALITY CHECK, PLEASE

So here we are. My grandparents and great-grandparents left behind persecution and poverty, and privilege and tempting governmental offers, and uprooted their lives to fulfill the crazy dream of reestablishing a home for the Jews. It's important to understand just how the Jewish pioneers approached this monumental job, how hard it was, and how much work they had to put in when they got there. But I also wanted to make sure you got an authentic picture of the reality on the ground *before* the establishment of Israel, because this is also a lost topic in modern political discussions about Israel.

You see, when my ancestors came to Mandatory Palestine, there just wasn't much there. Since the destruction of the Jewish state in the Jewish-Roman War around AD 70, and throughout the two thousand years that followed, there were always people living on that land: Arabs, Jews, Muslims, Christians, Druze, Bahais—a changing cocktail of religions, ethnicities, and nations, some of which are long gone (Hello again, Mamluks!). Though there was never a state there, as we relate to statehood today, there were indeed inhabitants throughout the years—just not that many. In fact, from the days of the Crusades (1095–1492), the number of inhabitants in that piece of land stayed pretty much the same. It fluctuated from around 205,000 people in the year 1500 to about 275,000 in the year 1800.[78] That's right—the entire place had about as many people as there are presently in Baton Rouge, Louisiana.

By 1890, that number had nearly doubled, to 532,000. While this may seem like a big leap, it represents almost no growth, especially compared to population trends elsewhere in the world. By comparison, the US population in 1800 was 5,308,483, and by 1890 it had jumped to 62,979,766—eleven times higher![9] Why was that? Why did the population stay pretty much the same for most of recent history? Forgive my bluntness but here goes: it's because the place was a nightmare.[10]

Mark Twain described it best in 1869 when he came back from his pilgrimage throughout the Holy Land, completely disillusioned:

> Of all the lands there are for dismal scenery, I think Palestine must be the prince. The hills are barren, they are dull of color, they are unpicturesque in shape. The valleys are unsightly deserts fringed with a feeble vegetation that has an expression about it of being sorrowful and despondent.[11]

Palestine was a rough area, dry and unfertile, and throughout history, people who tried to live there suffered from various diseases, like the black plague, typhus, cholera, and malaria. For a few hundred years, the Templars and the first Jewish pioneers tried to build something up north near Nazareth and the Hula Valley, only to be chased out by mosquitos and death. For a brief period of time, the child mortality rates neared 100 percent.[12] It was a super-dangerous hot mess.

Under the Ottomans' rule (1516–1917), and as that empire was slowly sinking, the place was an underdeveloped peripheral region, with high percentages of illiteracy and child mortality and no organized agriculture or industry. It received no resources from the Ottoman Turkish government or attention of any kind, really. These were considered malaria-infested lands, plagued and inhospitable. You could easily buy lands there, and at a bargain, from either the Turkish government or private Arab or Christian landowners, most of whom didn't live on the land and were absentee landlords living in less peripheral Ottoman regions. The land Degania was built on, for example, cost 128,974 francs for 6,448 dunams, approximately 20 francs per dunam[13] which is about $16 per acre at the time, $495 in today's US dollars. By comparison, in the entire US in 1905, land on average cost around $30 per acre, which is about $928 today. Since there was nothing of worth in the region, migration was allowed; however, for obvious reasons, only a few jumped at the offer.

By the time the first Zionists arrived at the turn of the century, there were *some* people in Palestine (mostly in the old cities and spread out in villages), but large tracts of the land were empty and highly inhospitable. This was the land that the Jews legally purchased from local landowners.

The pioneers got to work and transformed the land—rapidly. While the Arabs congregated in smaller towns and villages, the Jewish emigrants, including my grandmother Fania, focused on building kibbutzim and agricultural villages (moshavot) and did their darndest to make the place bloom. As explained in US congressional hearings (April 18–21, 1922) on the matter:

> Jewish agricultural colonies . . . developed the culture of oranges and gave importance to the Jaffa orange trade. They cultivated the vine, and manufactured and exported wine. They drained swamps. They planted eucalyptus trees. They practiced, with modern methods, all the processes of agriculture.[14]

The country as we know it today did not exist. The pioneers made it happen. The capitalists in the cities made it happen. The kibbutzniks made it happen. Each new kibbutz or little town or city dweller was a part of the Yishuv. They built Petach Tikva, Rishon Le'Zion, Afula, and dozens more *without* forcibly removing *any* people from *any* land. And in 1909, on an empty sand dune by the Mediterranean Sea, a bunch of pioneers drew seashells out of a box to divide plots and break ground on my beloved city of Tel Aviv, where I was born. My grandparents and great-grandparents made this happen. They were the ninjas of ninjas. They were a bunch of NinJews.

Suddenly, around this time—in part but not exclusively because of the Jewish efforts—the population grew exponentially. Under the

British Mandate, there were advancements in agriculture and industry (Thanks, Nachum Tishby!), and with more economic opportunities, there were clear migration trends of Jews and others. The Arab population grew more during this time than it had in the previous four hundred years. While some scholars think this was the result of a rapid natural growth, others point to immigration from neighboring Arab countries rather than an indigenous population boom of people who had been there for generations prior.

Why is this? Basically, the place was becoming economically appealing. There is further proof of this as thousands of Arabs migrated to Palestine from the region—Syria, Jordan, Egypt, and the Hejaz—in search of a better life only a few years prior to the establishment of Israel. The fact is that there was a huge migration of people, both Arabs *and* Jews, in those days. This does not mean that Arabs who legally owned land do not have a claim to it as well, regardless of *when* they arrived. It is, however, a sticking point in today's debate, when pundits and politicians discuss the "right of return." While some of the Arab people can truly claim that ten generations sat under the same family-owned olive tree, not everyone who claims to have been there for generations has actually been there for generations (more on this later).

Israel became a highly contested and valuable piece of real estate, but only through an organized (and legal!) effort. The official declaration of the State of Israel, which came in later years, was a bloody affair, as all wars are, and we are about to get to that in the next chapter. But the beginning was . . . formless and, yeah, *mostly* empty. As you may remember, when my safta Fania landed in Jaffa, she was greeted by both an Arab funeral and a Jewish holiday celebration, so, yes indeed, there were *always* Jews *and* Arabs (and Christians and every other religion) living in the land—just not that many, and with not much around to call a state.

Through the story of my family and the use of these infamous facts again, I need to express an inconvenient truth, but a truth nonetheless. The Jews did not "take Palestine." There was no Palestine for the taking. There was no state, no united governance, not much industry, or a healthcare system, or agriculture, economic or education systems. There was certainly no democracy, equality, safety, or prosperity for the people living there. The pioneers, my grandparents, turned much of the land from a place that was nearly uninhabitable into a flourishing community of agriculture and booming economic growth, a foundation for the state Israel is today.

They had no choice and nowhere else to go. This wasn't about exceptionalism. Rebuilding a homeland, a safe haven, was their only way to survive. And it became even more urgent as the crisis for the European Jews who stayed behind was worsening by the minute.

PART II

DO

CHAPTER SIX

A STATE IS BORN

ENOUGH IS ENOUGH

As the Jewish Yishuv in the British Mandate of Palestine was working toward a state to be, the Jews in Europe were growing desperate.

In the mid-1930s, my grandmother Hilda's family was living in the town of Teplice in what today is the Czech Republic. Wealthy and educated, the Schorr family had lived a privileged life until the Nazis took over Germany in 1933. As the danger mounted nearby, my great-grandfather Paul, who owned a fabric factory, moved the family out of rural Czechoslovakia into the capital city of Prague, thinking that Hitler would never make it that far. Clearly, he was wrong. They had about ten months of peace in the beautiful capital until the Germans invaded. The year was 1939.

How they got their visas to leave Prague and travel to Palestine remains a family mystery. According to my great-uncle Beno: "All I know is that one of the German officers was stunned by your grandmother's beauty. Father took her to visit the officer, and they came back later that day with the certificate." She was seventeen years old.

Only my grandmother knows what she did that day to get her family out of Czechoslovakia in the nick of time, and she has long since passed away. However, in those days people did anything and everything to get out, and for a very good reason. The Nazis were taking over Europe.

The Schorr family traveled through Poland and bid farewell to their relatives, not knowing this would be the last time they'd see them. When they arrived in the British Mandate of Palestine in 1939, they joined the approximately 449,000 Jews and upward of 861,000 Arabs who already lived in the land, including my grandmother Fania and my great-grandfather Nachum. They were the lucky ones. Everyone else from the family died at the hands of the Nazis.

This book is not about the Holocaust, and I feel like unless you're Tara Westover pre-education, you probably know enough about it by now. But for the sake of my master chronology, I'll say this: between 1941 and 1945, the Nazis systematically killed nearly six million Jews in what they branded "the final solution," and what the Jewish people would come to call the Shoah, or the Holocaust. Those who survived were stripped of their citizenship, land, and possessions. Even worse, in certain places, like Poland, Jews who returned to their former homes after World War II faced continued pogroms and persecution. By the end of that war, there were 210,000 to 250,000[1] Jewish refugees in camps all over Eastern, Central, and Western Europe; they were war-torn and had no identity papers or possessions. They were desperate to emigrate to Palestine, but the British capped Jewish immigration, turning refugees back to Europe (including the ones on board the famous ship *Exodus*).

The tensions between the Jewish Yishuv, the Arabs, and the British were escalating rapidly. There were riots, attacks, and counterattacks on all sides. The Arab residents of Palestine, whether they had just immigrated or had been there for generations, were not happy with the sudden return of the Jews. The Jewish residents were similarly unhappy with the British constraints on Jewish World War II survivors' migration, and focused their aggression on the British government. Great Britain, who'd controlled the land since after the First World War, was done with this Levantine drama. They announced that they were ready to terminate their mandate and leave. They kicked the can to a newly formed international body called the United Nations and, like the true gentlemen they are, politely asked to be excused from any further decision-making, thank you very much.

The end of the British Mandate in Palestine was part of a bigger international picture. Yes, it had to do with the fierce and bloody Jewish resistance, but it was also a result of other tectonic shifts. Political and economic pressure from inside and outside the British government pushed them to end many colonial endeavors around the world. One important part of their agreement to leave Palestine had to do with the British Empire giving up its hold on India. As soon as that was done (on August 15, 1947), the Brits no longer needed the region to defend the path to India, so they were thrilled to give up their Mandate over Palestine and just kept control over that oh-so-important route, creating the Suez Canal Zone (militarized, of course, until 1956).

The UK (and the US and the rest of the world) knew the Arabs were vehemently and aggressively against the existence of any type of a Jewish state,[2] and in order to *not* upset them they decided to simply leave the Jews and the Arabs to duke it out on their own, which they would soon do. This was the only time the British government folded one of its colonies without an official handover to another government. Sigh.

This left the baby-faced United Nations to put together an exploratory group to find a solution for the land, and for the Jews.

THE PARTITION

Acknowledging the horrors of the Holocaust and the need for the Jews to have a safe place, the UN created the United Nations Partition Plan for Palestine—a plan for how to divide the land between the Jews and the Arabs.

The plan included a Jewish state to be formed on about 55 percent of the land, and an Arab state on about 45 percent of the land. Though the Arab state was a bit smaller, the land was better quality, with greater access to water. It wasn't a perfect plan, but it was a plan! For a state!

The UN General Assembly put the proposal to a vote on November 29, 1947, and both Jews and Arabs waited for the verdict. My father, who was seven years old at the time, planted himself in front of his radio in Jerusalem and listened anxiously as the UN polled country after country. My safta Fania in Degania joined all members in the dining hall to listen to the live radio broadcast on the single kibbutz radio. My six-year-old mother used the opportunity to escape the "kids' room" and climb her favorite tree. The entire country held its breath. Thousands of years of exile were about to come to an end.

With a final vote of 33 for, 13 against, and 10 abstentions, the resolution for the creation of the State of Israel was adopted. Everyone in my family tells of the elation that erupted that night. Roars and cheers, tears and screams, hugs and kisses, and hundreds of thousands of Jews flooding the streets of Jerusalem, Tel Aviv, the villages, and the kibbutzim dining halls, dancing the hora until dawn.

At the end of the First Jewish Congress, Theodor Herzl wrote: "In Basel, I founded the Jewish State. If I said this out loud today, I would be greeted by universal laughter. In five years perhaps, and certainly in fifty years, everyone will perceive it." United Nations Resolution 181 for the creation of the State of Israel was adopted on November 29, 1947, fifty years to the day after Theo wrote those words.

The world had agreed to give back the land to the Jews. After two thousand years of exile, countless persecutions, a succession of empires, two world wars, and the horrific and unprecedented Holocaust, the Jews could return home. A state was granted, and it was assumed that a Jewish state would formally be created when the Brits announced the official end of their mandate on May 14, 1948.

However, while the Jews agreed to the UN plan, the *entire* Arab world rejected it flat out. As with any good deal, no side was totally happy. The Jewish leaders of the time—the Jewish Agency and the World Zionist Organization (which Theo Herzl had started)—expressed disappointment in the size of the future state; however they fully accepted the plan "in order to achieve peace and prosperity." Every single Arab country and every single Arab leader, on the other hand, rejected it immediately. They announced that not only were they not accepting the plan, but should Israel be created, they would go to war in order to wipe the new Jewish state off the map.

And so they did—the following day.

AND BEN-GURION SAID: LET THERE BE A STATE

In the months that followed the UN resolution, tensions between the two communities reached a new high, and by *tensions* I mean serious bloodshed. How, against this backdrop, did the creation of Israel move from a UN resolution to a reality? In order to achieve a state, a nation needs a leader. Fortunately, throughout the awakening of Zionism, one voice had emerged. A five-foot giant of a man.

People tend to think that we use our words to describe our world. But the truth is that we actually use our words to *create* our world. When it comes to the creation of countries, this concept is as real as it gets. How a country is declared into being *in words* is an actual blueprint for its future society. This was true for the American Declaration of Independence, and it was true for its younger sister, the declaration of independence for the State of Israel.

David Ben-Gurion, the man who would become Israel's first prime minister and its minister of defense, was a man of words *and* actions. He was, and still is, considered the architect of the Jewish state and the Israel Defense Forces. Born in Poland to a Zionist family, Ben-Gurion started his political activism at the ripe age of fourteen. In 1906, at the age of twenty, he migrated to Ottoman Palestine and dedicated his life to rebuilding and then protecting Israel. His résumé is dizzying, so I'll try and be brief.

DBG was a writer, a farmer, a journalist, a revolutionary, an activist, a genius politician, and a brilliant military strategist. Among his official positions, he was the executive head of the World Zionist Organization and the head of the Jewish Agency. In 1915 he traveled to New York to spread the word of Zionism, and when he realized the Americans were not yet aware of the emerging Zionist movement and its activities to rebuild Israel, he took it upon himself (along with his friend Itzhak Ben Zvi) to publish two books—*Yizkor* and *Eretz Israel*—describing the transforming reality on the ground. He founded the political party the Workers of Zion and in 1930 helped merge it with the Young Worker Party to create Mifleget Poalei Eretz Israel (or Mapai), the Party of the Workers of Israel, which became the dominant political party in the Zionist movement and later in Israel, a precursor to the Labor Party. As a result of those relentless efforts, DBG became the de facto leader of the Jews in the Yishuv and the man who brought Herzl's vision to life.

After the UN resolution, David Ben-Gurion knew he had very little time. Now that the Jews had been granted a state, the Brits were heading out within half a year, and the Arabs from inside and outside were plotting a war. A new reality needed to be created ASAP.

The Yishuv, Ben-Gurion, and the rest of the world knew that as soon as the British Mandate ended, the neighboring Arab countries would invade and attack in order to prevent Israel from ever being established, so the overlap needed to be swift. The Arabs were hell-bent on never allowing the UN Partition Plan to be realized, never allowing a Jewish state to be created, and they vowed to kill the Jewish settlers, pioneers, Holocaust survivors, and my entire family. They didn't hide it; they announced it openly. But Ben-Gurion was undeterred, and he bulldozed toward an official declaration.

The first question was: How would the new state defend itself? The Jewish Yishuv, now led by Ben-Gurion, had been working over the past fifty or so years to build a foundation for a state and a military. Since the whole world knew a war was going to start as soon as the British Mandate folded, creating a united military was priority number one. The Haganah was the largest military arm of the Yishuv, numbering approximately forty-three thousand men. There were two other smaller militia groups that originated from the opposing Revisionist Zionist movement: the Etzel, which numbered about three thousand men, and the Lehi, with a few hundred men. Both these groups, the Lehi especially, caused major headaches for both the British and the Jewish leaders. They were considered by the British, and periodically by the Yishuv, as terrorist organizations. It was now DBG's job to bring all three of these competing organizations—the Haganah, the Etzel, and the Lehi—together.

The second question was: What would be the name of the new country? Judea was rejected, to make it clear that one did not need to be a Jew in order to be an Israeli. Zion was also ruled out, for a person could be a Zionist without living in Israel. The name Israel was proposed. It appears in the Old Testament approximately two thousand times, yet it is still inclusive in its nature. Ding ding ding! We have a winner.

The third question was: What were Israel's founding principles?

The Israeli Declaration of Independence was directly influenced by the American Declaration of Independence. The first draft was cowritten, with legal scholar Mordechai Beham, by American veteran, Purple Heart recipient, and Columbia graduate Rabbi Harry Solomon Davidowitz[3]—but it was too heavy on "divine providence" and the like. For the next draft, all references to God were taken out to make it clear, yet again, that this was to be a secular country, not exclusively Jewish, but open to all religions. Ben-Gurion edited the final draft himself on the morning of the declaration, creating the democratic blueprint for the re-created Jewish state.

The vote to jump into the waters of nationhood and officially declare a state was decided in the "Cabinet of the People" (the precursor to the Israeli government) after an extensive and heated debate, only one day before the Brits were about to leave. They made the decision to create a state and do it immediately.

Friday, May 14, 1948, the last day of the British Mandate, was a very serene day. The Brits knew full well that a war was about to break out, and since the Arabs refused a state, they just left without any formal handover. The videos are quite charming in their reserved British elegance. Sir Alan Cunningham, the last high commissioner for Palestine, observes the remains of the British military in the port of Haifa and watches the guards as the Union Jack is carefully taken down and neatly folded. He boards a small boat and dramatically salutes as that boat slowly leaves the Holy Land behind, en route to a bigger warship anchored nearby, on which he waits until midnight and then gets the F out. What a highly civilized way to fold an empire, I say.

On that same Friday, May the 14th at 16:00 by the military clock, eight hours before the midnight that ended the British Mandate, David Ben-Gurion stood on Rothchild Boulevard in Tel Aviv, in front of the Cabinet of the People, a picture of Theodore Herzl behind him, and read out the Declaration of Independence, formally announcing the establishment of a Jewish state in the land of Israel. After two thousand years of diaspora, the Jews had a national home again.

He described a country established by a group of liberal, mostly secular, persecuted, and idealistic people who had nowhere else to go. The new country, he said, was established, true to Herzl's vision, as a Jewish and democratic state, without any discrimination based on religion, race, or sex.

> ERETZ-ISRAEL (Hebrew—the Land of Israel) was the birthplace of the Jewish people. Here their spiritual, religious, and political identity was shaped. . . . After being forcibly exiled from their land, the people kept faith with it throughout their Dispersion and never ceased to pray and hope for their return to it and for the restoration in it of their political freedom.
>
> ACCORDINGLY WE, MEMBERS OF THE PEOPLE'S COUNCIL, REPRESENTATIVES OF THE JEWISH COMMUNITY OF ERETZ-ISRAEL AND OF THE ZIONIST MOVEMENT, ARE HERE ASSEMBLED ON THE DAY OF THE TERMINATION OF THE BRITISH MANDATE OVER ERETZ-ISRAEL AND, BY VIRTUE OF OUR NATURAL AND HISTORIC RIGHT . . . HEREBY DECLARE THE ESTABLISHMENT OF A JEWISH STATE IN ERETZ-ISRAEL, TO BE KNOWN AS THE STATE OF ISRAEL. The state of Israel will be open for Jewish immigration and for the Ingathering of the Exiles; it will foster the development of the country for the benefit of all its inhabitants; it will be based on freedom, justice and peace as envisaged by the prophets of Israel; it will ensure complete equality of social and political rights to all its inhabitants irrespective of religion, race or sex; it will guarantee freedom of religion, conscience, language, education and culture; it will

> safeguard the Holy Places of all religions; and it will be faithful to the principles of the Charter of the United Nations.

The Declaration of Independence also included a very specific call to the Arab residents of the state-to-be. Ben-Gurion read:

> We appeal—in the very midst of the onslaught launched against us now for months—to the Arab inhabitants of the State of Israel to preserve peace and participate in the upbuilding of the State on the basis of full and equal citizenship and due representation in all its provisional and permanent institutions. We extend our hand to all neighboring states and their people in an offer of peace and good neighborliness and appeal to them to establish bonds of cooperation and mutual help with the sovereign Jewish people settled in its own land. The State of Israel is prepared to do its share in a common effort for the advancement of the entire Middle East.[4]

Ben-Gurion ended the declaration with a gavel, pounding the table and dramatically announcing: "The state is in existence; this meeting is adjourned!" As he completed his speech, the country erupted in cheers, roars, and tears. These are the words Israel was founded upon, and they have remained the compass of the nation throughout its trials and tribulations.

Every nation needs a Ben-Gurion. The man knew how to communicate, lead, inspire, and unite. He took a fractious group of people and turned them into one nation. He was willing to take stands and make strong choices, sometimes against his fellow Jews, in order to achieve that goal. Eleven minutes after the establishment of the state, US President Truman recognized Israel, followed by recognition from Guatemala, Iceland, Nicaragua, Romania, and Uruguay. Three days later the Soviet Union did the same. Israel became one of only a few issues the US and the USSR agreed on at the time.

The surrounding Arab countries, however, felt differently. As the newly coined "Israelis" took to the streets to celebrate, the armies of Syria, Jordan, Egypt, and Iraq, with the help of Saudi Arabia and Sudan, prepared to invade the freshly baked state.

As Arab leaders had promised, a massive war broke out the next day: the War of Independence.

A TOTALLY UNEXPECTED INTERLUDE

I want to pause quickly for a quick recap of events—a rundown from the beginning of Zionism to the establishment of Israel, just to make sure we're all on the same page. Now, this is something you don't see every day in a history-ish book, do you? Ready? Go!

- The desire and need to rebuild the Jewish state morphed into a political program with concrete aims after the first Jewish Congress in 1897, organized by Theodor Herzl in Basel. Around that time Jews started trickling down to Ottoman Palestine, coming from far and wide to buy land and settle wherever they could. They joined a small Jewish community that had lived there for generations.

- After World War I, Great Brittan and France carved up the Middle East (the Sykes-Picot Agreement), and Great Britain got the British Mandate for Palestine from the Turks—despite their earlier promises to give the Arabs a state in the Hejaz and the 1917 Balfour Declaration that officially promised a "national home for the Jewish people." Nevertheless, for the next thirty years, hundreds of thousands of Jews emigrated to British Palestine and started creating the infrastructure for a future state (based on the League of Nations' intention to secure a homeland for the Jews).

- They were either motivated by ideology or pushed out of their countries by a rising antisemitic tide in Europe and the Arab world.

- From 1939 to 1945, World War II raged and the Nazis killed nearly six million Jews.

- Starting in 1945, hundreds of thousands of Jewish refugees wanted to immigrate to Israel, but the British limited the number of Jews they allowed to enter the country. The Jewish Yishuv did not like this one bit and started resisting the Brits.

- In 1947, the Brits decided to wash their hands of their mandate in Palestine along with other colonial interests, and the UN decided to partition the land into a Jewish state and an Arab state. The Jews agreed; the entire Arab world disagreed.

- In 1948, a few hours before the Brits officially left, David Ben-Gurion declared, "I announce the establishment of a Jewish and democratic state, the State of Israel," and a state was born.

- The following day, every one of Israel's Arab neighbors joined forces with the local Arabs of Palestine and attacked the newly founded state.

LET THERE BE BLOOD

The Arab residents of Ottoman and British Palestine were mostly unhappy with the changes I have described above. Despite the inhospitable climate and underdeveloped landscape, this was their home and they did not like the Jewish immigrants becoming their neighbors. I can sympathize. You've lived there for generations, or your family just emigrated from another neighboring Arab country, and suddenly the Jews are back. Even though the lands were legally bought from Brits, Turks, Bahais, Christians, or Arabs, it was still a major change for the neighborhood. It must have been shocking. The animosity between the new Jewish immigrants and the Arabs started pretty much from day one, and the new Jewish villages and kibbutzim suffered attacks from Arab villages. Unfortunately, the local Arab population was not doing great on its own, even without the Jews. They were extremely disorganized, fractured, and divided into clans, tribes, and family allegiances, with high rates of illiteracy and poverty. The power was held by a group of wealthy families collectively called the *Ayan*, or Nobility, and they heavily depended on Great Britain for social and economic services. Historian Benny Morris vividly describes the infighting and general mess:

> Their power, influence and connections were usually local rather than national; their obligations were to family, dependents, town, and district, in that order. It was a highly regional, oligarchic structure.[5]

They didn't have one voice or an organized structure, whereas the Jews had Ben-Gurion, who was focused on exactly that: one democratic nation, one power structure, one state. From the get-go, Ben-Gurion relentlessly tried to reach a peace deal between the Arabs and the Jews. He wrote all about it in his book *My Talks with Arab Leaders*. In it he describes the efforts he and his partners put into achieving peace, to no avail. Ben-Gurion writes:

> The assumption we all made in the Zionist movement at the time was that we [the Jews] bring blessings to the Arabs in the land and therefore they will have no basis to resist us. In the first conversation I had with Musa Alami [a prominent Palestinian leader] along with Moshe Sharet [a prominent Jewish leader who would later be the second prime minister of Israel] . . . that assumption was undermined when Alami told me the following: "I choose that the land would be desolate and poor even for a hundred more years, until us Arabs will be able to develop it ourselves."[6]

Well. That attitude was not going to fly, especially not with a group of people coming out of the Holocaust and pushed out of their Arab countries; the Jews just didn't have the luxury of time. The country had to be built *now*, not in a hundred years, thank you very much. And so, the Arab attacks on the Jews continued.

There were so many waves of attacks on the Jewish Yishuv throughout the years that they are collectively called "The Incidents." There were incidents in 1920, 1921, 1929 (in which sixty-seven Jewish residents of the ancient Jewish community of Hebron were murdered by their Arab neighbors), and 1936–1939. There was a constant drip of violence in the shape of massacres, sniper attacks, and good old robberies. In addition to the general diseases, the heat, the harsh and barren land, and the malaria-bearing mosquitoes, there was deadly danger from angry mobs.

Because the animosities between the communities had been going on for a while, the War of Independence is actually divided into two parts:

- November 1947 to May 1948—from a day after the UN resolution to before the declaration of Israel's statehood. This period is considered a civil war, since both warring sides were more local militias, not official state militaries.
- May 15, 1948, to July 1949—starting a day after the establishment of Israel, when neighboring Arab countries invaded the new state.

Everyone, including the UN and US, Russian, British, and Jewish leaders, made the correct assessment that all neighboring Arab countries would invade Israel as soon as it was created. New documents uncovered from US envoy to the UN Ralph Bunche show the UN committee's conclusion that an Arab state would *not* be established and that the UN would need to ensure that a Jewish state could survive against the Arab violence that was bound to ensue (not that they did). The war came as a surprise to just about no one.[7]

On May 15, as the newly minted "Israelis" were sleeping off their first Independence Day partying hangovers, all those Arab armies that had been preparing for just this day (Syria, Jordan, Egypt, and Iraq, with the help of Saudi Arabia and Sudan, and now with the assistance of Lebanon) invaded the new state in order to destroy it. They joined two other invading Arab forces that already operated in the territory: a militia created by the Arab League called the Arab Liberation Army (ALA) and a few battalions of Muslim Brotherhood volunteers from Egypt. The invading countries, certain of their victory, called for the Arab residents of Israel to vacate their towns and villages until the fighting had finished and every Jew had been killed. They attacked Israeli communities and put a choke hold on vital resources. My dad, eight years old and under siege in Jerusalem for months at a time, had nothing to eat and relied on pigeons that he and his younger brother Rafael would shoot down with slingshots. Both sides suffered tremendously.

It seems unfathomable today that baby Israel would win that war. But Ben-Gurion was well prepared. A year before Israel was established, he had designated time to learn everything he needed to know about defense, creating what he called a "seminar," interviewing dozens of military experts in order to become one himself. He concluded that the main threat to the Yishuv was not the British and the local Arab animosities but rather the inevitable invasion by surrounding countries. He was right. The Israelis were ill-equipped, small in size, and poor, but they were as prepared to mount a defense as they could have been. The Arab nations, despite being huge in size and in numbers, were not as organized. The Israelis had one unified effort, one central command. They were able to purchase weapons fast, and, paradoxically, having to defend a small territory allowed them to mobilize quicker and be more agile. But the most important difference was motivation. The Arab countries were fighting a thorn in their butts, while the Jews were fighting to survive, to prevent another Holocaust.

After ten months, the ragtag Israeli army had pressed its advantage, and in July 1949, all the invading Arab nations had retreated and signed *temporary* truces with Israel. The armistice lines, known as the Green Line, established the first de facto (and de jure) borders of the State of Israel. Ironically, as a result of the Arab invasion, Israel now controlled not only the area that the UN had originally set aside for the Jews in the Partition Plan but an additional one-third of the former British mandate's land, including West Jerusalem, the Galilee, and the bigger parts of the Negev desert. The local Arabs did not use this opportunity to go back to the UN Partition Plan to ask to establish their own state, and so an Arab-Palestinian state was never established. Instead, Egypt took the Gaza Strip, and Jordan took the West Bank, even though the Partition Plan allocated these territories to the local Arabs (the Palestinians) for a state of their own.

As the Arab world licked its wounds, Israel was finally able to turn its attention to state building. Ben-Gurion's Mapai Party won the most seats, he became Israel's first prime minister and minister of defense, and the brand-spanking-new Israeli government and Israeli people got to work. About a million Holocaust survivors from Europe and Jewish refugees expelled from Arab countries were flocking to the shores of their old-new country. Within two years the population more than doubled, and infrastructure had to catch up with the number of people needing a place to call home. Everything needed to be built from scratch: bridges and roads, schools, banks, healthcare, food supplies, industry, and a standing army.

Two weeks after Israel was created and as the War of Independence was still raging, Ben-Gurion created the Israel Defense Forces, the IDF, and called all former militias to officially join together. A small fraction of the previous militia groups, the Lehi and the Etzel, wanted to maintain some independence. In June 1948, in the middle of the war, the Etzel bought weapons and brought them to Israel aboard a ship called *Altalena*, breaking a UN-imposed weapons embargo. As the ship arrived offshore, negotiation started between the leader of the Etzel, Menachem Begin, and the Israeli government. The Etzel demanded that 20 percent of the ship's weapons be left in the hands of their militias. Ben-Gurion refused; there was only one military from now on. Etzel and Lehi fighters entrenched themselves on the beach in Tel Aviv. Tensions were at a peak. After two days of back-and-forth, attempts at negotiations, and periodic shootings, Ben-Gurion commanded the ship to be bombed. And it was. *Altalena* went up in flames in front of one of my favorite beaches in Tel Aviv. Sixteen Etzel and Lehi members and three IDF members were killed in the fighting.

This story is horrific, and it's still an open wound in the Israeli consciousness. However, it is also a story about the heavy price of unity. It is about creating one authority, one voice, one military, one state. Ben-Gurion and Begin both had the same ultimate goal; they just wanted to go about it differently. Begin, despite having lost this battle, warned his people against a civil war, and a civil war was prevented. He knew when to push and when to back down, and now, he realized, was the time to join Ben-Gurion and endorse the merging of former militia fighters into the IDF.

While the Israelis focused on unifying and building, the Arab world continued resisting the UN resolution and the Jewish state, which meant resisting the creation of a Palestinian state as well.

Israel did not want or start the War of Independence, but she fought hard, and she won against the odds. In recent years, that win, despite being unquestionably a defensive act from the beginning, suddenly became a controversy. It was also the birth of the Palestinian refugee problem.

THE NAKBA

A year after the Arab invasion to destroy the new State of Israel, the Arab armies withdrew. In the course of the fighting, between 700,000 and 750,000 Arab residents of the land were permanently displaced. Some left because the Arab countries told them to; others fled due to the brutal realities of war.

The first to leave were the wealthier Arab families who didn't want to get caught in the fighting. A full-on exodus started in the midst of the main Arab invasion as Arab leaders started calling on their brothers to evacuate, avoid the fighting, and return after the destruction of Israel. They first sent out the women and children, and the men followed soon after.

The war was bloody and brutal. And although the Arabs instigated it, not all Jews fought nice. The official army of the state-to-be, the Haganah, did its best to keep everyone at bay, but when the fog of war took over, local fights erupted, blood was spilled, and atrocities were committed, such as the massacre in the Arab village of

Deir Yassin. On April 9, 1948, Lehi and Etzel militia forces attacked the village and killed between 81 and 120 of its residents (reports vary), among them innocent women and children. It was an abominable event that horrified Jews and Arabs alike. The leaders of the Yishuv were quick to condemn it. The Jewish Agency sent a consolation letter to King Abdullah of Jordan calling the event "barbaric," "brutal," and one "which goes against the Jewish spirit." The main newspaper, *Davar*, condemned the atrocity and the chief rabbinates of Israel called it "a vicious act." The massacre rightfully horrified the Arab population and caused many more to flee their homes in fear for their lives.

Historians still debate exactly how many Arabs fled on their own and how many were pushed out by the Israeli army. And, yes, let's be clear: In that war, which was not wanted or started by Israel, there were Arabs who indeed got pushed out. Naturally, after years and years of hostilities and bloodshed, in the middle of an all-out war that took place only three short years after the Holocaust, the Jews weren't in any mood to be slaughtered again. As historian Benny Morris clarifies:

> The Jewish community in 1948 had two possibilities: Either that the Arabs would commit genocide against them—and I have no doubt that an Arab victory in 1948 would have ended with mass slaughter of Jews—or the Jews, to defend themselves, would expel Arabs, or at least prevent those who fled and were expelled from returning. The Jews chose not to be massacred, and rightly so. But even ethnic cleansing according to the meaning of the term as it has been defined in recent decades, based on the actions of the Serbs in the 1990s in Bosnia . . . was not carried out here. What happened here was a struggle between two peoples who both claimed the right to the same land.[8]

As a side note, Benny Morris is called both an anti-Zionist and a Zionist propagandist, depending on whom you ask, which is a strong indication that he's actually plenty balanced.

Today, anti-Israel groups use the 1948 war to blame Israel for ethnic cleansing. But that's a claim that borders on slander. In fact, let me quote Morris again: "As late as March 24, 1948, the high command of the Haganah had instructed all its units to recognise the full rights, needs, and freedom of the Arabs in the Jewish state without discrimination, and a striving for coexistence with freedom and respect."[9]

These were the orders. Did some commanders on the field push people out? Yes. Were offensive atrocities committed in a defensive war? Yes. Was it right? No. Is this systematic ethnic cleansing? Give me a break. If this was the definition of *ethnic cleansing*, then every country that has ever gone to war (or been forced into war) would be guilty of it. The claim of ethnic cleansing is particularly ridiculous given the fact that not all Arabs left or got pushed out. In fact, some 150,000 Arabs heeded Ben-Gurion's invitation for democracy and equality written in the Declaration of Independence, stayed put in their homes, and became Israeli citizens, enjoying full rights in the new state, for themselves and their descendants. As far as ethnic cleansing goes, that would seem like one major fail.

Israel was created, then fought and won the war, and the Jewish state was a done deal. On the other hand, an Arab state, as granted by the UN, was not created, by choice of the Arabs, not the Jews. As for the 700 to 750,000 displaced people who lost their homes and valuables, they went for help to those neighboring Arab countries, where they were stuffed into refugee camps. The very same countries that had started the war, that had encouraged these people to abandon their homes, now refused to grant these refugees any help or rights. In some cases, most notably Lebanon, Palestinians were denied citizenship and were (and still are) banned from working in numerous industries. Instead of relocating these poor people or helping them start a new life, even for the time being, the Arab countries forced them into camps for what is now three to four lost generations.[10] They intentionally cemented the refugee problem, using these people as pawns in their game to continue a campaign of hatred and war against Israel on the international stage, one that has continued to the present day.

Meanwhile, after the War of Independence, these same Arab countries who refused to properly take care of their Arab refugee brothers, expelled their own Jewish populations. In the years to come, approximately 850,000 Jews would be expelled from countries in the Middle East,[11] leaving behind their homes and their possessions. In the following decade, they'd be encouraged to leave or brutally kicked out of Morocco, Yemen, Algeria, Tunisia, Libya, Iraq, and Egypt, and many of them would find safety in their old/new land: Israel.

My parents grew up in this reality, and nothing had changed by the time I came into the world. As a little girl, I was told about the heroism of rebuilding the Jewish state, but also understood the price that was paid for it. My parents taught me that the War of Independence was messy. I wasn't told a skewed version of the truth; I was told the truth. I wasn't told "There were *no* people there" or "*All* Arabs just left voluntarily." I was told that both people deserve to live side by side in peace and we must find a way to reach that peace with our Arab neighbors.

About twenty years ago, I started hearing this new term floating around: the Nakba. The Disaster. What was that mysterious word, and how did the liberal me know nothing about it? My lefty friends told me that *nakba* in Arabic means "catastrophe," or "disaster," and this "new" word was being used for a national holiday, on May 15, to mark the day all Arab countries invaded Israel in order to destroy it. I must say I was amazed. Not so much by the obvious pain of the displaced, but by this sudden rebranding.

I went on a search to find the origins of this newly introduced concept, and what I found was interesting, to say the least. The term *nakba* was first used in the context of Israel in a pamphlet written by Syrian professor and intellectual Constantin Zureiq on August 5, 1948, as the war was still raging. Surprisingly, in that pamphlet, Zureiq does not refer to the Nakba as something the *Israelis* did to the Arabs but as a self-inflicted and humiliating wound caused by the Arabs themselves. Just so we're clear, Professor Zureiq was not some Jew-loving pro-Zionist. In fact, he couldn't have been clearer about his position when he referred to Israel as "the Zionist enemy" (a term we will continue to hear from the Ayatollah of Iran, the leaders of Hezbollah, etc.). And yet Professor Zurieq very clearly defined this disaster as one that befell the Arabs *by their own doing*, a humiliation they should take responsibility for. Just read the origins of the term *nakba* in Zureiq's own words:

> When the battle broke out, our public diplomacy began to speak of our imaginary victories, to put the Arab public to sleep and talk of the ability to overcome and win easily—until the Nakba happened. . . . We must admit our mistakes . . . and recognize the extent of our responsibility for the disaster that is our lot.[12]

This fact was pretty well-known in the Arab world at the time, as Arab leaders avoided even using the term *nakba* altogether:

> Furthermore, in his 1956 book *Facts on the Question of Palestine* (*Haqa'iq an Qadiyat Falastin*), Palestinian nationalist leader Mohammed Amin al-Husseini kept his hands off the term Nakba as it "was widely associated at the time with a self-inflicted Palestinian Arab disaster—either through land sales to Zionists, failure to put up a fight, or the issuing of instructions to the people to leave."[13]

So how, I wondered, did this term suddenly resurface to infiltrate the liberal zeitgeist? Well, branding is everything, and Yasser Arafat knew it. Arafat was the founder of Fatah, a terrorist organization which started out committed to destroying Israel and slowly softened its edges (or at least pretended to do so). When Fatah overtook the Palestine Liberation Organization (PLO) in 1968, the Palestinians gained for the first time an official representation. It was also Arafat who recognized the need for a sticky national story and in 1998 announced May 15 as Nakba Day, a national day of commemoration, mourning, and protest. This little word, *nakba*, caught on like wildfire, rewriting its own meaning and the history of the War of Independence along with it.

I am not for a second dismissing the pain that war and displacement has caused the Arabs. However, it is infuriating to see over and over again history being twisted into a perceived underdog story. Palestinians and their supporters, including many on the American left, some of whom are my close friends, use the word *nakba* to describe a disaster that just *happened* to the Palestinians, like some natural disaster, a hurricane, or, dare I say, a premeditated holocaust. One that was inflicted upon a nation out of the blue and without any provocation. But that day, which was indeed disastrous for Arab Palestinians, Syrians, Iraqis, Egyptians, and their allies, was not an act of God. It was a military and political defeat that was the result of bad choices made by bad Arab leaders.

Israeli ambassador to the United Nations Abba Eban described it best when he addressed the UN on November 17, 1958:

> The Arab refugee problem was caused by a war of aggression, launched by the Arab States against Israel in 1947 and 1948. Let there be no mistake. If there had been no war against Israel, with its consequent harvest of bloodshed, misery, panic and flight, there would be no problem of Arab refugees today.

> Once you determine the responsibility for that war, you have determined the responsibility for the refugee problem. Nothing in the history of our generation is clearer or less controversial than the initiative of Arab governments for the conflict out of which the refugee tragedy emerged. The historic origins of that conflict are clearly defined by the confessions of Arab governments themselves: "This will be a war of extermination," declared the Secretary-General of the Arab League speaking for the governments of six Arab States. "It will be a momentous massacre to be spoken of like the Mongolian massacre and the Crusades."

The Palestinian cause is full of pain; however the Nakba is a branded term, used to attribute victimhood and heroism to a loss in a war that was initiated by that same losing side. If the Arabs had agreed to the United Nations Partition Plan, no war would have happened, no Nakba would have happened, and maybe we would have been living in peace ever since.

But they didn't.

UNRWA: IF IT AIN'T FIXED, BREAK IT

In December 1949, after approximately seven hundred thousand Arab Palestinians were displaced and the very Arab countries who started the war refused to offer them any serious material assistance, the UN General Assembly passed Resolution 302 (IV) creating the United Nations Relief and Works Agency for Palestine Refugees in the Near East, also known as UNRWA. This was to be a special agency in the United Nations dedicated exclusively to the Palestinian refugees, the only nation in the world to have its own specific agency.[14] The 1949 UN resolution to create UNRWA stated that "constructive measures should be undertaken at an early date with a view to the termination of international assistance for relief."[15] In other words, this solution was temporary, with a mandate to be "reevaluated" each year. Seventy plus years later, UNRWA is now a huge organization with an annual budget (donated by the international community) of about $1.2 billion and a staff of thirty thousand. How did a temporary agency become so, well, permanent?

In 1949, when UNRWA was first created, the world was in turmoil. After the Second World War, dozens of countries were changing, borders were being redrawn, and people were dealing with the aftermath of war, genocide, and displacement. There were roughly 11 million refugees worldwide, 700,000 of whom were Palestinian. The 10,300,000 non-Palestinian refugees were funneled into UNHCR (United Nations High Commissioner for Refugees, created in 1951), the UN agency dedicated to resettling and integrating refugees and/or stateless peoples.

While UNHCR is constantly working on getting the global number of refugees *down*, with UNRWA the numbers go up, up, up. After the 1948 war, there were approximately 700,000 displaced people. Now UNRWA has 5.6 *million* "refugees" registered in their books. How is that possible?

Well, the primary issue stems from how UNRWA defines a refugee. The 5.6 million "refugees" include, for example, Palestinians living in Gaza and the West Bank (can you be a refugee from Palestine when you currently live in . . . Palestine?)—many of whom have Jordanian citizenship (though the international community generally agrees that you can't be considered a refugee, or "stateless," if you have citizenship in any state). And here is the worst part: UNRWA *automatically* counts as refugees Palestinians who are now three to four generations removed from the 1948 conflict (which is not the case for *any other refugees* who've passed through UNHCR, which will review case by case and make some exceptions if need be).

Instead of helping people move forward, UNRWA keeps the Palestinian people in an eternal loop of displacement. Instead of solving the problem in any meaningful way, they have overseen the problem's exponential growth. Among the people UNRWA counts as "refugees" are those like Mohammad Hadid. Mohammad Hadid is the mogul real estate developer and father of supermodels Gigi and Bella Hadid. He was born in Israel in 1948, and during the war his family left and became refugees; they moved to Damascus, Tunisia, Greece, and then Washington, DC, where Mohammad became a huge success. Despite all that (and unless he actively asked to be removed from the books!), he is still registered with UNRWA as a refugee, and is counted toward a "problem" that needs to be "solved." His stunning daughters Gigi and Bella, though born in the US, can still go to Syria, register with UNRWA, and also become a part of the "Palestinian refugee problem." UNRWA doesn't track the whereabouts or development of any of their "registered refugees," and never removes anybody from their lists, so one can become a multimillionaire LA mogul and still be counted toward the "refugee problem."

UNRWA is like a generational membership club, sponsored to the tune of $1.2 billion by the international community.[16] So why is that?

When the agency was formed, the world assumed that settling the refugees would not be that much of a problem. They, after all, were all Arabs, and they were surrounded by Arab countries who had made the Palestinian plight central to their sociopolitical agendas. But pretty quickly it became clear that UNRWA was a complete and utter failure. Only three years after its creation, David Fritzlan, the US chargé d'affaires in Jordan, sent the following cable to the US State Department: "For some time, I have been disturbed over the failure of UNRWA to accomplish anything substantial in Jordan in the form of refugee resettlement. The result [is] that vast sums of money were being invested month after month just to sustain the refugees, with no parallel effort to make them independent and remove them from the list of aid recipients." The Arab states, noted Fritzlan, needed to explain to the refugees that "despite their promises . . . it was unlikely that many of them would ever return to their former homes." But the Arabs were doing none of this, said the US chargé d'affaires. Despite pretenses of support for the refugee rehabilitation efforts, the basic policy of the Arab League was to frustrate them. "The purpose of this policy," concluded Fritzlan, "[is] simply to keep the Palestine problem alive in the hope of bringing about the downfall of Israel."[17]

Fritzlan bluntly complained that Arab countries were taking the UN's money with no intention of solving the refugee crisis. By 1958, the US and the UK had had enough of UNRWA. They knew that the agency had failed to fulfill its original purpose and were working toward dismantling it, when they experienced a scene that would have made Don Corleone proud:

> The Saudi ambassador in the United States invited himself to the State Department in Washington, DC, to make an offer that could not be refused. . . . [Saudi ambassador] Abdullah al-Khayyal began the meeting saying that he was there representing all Arab ambassadors, in order to underline the price to be paid if the United States were to refuse his demand. He said he was convinced that the United States was interested in a close relationship with the Arab world. Washington, he said, must avoid a repetition of past mistakes. The abolition of UNRWA, he added, "would have bad echoes in Arab countries."[18]

When US undersecretary of state Christian Herter, a Massachusetts Republican, inquired as to what, exactly, the US's past mistakes were, Khayyal replied, "Supporting the UN partition plan."[19]

In other words, by supporting the existence of the State of Israel, the US and the UK had crossed the Arab world and now, if they wanted oil, or allegiances, or strategic military intel, they had to pay for it. When Herter asked Khayyal to sit down with the Israelis and help find a solution, Khayyal answered that no one would talk with the Israelis. Full stop.

Effectively, the international community started paying protection to the Arab world, which has now reached $1.2 billion a year.

The pitch to the international community continues to be laced with thinly veiled threats of the horrors to come if countries *don't* pay. Take, for instance, these words from former UNRWA spokesman Chris Gunness:

> We hope donors will give generously, because, make no mistake, nothing short of stability in the Middle East is at stake. . . . At a time when extremist groups are in recruitment mode, it's surely not in anyone's interest to have half a million children not in UN schools but on the streets. . . . Is it really in anyone's interest to have one million hungry, angry people in Gaza?[20]

The refugees themselves don't even like this language. "It's really offensive to us," says Mohammad Abu Srour, from the Aida refugee camp. "UNRWA should be seeking money based on respect, morality, humanity, and human rights. . . . You cannot threaten people saying that other people will become terrorists to achieve your goals. It's a cheap way to do that."[21]

And he is right! The refugees need respect, morality, humanity, and a possibility for a better future. And the only way to express this is to help them create that *future*, not keep the problem alive. But UNRWA isn't interested in that. Instead of using its billion-dollar fund to help refugees establish stable, independent, and fulfilling lives, they help to perpetuate the problem. It is true that UNRWA does provide crucial assistance such as food, education, and healthcare to millions of people; however, this should be the job of a government, not a UN entity. In addition there is in fact a huge problem with UNRWA's education system. The organization has created its own textbooks and curriculum or uses the "host" countries' books, without proper UN oversight. Children under UNRWA are taught antisemitic propaganda and encouraged toward violence and martyrdom. UNRWA textbooks teach fourth graders to count by counting suicide terrorists (*shaheeds*), and for eleventh graders they describe the Munich Olympic massacre as "a strike against Zionist interests abroad." A shocking and detailed report on the matter by the NGO IMPACT-se was presented to the UN Committee on the Elimination of Racial Discrimination (CERD) in August 2019, which propelled condemnations and investigations from the UN, the US, and the EU, to name a few.[22] As former UNRWA general counsel James Lindsay stated in a hearing in the forty-second session of the UN Human Rights Council on September 23, 2019, the organization needs to either "evolve or dissolve," and when it comes to UNRWA, "the General Assembly has elevated politics over morality."[23]

In effect, UNRWA became a part of the problem, not at all the solution, all paid for by you.

Here is the nugget: settling the refugee problem would mean ending the war against Israel, and as of now, the Palestinians (and many in the Arab world) have been refusing to do so. The best way to keep the war with Israel alive is to maintain a perpetual "refugee problem" under UN legitimacy, which maintains an international concept of "right of return," at the cost of many hopeless generations. As long as the "refugee problem" is around, they can continue to believe that (1) the war with Israel is not over, and (2) they can still win it.

The Palestinian refugees are now a sticking point in any peace talks and a talking point on every college campus. They've been used as an excuse for a long and winding road that's taken Israel from one war to the next and one failed peace process to another.

CHAPTER SEVEN

A TUG OF WAR AND PEACE

FORMATIVE MEMORIES

There were a lot of fun things to do when I stayed with my safta Fania in Degania, but my favorite was the first thing to welcome me at the gates of the kibbutz. It was a rusty, menacing tank. Not some art installation or commemorative statue, but an actual Syrian army tank. The tank has been standing at the same spot since one fateful night in 1948, when it was stopped by five kibbutz members and one Molotov cocktail (or maybe a shell bombing, or maybe both). The photos from that fight are indeed horrifying: the tank was stopped literally at the entrance to the kibbutz, on the edge of a freshly dug trench.

I loved that tank as a child. The steel beast was a vivid and tangible reminder of the victory of the "few versus the many," the heroism of the pioneers, the dangers they faced, and how close of a call it was when they looked death smack in the eye. My cousin, the rest of the kibbutz kids, and I used to play on the tank as if it were a jungle gym. Which, of course, was the intention. That tank was left there for generations so that kids would understand the price we paid, and continue to pay, for having our own state. Imagine having that on your childhood playground!

I grew up with the ethos of war, and it has inserted itself into every aspect of my life since I was a child. I distinctly remember the year 1982. I came home from school and was thrilled to find my mom in the living room. My mom, a high-powered career woman, was never home at that hour. I ran to give her a hug, when I saw the tears on her cheeks. She was home early to break the news to my eighteen-year-old sister, Mira, that her boyfriend Rami, the guy she was going to marry, had been injured in Lebanon. I had no idea what was going on at the time; I just knew that something really bad had happened.

My beautiful older sister Mira was in absolute hysterics. She was running up and down our apartment, howling. My mom was chasing after her, trying to calm her down. In a broken voice she yelled after her older daughter, "It's just a scratch, it's just a scratch!" My mom was trying to grab my sister, hug her, but Mira wasn't having any of it. She was inconsolable. "*You're lying!*" she yelled at Mom. "*I know this is not just a scratch!*"

Mira was right, of course. I have no idea how she knew, but she knew. My mom was trying to break the news to her slowly, but at the time Rami was already in a coma. He died the next day.

As the tragedy unfolded, I fell to the floor in the hallway and tried to make myself as small as I could. I curled up and leaned against the corner of the front door, mouth shut hard, eyes wide-open, staring at my family crumbling, panicked and paralyzed. The horrific scene burrowed into my soul. I was seven years old. Rami was a part of our family. He used to toss me up in the air and play with me like a kid himself. And now he was gone.

That moment was a pivotal one in my emotional development.

A child who witnesses a scene such as this can become either highly un-functioning or overly functioning, and I chose the latter. In that instant I realized that shit can hit the fan at any moment, and massive drama can come knocking, unannounced, to smash reality to pieces. In an instant I made a subconscious decision: "I will not fall apart like this. They will never have to worry about *me* like this. I will be strong. I will be fine."

For the most part, I was and I am. I became strong and averse to drama. I have learned how to detach and disassociate. For years I would tell friends I was "GREAT!" when they asked me how I was doing, even when I wasn't doing great at all. It took me years of therapy and a plethora of self-help books, classes, and seminars to get back in touch with my emotional range, acknowledging pain when it comes up and giving it space and respect. This is still something I struggle with. I will forever have to practice checking in with my emotions when I feel like something threatening is coming and I automatically want to check out.

I'm telling you this at this point because this is the part of the book where I am going to talk about Israel's wars from its establishment through today. Over the years I have learned that even people who know nothing about Israel will associate the country with conflict. One of the first questions people ask me about Israel is "Isn't it dangerous?" And even though the country feels as safe as Venice Beach (if not more so), I get where the question is coming from. Israel has had its fair share of wars, and the international media eats them up. After all, "if it bleeds it leads."

But there is a long-lasting psychological price humans pay, hiding behind the headlines, and it plays out in every Israeli and Palestinian household.

This chapter is also meant to illustrate how the "recent conflict" is not recent at all. It isn't dependent on this government or another, with this policy or the other. The main thing to understand, both when talking about the wars and the regional psychology for peace attempts, is that Israel has always fought for her existence, but her enemies have changed throughout the years. And this is the key: The conflict is *not* between the Palestinians and the Israelis. It's between the *Arab world* and Israel.

THE TUG

The conflict between Israel and the Arab world is commonly divided into three time periods:

- **Bi-Communal Conflict (1860–1948)**. The years before the establishment of the state were more of a civil war between Arabs and Jews. For the most parts the Arabs did not want the Jews to come back, and initiated attacks against the Yishuv despite the fact that there were no large-scale territorial disputes or Palestinian displacements. Of course, not all Arabs were against the Jews coming back. The sheik of the Galilee and prince of Nazareth Daher Al Omar pleaded with the Jews to return and resettle their land all the way back in 1738, and there was a moving article in the official Mecca newspaper describing the "Jewish brethren returning to their land" in 1918. But for the most part there were constant attacks and counterattacks, and periodic massacres of Jews in Ottoman and British-mandated Palestine.

- **Interstate Conflicts (1948–1973).** When the State of Israel was established, the local animosity turned into an organized effort by all neighboring countries for the full defeat and destruction of the new Jewish state. These were three decades of classical interstate wars, wherein the main threat to Israel was the mighty military forces of Egypt as well as Syria and to some extent Iraq,

Jordan, and Saudi Arabia. These three decades were also when the Cold War was at its peak and Israel and the Arab world became, to some extent, proxies of the United States and the Soviet Union, respectively.

- **Non-State Actor Conflict (1973–present).** From around 1973 until today, the Middle East conflict has been dominated by non-state actors: terrorist, guerilla, and insurgent organizations sponsored by other nations and used as proxies to wage war. The Palestine Liberation Organization was formed in 1964 with the intention of establishing a Palestinian state over the entirety of Israel and to do so by an armed conflict. It has transformed and split throughout the years, and it is no longer the dominant player; instead, we have new actors like Hamas and Hezbollah, paid for by the emergence of Iran as a new wannabe regional power, also hell-bent on Israel's destruction and Shia/Arab world domination.

In the Israeli psyche (and arguably in reality), all of the above periods of conflict are inseparable. Despite having different enemies from different countries with different agendas at different times, Israelis see them as one massive enemy that is committed to their destruction. The names have changed, but the through line is clear. They want us out, and they want us dead.

The lack of a peace agreement in the region at this moment is not for lack of trying. Many attempts have been made throughout the years, but in order for a real change to occur, both Israelis and their enemies will have to shift their thinking.

But before we discuss that elusive solution, let's break down the more recent wars and attempts at peace.

- **The War of Independence (November 1947–July 1949).** See chapter six. Israel was formed; Arab nations invaded. This war ended in a truce—not a peace agreement—and the Green Line was created. In the years that followed, the Egyptian Army formed a special unit, the Fedayeen, and launched terrorist attacks against civilians on an almost daily basis.

- **The Sinai War (October–November 1956)**. Egyptian leader Gamal Abdel Nasser was spoiling for a second round with Israel. Egypt also blocked two crucial waterways for Israel (the Tiran Straits and the Suez Canal) and encouraged Fedayeen attacks. This motivated Israel to join the French and Brits for a failed attempt to try and take back the Suez Canal. This was mostly a French initiative, but the Brits wanted the canal, and the Israelis wanted to stop the Fedayeen (and open the waterways and halt Egypt's arming), so everyone had an agenda.

- **The Six Day War (June 5–June 10, 1967).** The infamous Six Day War was named for its speed and precision.

  Against the background of Syrian support for Palestinian militias attacking Israel from the north, Egyptian President Nasser warned Israel against moving its forces. As it later turned out, Nasser was fed fake news by the Russians: that Israel was about to attack Syria. To this day, no one knows who sent these messages or why. But this fake intel caused a crisis, in which Egypt, Syria, and then Jordan planned to attack Israel. Tension was boiling, the Tiran Straits were blocked, and Egypt asked the UN forces separating it from Israel to leave. Israelis were awaiting an Arab blow as the military noose around Israel was tightening and Israeli intelligence uncovered the plans for yet another joint Arab attack on Israel.

  On June 5, 1967, Israel sent 185 fighter jets as a preemptive strike to destroy the Egyptian, Syrian, and Jordanian air forces and air bases. Syria, Jordan, Iraq, and Egypt immediately activated their planned attack, and Libya, Lebanon, Saudi Arabia, Sudan, Morocco, Tunisia, and Algeria threw in, too. It was an all-out, all-Arab planned battle to get rid of Israel once and for all.

Within six days, Israel won the war in a stunning victory. Once again, the military not only defended its land but also conquered new territory. Up north, Israel took the Golan Heights from Syria. In the south, it took the Gaza Strip and the Sinai Peninsula from Egypt. And in the east, it took the West Bank (or Judea and Samaria) from Jordan. This last chunk of land was already disputed, as Jordan had taken it nineteen years earlier in the War of Independence. Although it officially annexed it, the international community on the whole (excluding Iraq, Pakistan, and Britain) did not accept Jordan's sovereignty over it. Nonetheless, the West Bank is at the heart of the international debate you've heard about Israel through the years, and we'll focus on that in the next chapter. This expansion to the east included the crown jewel of Israel—the Old City of Jerusalem. After two thousand years of exile, Israeli paratroopers marched through the ancient gates and stood by the walls of Temple Mount. The Jews had finally returned to the holiest place in Judaism.

- **UN Security Council Resolution 242 (November 1967).** Five months after the Six Day War the United Nations Security Council adopted a revolutionary resolution: land for peace! This was the first time the possibility of actual peace between Israel and its neighbors was created. Israel adopted the resolution within a month, signaling to the world its intentions to use occupied land as a bargaining chip in negotiating for peace.

- **The War of Attrition (June 1967–August 1970).** The Egyptians wanted the Sinai Peninsula back, but instead of going for a peace agreement based on the above UN resolution, they initiated numerous attacks on Israeli forces, mostly by artillery and seaborne raids. Israel responded in force.

- **The Yom Kippur War (October 6–26, 1973).** This was one of the worst wars in the history of the country. It was around 2:00 p.m. on Yom Kippur. My sisters were out riding their bicycles on the empty streets of our neighborhood (out of respect to ancient traditions of this holy day, Israelis voluntarily refrain from driving on Yom Kippur, and the streets are swamped with kids riding their bicycles on the empty roads), and my mom was at home recovering from a stomach operation. The phone at the apartment rang, and on the line was my mom's best friend, Rachel. "*Yael!*" she yelled. "*Take the girls and run to the shelter! Now!*" And then she hung up the phone. Rachel worked for the Ministry of Defense, and my mom knew right away that, whatever this was, it was serious. She ran downstairs to look for my sisters, yelling at the neighbors to run for shelter, now in full panic and bleeding through her bandages. My mom managed to find my sisters and convinced a handful of neighbors to open the shelters and get in. An hour after she got that call, sirens blasted through the country. Egypt, Syria, and Iraq, with active assistance from Libya, Algeria, Morocco, Saudi Arabia, and Jordan, coordinated an attack on Israel, and this time surprised everyone. The attack came on Yom Kippur, the holiest day in the Jewish calendar, and caught Israel completely off guard. The Arabs came incredibly close to achieving their goal of destroying the country. Israel eventually and just barely won the war, but it was a close call for the survival of the country and left the Israeli people reeling in shock and anger for a long time.

- **Camp David Accords (1978).** The framework agreements signed at the Camp David Summit by President Jimmy Carter,

Israeli prime minister Menachem Begin, and Egyptian president Anwar Sadat. This led to Israel giving back the land it had captured from Egypt in 1967—the Sinai Peninsula—in exchange for a peace agreement with Egypt. A cold yet stable peace between the two countries has been holding since. Egyptian president Anwar Sadat paid with his life for this heroic and brave move when he was assassinated by a member of the Egyptian Islamic Jihad in 1981.

- **The First Lebanon War (June 6–September 29, 1982).** Starting around the late 1960s, the Palestine Liberation Organization settled itself inside Lebanon on the northern border of Israel and launched attacks on Israeli civilian targets. After approximately 270 terrorist attacks and a failed assassination attempt on the Israeli ambassador to the United Kingdom, the Israeli military rode into Lebanon to remove the PLO. The war was named "Operation Peace for Galilee" and would be debated for years to come, as it became clear that the minister of defense, Ariel Sharon, "failed" to update most of the Israeli government on his plans to not only clean out the PLO but make it all the way to Beirut. Sharon's miscommunication (on a good day) or deceit (on a truthful day) caused Israeli public opinion to turn against the government. This was also the war in which my sister's boyfriend Rami Shalgi was killed.

- **The First Intifada (1987–1993).** The First Intifada, also known as the "Shaking Off," was a Palestinian popular uprising against the Israeli occupation of the West Bank and the Gaza Strip (which, you'll remember, Israel took from Jordan and Egypt in the Six Day War, after they took them in the War on Independence). Palestinians fought mostly by throwing stones, burning tires, and hurling Molotov cocktails, primarily within the 1967 borders in the West Bank.

- **The Gulf War (August 1990–February 1991).** In which I was personally attacked by Saddam Hussein. I was a teenager in Tel Aviv when Iraq invaded Kuwait, and when the US came to Kuwait's aid, Iraq responded by sending Scud missiles into Tel Aviv. As one does. I was at a friend's house when the sirens went off. The radio instructed everyone to go into bomb shelters, so we did. We were told this might be a gas attack, so while Iraqi missiles exploded around us, we duct-taped the cracks around the windows and doors to prevent the mustard gas from leaking in. We were all terrified and also puzzled by this war. What did we have to do with Iraq invading Kuwait and why were we being attacked for it? Those attacks lasted a few devastating weeks and freaked me right out. I had to go to school carrying a gas mask in a cardboard box, which I decorated with bright colors and lace. It didn't help alleviate my fears; these were scary times.

- **Madrid Conference (1991).** Heads of state from the United States, the Soviet Union, and Spain joined representatives from Israel, Syria, Jordan, Lebanon, and Egypt. This was the first time indirect communications occurred between the Israelis and the Palestinians. Though the PLO (still committed to destroying Israel) was not "officially" involved, they were a part of the Jordanian delegation, negotiating on behalf of their people.

- **Oslo Accords (1993–1998).** Secret negotiations in Norway between Israeli academics and PLO leaders paved the way for recognition of the Palestine Liberation Organization as the official representative of the Palestinian people. The Palestinian Authority was created, and Israel began a withdrawal from the West Bank and Gaza. The Oslo Accords won Israel's prime ministers Yitzhak Rabin and Shimon Peres, and the PLO's Arafat, the Nobel Peace Prize. But a few years later, the

Oslo Accords fell apart for reasons we will get to shortly. These agreements were not welcomed by the right wings on both sides, and Hamas upped its terrorist attacks on Israeli civilians, including a bus exploding right by my apartment in Tel Aviv.

- **Israel and Jordan Peace Agreement (October 26, 1994).** After years of clandestine communications, a peace agreement was signed between Israel and Jordan. It settled borders, land, water, and agriculture, and ended with a legendary picture of King Hussein of Jordan lighting up Israeli prime minister Yitzhak Rabin's cigarette. Much like the agreement with Egypt, this is a cold yet stable treaty. Jordan did not request the West Bank back as a condition for peace, so the territories stayed in Israeli hands.[1]

- **The Assassination of Yitzhak Rabin (1995).** This wasn't a war or a peace accord, but many point to it as the moment the peace movement died. A month after signing the second part of the Oslo Accords, Rabin was assassinated by an *Israeli* ultranationalist who rejected that deal, and the entire idea of land for peace. I was at a concert that night, and since these were the pre–cell phone days, news traveled slowly. An unpleasant murmur started passing through the crowd, and all of a sudden a man burst through the doors and started yelling: "They shot him! He's dead!" Rita, one of Israel's national singers, froze onstage and slumped down, grabbing her head in her hands. The crowd, me among them, gasped, stood up, and ran out. I drove home dazed and in tears, as did all other drivers standing in traffic around me. It was one of those moments in life when you can see a devastating historical turning point right in front of you.

- **Camp David Summit (2000).** Israeli prime minister Ehud Barak and US president Bill Clinton attempted to finish what

Rabin and Peres started and worked toward signing a full peace agreement to establish a Palestinian state. Barak agreed to almost all of the Palestinians' demands, but Arafat refused to sign. This episode continues to be cited as the moment when an individual (Arafat) had the opportunity and the global support to make a real change for his people and did not take it.

- **Second Intifada (2000–2005).** This uprising started when former defense minister Ariel Sharon visited the Temple Mount, which includes the Al-Aqsa Mosque. The Second Intifada began as a series of disturbances but would soon be defined by Palestinian suicide bombers indiscriminately killing Israeli civilians. Israelis responded by retaking parts of the West Bank and Gaza, at times in heavy fighting. Hell broke loose.

- **Arab Peace Initiative (2002).** Saudi Arabia published the Arab Peace Initiative, which, for the first time, laid out the terms that the entire Arab League offered in order to accept Israel as a country. The initiative, though encouraging, had major problems for Israel, specifically regarding borders and refugees. In addition the Arab nations refused to agree to an "end of demands" clause, such as the one that exists in almost every plain contract anywhere in the world (more on this point in a bit). Even though Israel refused to accept the terms, the initiative paved the way for unofficial communication and cooperation between Israel and the Gulf states (one of the worst-kept secrets in the region), which led to the Abraham Accord in 2020.

- **The Second Lebanon War (July 12–August 14, 2006).** Enter Hezbollah. Israel had cleared the PLO from the south of Lebanon, so Iran created and is still sponsoring Hezbollah, which is both a terrorist organization and a political party (and part of the Lebanese government!). The organization is deployed on Israel's northern border and is devoted to, yet again, her destruction. In the summer of 2006, Hezbollah launched an attack on Israeli soil in which three soldiers were killed and two kidnapped, and it sparked a war. Hezbollah fired thousands of missiles on civilians in the north of Israel, and the war lasted for thirty-four messy days. Despite heavy criticism within Israel, which led to the resignation of the IDF chief of staff and other officials, this war is credited with deterring similar attacks on Israel for years to come.

- **No Wars (2005 to present).** You may be surprised to hear, but there actually hasn't been an "official" war in recent years. Having said that, there have been many terror attacks, rocket and mortar-shell attacks, military operations, and bloodshed—most notably, three rounds of fighting between Israel and Gaza-based Hamas, and Israeli armed efforts to contain Iran's military efforts, base building, and arming of militias in Syria.

- **The Trump Peace Plan (2019).** This was the recent stab at a peace agreement between Israel and the Palestinians, and the verdict is still out on whether or not it'll be the basis for anything in the future. Jared Kushner designed the proposal with strong economic incentives for the Palestinians. It's not a bad idea, but the fact that the Palestinians have not been involved in that plan is a terrible one. The Trump administration did invite the Palestinians to come to the table over and over again, but they declined repeatedly. (They viewed, not without justification, the Trump administration as biased toward Israel.) The other thing we know is that the more time passes, the less is on the table. This plan is not that different from past plans (two states for two nations—aka, the Two-State Solution), but the territory for a future Palestine is getting smaller by the minute, for reasons we will explore in a bit.

- **The Abraham Accord (2020).** In a swift and unexpected development, Israel, the United Arab Emirates, and Bahrain took their not-so-secret relationship public, and signed a peace deal. A few months later, Morocco, Sudan, and other countries started making noises of creating an official relationship with Israel (Whassup Saudi Arabia!). This is a fantastic development, as it is the first time Arab countries are acknowledging publicly what everyone in the region knows but rarely admits: Israel is not the biggest threat in the Middle East. The Iranian regime is.

And we're done! This was a lot to take in, but here is the main takeaway: Israel has always been on the defensive, since before it was established and continuing to this day. There is a famous saying in Israel, which Prime Minister Benjamin Netanyahu read in a speech to the Israeli parliament and which is attributed to Golda Meir: "If the Arabs put down their weapons there will be no more war. If Israel puts down her weapons, there will be no more Israel." Let's hope this changes, and the quicker the better.

YOU CAN'T ALWAYS GET WHAT YOU WANT; JUST GET WHAT YOU NEED ALREADY!

Mick Jagger is a clever man, and the above words are as true for rock stars as they are for the Middle East. A successful peace agreement between Israel and the Palestinians is the Golden Fleece of international affairs, and almost every American president since the 1970s has rushed toward it like Jason and the Argonauts. But the conflict has yet to be resolved, and so the fighting continues. Why?

There are many reasons for the lack of peace between Israel and the Palestinians, but three issues are especially thorny:

1. **Security.** The first problem is the continuation of attacks by terrorist organization proxies. Every time a peace process starts, radicals on both sides resist the attempts, but it's typically only radicals on the Palestinian side who express their resistance by killing people (Israelis)—whether it's bombs exploding on buses in the middle of Tel Aviv and Jerusalem, or the constant rockets and mortars launched from Gaza into towns in the south of the country as in recent years. This causes fear and trauma among the Israeli population, which shifts the general public opinion in the country against peace and toward armed force. Common Israeli refrains include: Why would we negotiate with someone who is *still* trying to kill us? How can we trust that a sovereign Palestinian state will control its radicals and ensure the safety of Israel if it can't control its radical groups now? Of course, when Israelis send soldiers into Gaza or the West Bank to deal with violent radicals, innocent Palestinians are killed, property gets destroyed, and the cycle of violence and revenge continues, which is exactly what these radicals are after.

2. **The Right of Return.** As I explained in chapter six, 700,000 to 750,000 Arabs were displaced by the War of Independence and were put in refugee camps under UNRWA control. Since UNRWA has enabled refugee status to be inherited, there are now 5.6 million registered Palestinian "refugees." To be clear, we are now discussing the "rights" of *5.6 million people* to return *not* to the Palestinian territories or to an independent State of Palestine to be created in a two-state solution peace agreement, but *into Israel*—a country whose *entire population* is only about 9 million people. Why would you negotiate for a Palestinian

state to call your own, and then demand that millions of your fellow citizens move *into Israel*? Let me repeat that. The peace talks are all about creating a two-state solution, arguably the only solution we can think of today that will create stability in the region. However, in order to agree to a two-state solution, the Palestinians demand the Right of Return, which requires that Palestinian refugees, three generations removed, return not to a negotiated, new, and independent Palestine, but into *Israel*. To call this demand absurd would be an understatement.

3. **No Further Demands.** The third issue is probably the hardest of them all: putting a final end to the conflict. On November 21, 2017, the one-hundredth-year celebration of the Balfour Declaration, which promised the Jews a national home in their ancestral land, Prime Minister Benjamin Netanyahu spoke in front of the Israeli parliament and lamented, "Sadly I must say that I have yet to meet a Palestinian Sadat who will declare out of his own will the end of the conflict, acknowledge Israel's border, and support our rights to live peacefully and safely." No matter what you think of Bibi, even his critics would agree that he's not wrong about that. Whenever a peace agreement is proposed, it has the same gaping hole—the Palestinian leadership will not include language for "no further demands." This is exactly what it sounds like: a promise that the negotiations are finished and the parties promise to have *no further demands* from one another. Almost every single contract signed on earth has a clause to this effect. It marks the conclusion of horse-trading and a finality to the matter at hand. And yet the Palestinians *will not* include such a clause. The refusal to state, in no uncertain terms, that an agreement to create a safe and secure Palestine next to a safe and secure Israel is dependent on no further demands gives the Israelis an uneasy feeling. It is the definition

> of negotiating in bad faith. It's as if the negotiations are for some half-baked agreement, a midpoint to reaching some unstated, larger goal. It can make even the lefties a bit queasy.

Israel is guilty of many things, but it has attempted to make peace over and over again. Israel accepted the UN's Partition Plan in 1947. It adopted UN Resolution 242, Land for Peace (which it implemented when it signed the peace agreement with Egypt). It reached out to the Arabs many times, including in 1948, 1967, 1994, 2000, 2008, 2019, and 2020. These peace offerings were presented and refused, time and time again.

Why, for some of the Arab world, is Israel's biggest "aggression" not its actions or unfavorable government but its mere existence? Let's get meta for a second. The Arab world comprises twenty-two states and over 5 million square miles. Israel is 8,522 square miles. Why would the Arab world insist on adding 8,522 square miles to its 5 million? The answer may be tough to digest. In addition to the political reasons I mentioned above, there has been one other mega reason for why some in the Arab world have resisted the existence of Israel, and I'm going to touch on it oh so very gently: religion.

In the fundamentalist interpretation of Islam, once a land is under Muslim law it belongs to Islam and can never be given to nonbelievers, so a land that was once Muslim is forever allowed to be invaded by Muslims. This refers to Israel in a pretty obvious way. Historically, this extremist interpretation of Islam has been a huge roadblock to peace. Jerusalem is the third holiest city in Islam, and the neighborhood committee simply did not want Jews having anything to do with it. They didn't care that the remains of the *second* Jewish temple predated the Prophet Muhammad's ascension from Al-Aqsa by approximately eleven hundred years. Nor that the word *Jerusalem* is mentioned in the Old Testament 659 times and exactly zero times in the Quran.

Having said all that, I am still an optimist. Pragmatic leaders on both sides can always overcome both an extreme religious interpretation and a concerned public and create a new reality, if they so choose. In April 1974, right after the Yom Kippur War, 89 percent of the Israeli public said that they were extremely worried about Israel's security. But Israeli Prime Minister Menachem Begin and Egyptian President Anwar Sadat continued their clandestine talks through international leaders (among them Henry Kissinger) in order to set the stage for a "lasting peace."

On the 19th of November, 1977, Sadat came to Israel. He was the first Arab leader to visit Israel and was received with an official governmental welcoming committee at the airport. From there, he was whisked straight to Jerusalem to meet with Israeli Prime Minister Menachem Begin. Both leaders spoke on the parliament stage the next day and committed to end the cycle of wars between their nations. Sadat said he was willing to "come to an enemy state while still in a state of war in order to break the walls of animosity between the nations" and promised that "Israel will be able to live among the Arab nations in peace and security." Begin said, "I will say a prayer that the Gods of our mutual fathers will give us the wisdom to overcome difficulties and obstacles. . . . And God willing we will reach the coveted day our people pray for—peace." This was a day of extraordinary magnitude. Here was an Arab leader who had *just* tried to exterminate us extending his hand in peace!

Two months before the signing of the peace agreement with Egypt, the Israelis were still skeptical. Sixty-six percent of the people did *not* believe Egypt was interested in a peace deal that would keep Israel safe. However, only a month after the signing of the agreement, 75 percent of the public believed it.[2] Talk about a swift transformation of public opinion! So things *can* happen in a hurry when the right leaders appear.

The rest of the Arab world saw the move as an inexcusable betrayal. Egypt was kicked out of the Arab League; Palestinian leader

Yasser Arafat claimed, "False peace will not last."[3] As I mentioned previously, Sadat paid with his life for this monumental peace agreement when he was assassinated by a member of the terrorist organization Egyptian Islamic Jihad on October 6, 1981.

As you can see, a peace agreement in the region is dangerous, unpopular at first, and more complex than it seems. But it *can happen*—if both sides are willing participants. So I will go back to the words of wisdom by Mick Jagger. If some Arab countries would like to see Israel gone, well, you can't always get what you want. If some Israelis would prefer to own an Israel that stretches from sea to shining river, well, you can't always get what you want. But if these nations would think of what we *need*, we can and will reach a resolution. The world needs to understand that the conflict is not Israeli/Palestinian; the entire Arab world is implicated and should take part in reaching a solution. From the perspective of Israel (and pretty much every world leader who has studied this topic) the solution *cannot* include the return of 5.6 million people to a country of 9 million people. It *must* include an "end of demands." And it *must* affirm Israel's right to exist in safety and security. And when the Israelis see that willingness and believe they will be safe, a change will come, and it'll come quick.

Every person in the region, on both sides of the conflict, has suffered. Every family has trauma. My family has a few of them. It wasn't just the death of Rami that shaped who I am in a profound way; it was a massive price my family paid before I was even born.

And when I learned what that price was, I also learned that my beloved safta Fania was not my grandmother at all.

EVERYBODY JUST WANTS TO BE WANTED

I was probably around five or six years old when I noticed that each year, sometime before my birthday in May, my mother and my sisters were enveloped by grief. My mom and my older sisters, Mira and Michal, would sit in the kitchen or the living room, in front of the radio or the TV, hug, or cry, or sleep, or do all of the above, and for reasons I was unable to comprehend, I wasn't a part of it. They were so taken over by despair that I would run upstairs to my friend Nurit's apartment and hide, hoping the day would pass as quickly as possible and I could get my family back. The sadness was unbearable.

Later in my childhood I found out what had happened. That's when I learned that the young and handsome uniformed man in the black-and-white picture hanging above my mother's bed was my mother's first husband and the father of my two older sisters. His name was Isaac Artzi, but everyone called him Aki. Aki was a fighter pilot, and his plane was shot down by the Egyptian Army in the War of Attrition on December 1, 1967. The airplane, a French-made Vautour number 31, got hit and exploded in midair, sunk into the waters of the Suez Canal, and was never recovered. The bodies of Aki and his navigator, Elchanan Raz, were never found. My mother was twenty-six years old when she became a widow, left with a toddler and a baby: three-year-old Mira and eighteen-month-old Michal.

By all accounts, Aki was an extraordinary man. A kibbutz boy, IDF fighter pilot, and as handsome as a Levi's male model from the nineties, with those huge bright eyes that looked out at me from the picture above my mother's bed. *His* mom was my beloved safta Fania, my grandmother from the kibbutz. I'd had no idea. I just grew up thinking everyone has three grandmothers so I had safta Dina (Tishby), safta Hilda (Yavor), and safta Fania (Artzi). Safta Fania was my favorite person in the world, and all of a sudden I realized she wasn't who I thought she was and that I was actually an outsider to that entire side of the family.

This story is awful for all the obvious reasons. My young mom having to get her life back on track for her daughters. The fact that she never had any closure, since Aki's body was never recovered. And my sisters, growing up without a dad. They all had to survive financially and emotionally after this life-defining trauma. My experience, on the other hand, living on the periphery of that event, was nothing more than collateral damage.

When I first learned what happened, I did what I always did and hid my feelings, even from myself. After all, *they* were the ones who'd suffered, not me, and therefore I put on my best face and got on with it. Just like I did when Rami was killed: "Don't worry about me. I'll be fine."

I managed to play my part every single day of the year except one: Memorial Day for the Fallen Soldiers of Israel and Victims of Terrorism. Israel is a tiny country, and since military service is mandatory for most citizens, everyone knows someone who died in battle or in a terrorist attack. Memorial Day is painful, communal, and very personal for everyone. The day starts with a heartrending siren at 8 p.m., which lasts for one minute and is heard all over the country. During that minute, the whole country stands still. People stop whatever it is they are doing—working, eating, playing with their kids, even driving. They get out of their cars in the middle of highways and stop for a moment of silence, bowing their heads in honor of the dead. Memorial services take place all over the country, from the main ceremony in Jerusalem, which is attended by the prime minister, the president, and government officials and broadcast on national TV, to community services everywhere else. The next morning at 11:00 another siren is heard, this time lasting for two minutes, and again everyone stops whatever they're doing. During those twenty-four hours, the country is awash in grief. Stores and restaurants are closed, the radio plays somber music, TV networks broadcast movies commemorating the fallen. It is virtually inescapable, even for a little girl, especially when it's right at home.

When I became a teenager and started singing professionally, I would participate in my high school memorial service, which was a big thing in our neighborhood. I would practice the beautiful sad songs and take pride in performing them for my community. I would only choke on my tears later at night, when I was alone. And I didn't understand why. Why was I crying for something that didn't happen to me? Why did it feel like this *was* my pain when it wasn't?

I pushed those dark questions into a small pocket of my mind until I moved to the United States and experienced the culture shock known as the American Memorial Day: a day of barbecuing burgers with your friends. At first, I was offended by this version of remembrance (or lack thereof), and then—relieved. I didn't have to go through this nightmare again if I didn't want to. Naturally, one could choose to follow the moving military observances of Memorial Day; however, living in a country in which serving in the military is an admirable individual choice rather than a lifesaving necessity for the nation gave me the option. I could either mourn or go out to buy a discounted mattress. Problem solved.

But the problem was not solved, and I didn't just get on with it. As the saying goes, "Wherever you go, there you are," and whatever that pain was, it didn't go away when my geographic location changed. I found that out when I was asked to host an Israeli Memorial Day service in Los Angeles. I said yes, of course, but to my horror, when the day arrived, I was nearly unable to get onstage. Uncontrollable tears and anxiety chased me all the way from Tel Aviv to the backstage of the auditorium at the American Jewish University on Mulholland Drive. Something was not right.

It took me years to uncover the psychological scar I was carrying. Hidden, nuanced, and deep. When I was twenty-seven years old, I participated in a training and development program called Landmark Education. In the program you learn a bunch of "distinctions" to help you get clarity about various life issues. One of the main distinctions is "what happened/what did you make it mean." In a nutshell, the core of this distinction is that something happens to us in life, and instead of seeing it for what it is, we immediately give it a meaning—unconsciously and constantly. We come up with these meanings very quickly, and then we just run with them, completely unaware that we just made that meaning up.

I started looking at the most painful times in my life and breaking them down through the lens of the distinction "what happened/what did I make it mean." I worked on my issues, starting with the obvious ones. A girlfriend looked at me funny in middle school—what did I make it mean? Oh, that I'm not cool enough. Ha! I get it. Maybe she was just hungry? Okay, next. My parents got a divorce—what did I make that mean? Oh, that I don't need a man. That's not true either! And on and on. But then I remembered Memorial Days. Why was I so sad about something that didn't happen to me? What did I make Memorial Day mean? My mom and sisters were devastated. . . . What did I make that mean? Aki died. . . . What did I make all this mean about *me*? The realization took my breath away.

What I had made Aki's death mean was that I was nothing but a mistake. I made it mean that I was not wanted. I made it mean that they would have preferred me not to be alive. After all, if Aki hadn't died, I wouldn't have been born, and since they were so freaking sad about him being dead, clearly they didn't want me around. But I *am* around and will forever remind my mother that *he* is not.

I have lived my entire life thinking that I was a mistake and that my mere presence makes my mom relive her disaster.

My reality opened up like the end sequence in *The Matrix*. Every decision I ever made had come out of that hidden "conclusion" I came to as a child. Crying uncontrollably on Memorial Days had nothing to do with Aki. I wasn't crying for a man I didn't know. I was crying for myself, feeling lonely and unwanted.

I am not telling you this to be dramatic. I am well aware that other people have it way worse than I do. That growing up without a father like my sisters did, losing your entire family or home, or getting injured in a war is way worse. But I am telling you this to illuminate that people and nations pay for wars in various ways. The costs are complicated and hard to decipher, and can be carried down for generations. Being born to a family who lost someone this way has shaped who I am. And it is shaping every person in every nation going through war now and forever.

I am so grateful for the inner work that I have done throughout the years, no matter how ugly and painful it was. I now understand that my mom's sadness on Memorial Day had nothing to do with me. My sisters didn't do anything wrong, and they all do love me. Once I saw that, I asked to get on a Los Angeles–to–Tel Aviv conference call with the three of them to tell them exactly that. To explain why I was resentful at times and to apologize for never coming with them to Memorial Day services in Aki's air force base, even when it became a family outing joined by everyone including my sisters' husbands and my nieces and nephews.

I also know that I did, in fact, have three grandmothers, and that my safta Fania loved me deeply and for real. And what a rock star she was for adopting me like her biological grandchild, never letting me feel anything but love.

There is a saying in alchemy, "as above, so below," and an easy way to visualize this concept is to think of a tree. When we look at a tree, all we see is the trunk and the branches above the ground. However, underground, the tree's roots are a mirror reflection of that aboveground tree. By that rationale, a human's psyche is not dissimilar to that of their nation. I just wanted to be wanted, accepted, loved. Everyone wants the same—to be wanted, accepted and loved. And every nation wants the same as well.

Israel wants to be accepted. She wants legitimization and normalization of international relations, and she will not take anything short of that. This is the difference between the existing peace with Egypt, Jordan, and hopefully the UAE and Bahrain,[4] and the lack of one with the Palestinians. The leaders of these Arab nations, Anwar Sadat, King Hussein bin Talal, Sheikh Mohammed bin Zayed bin Sultan Al Nahyan, and Prince Salman bin Hamad bin Isa Al Khalifa accepted that Israel is here to stay, and they acknowledged it in writing. The peace with these countries is providing safety and stability for the region and for the world. Israel was accepted; land was swapped when it was called for; war was over.

People in Israel and on the Palestinian side understand the damage of years of fighting and are empathetic to one another's pain. True, there are radicals on both sides who will never accept the other side even if the price is bloodshed for many more generations, but the voices for empathy and acceptance are here and they are growing. In 1995, Buma Inbar lost his son in Lebanon. In 2006, he initiated the Israeli-Palestinian Memorial Day Services. Each year, on the eve of Memorial Day, families who've lost loved ones both on the Israeli and on the Palestinian side come together to remember those loved ones and remind us that "war is not a predetermined fate, but only a human choice." In 2019, the ceremony was attended by over nine thousand people, with only a few hundred people protesting against it.

War is never going to be a final answer; only peace can achieve that. And as legendary statesmen, former Israeli prime minister, president, and Nobel Peace Prize laureate Shimon Peres used to say: "I have seen war and I have seen peace. Peace is better."

CHAPTER EIGHT

SETTLEMENTS

WITH MY OWN EYES

One of the advantages of my military service as a singing and dancing IDF clown-soldier was the ability to travel the country. Throughout the two and a half years of my service, I got to go everywhere, north to south, day in and day out. I visited hundreds of military bases and met the most incredible people. We'd get to our home base in Tel Aviv in the morning, and as I was the commander of my troop, I would receive from my higher-ups the location of that evening's show. That piece of paper would determine the rest of our day, as each base or corps had its own unique characteristics. Air force bases meant new facilities and the best food the military could provide. Officers' courses were fun and exciting, but they meant dealing with over-the-top male energy, as these young boys hadn't seen a girl in months. No physical aggression ever occurred, of course; however, I do remember one night when the rowdy crowd started a series of too-obscene-for-print and utterly ungentlemanly chants. As the commander of the troop, I stopped my band in mid-show and put the entire audience on notice. Sorry, not sorry.

One fine summer morning I showed up at my base and received our daily schedule to find that we were to perform in Hebron. I wasn't too pleased.

As you'll remember, in the 1967 Six Day War, Israel took control over territories on its eastern border, west of the Jordan River (i.e., the West Bank). This land included the town of Hebron in the Judea Mountains, about twenty-two miles south of Jerusalem. On the outskirts of Hebron is the small settlement of Kiryat Arba, established in 1971. The little town is within walking distance of the Cave of Patriarchs, where Abraham, Isaac, Jacob, Sara, Rebecca, and Leah (better known as the patriarchs and matriarchs of the Jewish people, and therefore the mothers and fathers of Muslims and Christians, too) are believed to be buried. NBD.

Hebron is one of the most ancient cities in the world and one of the only towns in the Middle East that has been inhabited since biblical days, including a consistent if fluctuating Jewish community. Naturally, Hebron is a big deal for the Jews. It is also a big deal for Muslims. And since it's in a highly disputed location, it's basically a hot mess.

I received my orders for the Hebron performance with a heavy heart. First, I knew that since we were going to a dangerous place, I would have to be armed. I am somewhat of a pacifist and never aspired to become the Israeli incarnation of G.I. Jane. I'm actually a pretty decent shooter, but I never wanted to use my rifle outside of a firing range. And second, I knew my mom would be super-mad at me for going to Hebron.

You see, despite the personal losses my family has suffered, they always remained liberals. When I joined the IDF, my mom suggested that I refuse an order if I was sent to "the Territories"—the Gaza Strip and the West Bank. I opted to refuse *her* order. I didn't want to cause a fuss, and my curiosity was stronger than my mom's political opinions. So I grabbed my M16 rifle and we all got on the van to Hebron in the West Bank.

That day proved to be a pivotal moment in my political understanding of the region. Here we were, six nineteen-year-old kids who just wanted to sing and dance, driving in an armored van through what felt like a hostile Arab country. As we made our way through the old city, we were watched by Arab shopkeepers, women with their faces covered, wide-eyed children, and a few yarmulke-wearing settlers who walked around calmly, armed to the teeth. I was clutching my M16 for comfort as we made our way to the IDF base, which was literally a tiny room located in an inner courtyard of a few two-story Arab homes, flanked by balconies.

We unpacked our equipment, connected the PA system, and set up our microphones in the courtyard. There were only a handful of soldiers stationed on that base, no more than ten, plus the officer who'd requested that my particular troop come and perform for her soldiers. (This woman turned out to be none other than the future Israeli minister of justice and the queen of Israel's right wing, Mrs. Ayelet Shaked. We struck up a friendship throughout the years, despite our political differences.)

That night, we performed our show. The Israelis were gracious and lovely, the Arabs kept to themselves, and the day ended without any drama. But the entire time, I was extremely confused.

What on earth were we doing there? Hebron is indeed mentioned in the Bible, and even though Jews had lived there through the centuries, it was clearly an Arab town now and the residents clearly did not want us there. None of this made any sense to me, and I was determined to learn how and why Israel was there so I could shape an educated opinion.

So here we are. At this point in the book I've talked a lot about the Arab world's antagonism of Israel, but I have been missing one cardinal element. The S word. Settlements. So here it is.

HOW AND WHY

The settlements have become a red flag and one of the main reasons for antagonism toward Israel. In fact, the settlements have so poisoned international debate over Israel that they are now just another confusing element in a confusing region. Which is why we're here—to clear out some facts. But first let me take a pause for a sec. When I started writing this chapter, I became extremely uncomfortable. "The Settlements" refer to Jewish towns and villages located outside the 1967 borders (the Green Line), and since, as I mentioned before, I come from a liberal background, the general vibe around our dinner table was "settlements = *bad*." But there is a why, a how, and a who when explaining the settlements, so let's do that first, even if it makes my family uncomfortable.

The West Bank, which was taken by Israel after the Six Day War,[1] is under what is known in international legal terminology as *occupatio bellica*, or belligerent occupation: lands which were captured in war, are under military control, and were not officially annexed by the winning side. Israel's official position on the land is filled with technicalities. The first is regarding the land itself. Remember the status of the West Bank before the Six Day War? These lands were never recognized by the international community as officially part of any other country, so *technically* speaking they are not occupied by anyone, and were not captured from anyone.[2] Therefore, according to international legal precedents, Israel has no second higher contracting party to negotiate with, as in: "If the territories are not occupied, Israel cannot be an occupier." The second technicality is the various Israeli governments' positions on the settlements themselves through the years, and the international debate on whether they are even allowed to exist or not. Broadly, Israel's position on the settlements (which changes, depending on the government) is that, based on the Fourth Geneva Convention, of which Israel is a signatory nation, *occupatio bellica* allows a country to have people go live on that military-controlled land. As long as the land is not annexed and until it is negotiated in exchange for a peace agreement, there is no legal justification for forbidding settlement. The international community, however, disputes this claim and argues that international law, including the Geneva Convention, forbids an occupier from changing the status quo in an occupied territory. This is also, without judgment, highly creative legal mumbo-jumbo, since we are not dealing with some theoretical legal thought exercise but with human beings. But there we have it, a real-life manifestation of a legal gray zone sadly still going strong since 1967.

Now let's get to the how and why, which for a leftie like me was even harder to accept. I've already mentioned how tiny Israel is, but to understand *just* how tiny she is, try to imagine that on the eve of the Six Day War, the width of the middle of the country from east to west, from Jordan, an enemy country, to the Mediterranean Sea, was between 8.5 and 11 miles. That's it. That's shorter than a half marathon. That's the distance between where I'm writing this book in West Hollywood and the Santa Monica Pier, where we go chill at the beach. It's the distance from Manhattan's Battery Park to Central Park. It's really. Freaking. Close. It was an incredible security risk, as had been proven in 1967 and soon would be proven again in 1973.[3]

These were the lands that *would have* made up the independent State of Palestine had the Palestinians agreed to them. But they didn't, so they never formally "belonged" to them. After the establishment of the State of Israel and the subsequent 1948 war, Jordan took the West Bank, but there was no international recognition of these lands as officially belonging to Jordan, so borders were never settled. Then, in 1967, all the neighboring countries tried again to wipe Israel off the map, and as a defensive act Israel pushed through and, yes, took these lands. Since the end of the Ottoman era, the West Bank had never actually been "owned" by any state, but here it was now, held by Israel.

Suddenly, Israel found itself with an enlarged land, and various factions of society, both political and religious, started developing an agenda as to what should be done with these territories. I believe the technical term for this is *balagan*, the Hebrew word for "crapshoot."

After the Six Day War, Israel, having been under attack for forever, realized that this was an opportunity to once and for all create defensible borders. In other words, it decided to add strategic padding by building on the land it had recently acquired from Jordan and Egypt. This wasn't a colonial enterprise; this was about ensuring survival. There was a war, land changed hands, and the incredibly vulnerable Israel was building up its defenses for the next attack, which evidently wasn't far off. The only piece of land that Israel formally annexed was East Jerusalem. Up until 1948 and for over a century prior, Jerusalem had had a Jewish majority, and there was a broad consensus among Israelis that Jerusalem should once again be the capital of Israel. Even so, in negotiations in 2000 and 2008 Israel did offer the Palestinians the Old City of Jerusalem (excluding the Jewish Quarter) as a capital—and was refused by the Palestinians yet again.

The Gaza Strip is its own mess and we will get to it soon, but for now I will focus on the West Bank, which got complicated in a hurry. The first settlements to be reestablished were in parts of the West Bank that had had a Jewish population prior to the 1948 war, during which the residents had to flee or were killed. An unofficial agenda was created by Minister of Labor Yigal Alon, known as the "Alon Plan," to settle in some of the occupied territories in order to establish a buffer zone for future attacks. The plan was never formally adopted, but parts of it were implemented and settlements started popping up in unsettled areas around the West Bank. Despite the role of the West

Bank in centuries of Jewish history, though, Alon planned to give most of it back to the Jordanians and even proposed a Palestinian semi-state there. But the Palestinians and the Jordanians alike rejected the offers.

The first settlement in the West Bank was Kfar Etzion, which was reestablished by the descendants of the original members of kibbutz Kfar Etzion, who'd lived there before it was taken by the Jordanian military in 1948 and the remaining Jewish inhabitants, who had not fled, were massacred. They were followed by Rosh Tzurim, Alon Shavut, and Elazar.

In 1974 an organization was formed, Gush Emunim (the Block of the Faithful), which took a page out of the old Zionist pioneer handbook. They took the concept of rebuilding a homeland, and added a splash of religious zeal. Their spiritual leader was a charismatic rabbi named Zvi Yehuda Kook, and the movement actively worked toward settling in *all* the new territories. At first the group was small and considered fringe, radical, and somewhat irrelevant, as it frequently clashed with the government when it tried to illegally establish settlements on the land.

But with the slow collapse of peace processes through the years, and as the Israelis were becoming more and more disillusioned, Gush Emunim grew, and its members embedded themselves in all aspects of Israeli society, from politics to the military, from media to entertainment. The group was passionate, idealistic, pragmatic at times, and non-pragmatic at other times. They wanted the entire biblical land of Israel, including the West Bank (Judea and Samaria), to be Jewish, somewhat ignoring the whole other group of people who were living there. Or as former prime minister Levi Eshkol described it immediately after the Six Day War in 1967: "We only want the dowry—without the bride."[4] The dowry being the land, the bride being the nine hundred thousand Palestinian Arabs living in the West Bank.

When Menachem Begin of the right-leaning Likud Party became prime minister in 1977, many thought he would allow settlements to bloom freely. To everyone's surprise, this wasn't the case. In the first few years under his leadership, Likud held back the settlers and their demands and the Gush Emunim crew were not happy. When Likud won reelection in 1981, however, the settlement project became more and more institutionalized. The shift in Israeli public opinion about the settlements happened slowly, like a frog in boiling water, and the settlements continued a slow growth.

In the nineties, while the Oslo Accords peace process was in full force, Labor's prime minister Yitzhak Rabin reduced the governmental incentives for the building of new settlements that the Likud-led government of the 1980s had put in place. He declared that Israel would not "initiate or take any step that will change the status of the West Bank and the Gaza Strip pending the outcome of the permanent status negotiations." Please notice the word *permanent*. Rabin was negotiating in as good a faith as one can have in order to bring the conflict to an end—a *permanent* end.

In 1995, as a condition of the Oslo Peace Accords, the Palestinians and the Israeli government agreed to share power in the West Bank, which was divided into areas A, B, and C, which, on a map, look like slices of swiss cheese. The A area, which includes the big Palestinian cities and villages, went under full Palestinian control; area B went under Palestinian control, with Israel overseeing security; and area C is still under Israeli control. All this was agreed to be phased in toward a complete peace agreement to be signed within five years. Except a deal didn't get signed, and we'll get to that soon, too.

The Oslo process collapsed. Tensions between extremist groups reached new levels of horror, with Islamist terrorist attacks hitting civilians in towns all over Israel, and with some settlers committing murderous acts of their own. On the morning of February 25, 1994, a shocking attack was carried out by a Jewish settler from Hebron. He walked into the Cave of Patriarchs and opened fire, killing 29 and injuring 125 Muslims in prayer. Needless to say, the act was condemned from wall to wall within Israel, but horrific incidents like that also helped to hinder any possibility of peace.

In order to make peace a nation needs a unique leader, and by the same token, to screw things up royally, a nation also needs a unique leader. Unfortunately for the entire world, the Palestinians had just that second kind of a leader.

A FATAL TURNING POINT

The collapse of the peace negotiations took place in the year 2000, over twenty years ago, with the final death of the Oslo Accords. It ignited the Second Intifada and brought into existence the West Bank Border Wall, Security Fence, Separation Barrier, or whatever other name you want to call it based on your political views. The collapse of the talks accelerated the growth of the settlements, and since then the Jewish population has almost doubled. (There are 9 million people living in Israel, and only 463,901 Jewish settlers in the West Bank.) More so, the collapse of these talks served a deadly blow to Israel's center left and the Israelis of the "peace camp," and the majority of the country was left defeated and dumbfounded.

From 1992 to 1995, Israel was led for the second time by Yitzhak Rabin, the famed former military commander turned aspiring peacenik. Even he and his allies on the left were willing to tolerate some settlements as a buffer zone for security and a bargaining chip for a future peace deal. And so his government *did* keep on building in some of the largest settlements. He was trying to not ruffle any feathers with the settlers until a tangible peace deal was on the table and could be presented to that community. Rabin was assassinated in 1995, and it slowed the peace talks for the next five years, until a moment that seemed like an opportunity arrived in 2000.

As described in chapter seven, Bill Clinton invited Israeli prime minister Ehud Barak and Palestinian leader Yasser Arafat to Camp David to finish what Rabin and Peres had started years before: completing the Oslo Accords and signing a full peace agreement to establish a Palestinian state. Barak accepted almost all of Arafat's demands. According to a friend who was a member of the delegation to Camp David, the agreement was set and done. There was a Palestinian state, on upward of 90 percent of the land demanded, with the ability for the Palestinians to finally start building a country of their own. All Arafat needed to do was put his pen to paper and justify his Nobel Peace Prize. But he didn't. He said no.

Arafat refused to sign the deal. And not only did he say no, *while* Arafat was "negotiating" with Clinton and the Israelis out of one side of his mouth, polishing his Nobel Peace Prize and traveling the world on his private jet, he was also inciting, supporting, and coordinating an Islamist, radical, fundamentalist, deadly terrorist uprising in the West Bank and Gaza Strip. Intelligence agencies on the American and the Israeli side knew this but decided to push forward anyway, hoping Arafat would do the right thing when the moment came. But he did not.

Arafat proved the right wing of Israel right and walked away from the deal, igniting another bloody uprising in his wake. The final straw was Israel's capture of the ship *Karine A* in 2002, which was headed from Iran to Gaza loaded with fifty tons of weapons. The ship convinced the Americans that Arafat was, in fact, still a terrorist. They scaled back their relationship with him and much of the Palestinian Authority.

Arafat's actions took the region back decades. Israel was willing, ready, and able to dismantle settlements and leave the West Bank in exchange for recognition and a real peace. She had done this before and was going to do it again, and this time for good. But Israel failed. The Palestinians, on the other hand, showed that they preferred to dance with the right wing of Israel than to be a true partner to the peace camp.

When the talks collapsed, the West Bank erupted in blood. Terrorist attacks against Israeli citizens started again, and the IDF started using massive force to suppress them. The public in Israel turned against the Oslo Accords and became skeptical of the possibility of peace in general. And after one too many terrorists walked freely across the unfenced mountain terrain from Ramallah to Tel Aviv, covered in bombs and ready to explode themselves among the civilian population inside Israel, the separation wall around the West Bank was erected, cutting up Palestinian land and forcing millions of Palestinians to live under oppressive confinement.

And Arafat, in the meantime? Leaving the status quo as is has its perks. He allegedly became the ninth richest ruler in the world at the time. The international community paid the PLO, and then the PA, billions of dollars to support the Palestinian people. Needless to say, those billions did not make it to the Palestinian people, who still struggle with poverty. The International Monetary Fund (IMF) and the Mossad estimate that Arafat's personal wealth grew to the range of $6.5 billion. The IMF found $2 billion missing from the PA, and hundreds of millions of dollars skimmed from payments meant for PA salaries had moved through Swiss bank accounts registered under various names.[5] By the time of his death in 2004, Arafat had duped the Israelis and the international community and stolen his people's money systematically for decades.

As the director of Islamic Theology of Counter Terrorism, terrorism expert Noor Dahri writes: "Yasser Arafat was a fake hero, a lord of corruption and a true godfather of Palestinian terrorism."[7]

There were voices within the Israeli intelligence and political communities who warned at the time that a collapse of these talks would bury the peace camp for the next twenty years. They were spot-on. The peace camp had no plan B. We put all our chips on Arafat being the elected representative of the Palestinian people and that he would do the right thing for his and our people and for the future of the world. What a mistake.

That collapse, over twenty years ago, created a whole new generation of kids on both sides who don't view peace as a legitimate goal. The word *peace* itself became tainted and is dismissed with an eye roll, and the word *occupation* was weaponized by the hard right to judge "loyal" and "disloyal" Israelis. It is heartbreaking.

Arafat gave the Israeli right wing a gift that's kept on giving. It proved their point that the Palestinians aren't interested in a deal with Israel at all—that they don't want Israel to exist; they just want to keep the status quo and wait until Israel crumbles from the outside or within and they can take over the entire place. This was more than a betrayal. This was yet another *nakba*. A self-inflicted disaster of Israel's peace camp and the doves, liberals, and moderates who believed Yasser Arafat.

I am still a liberal, and I still believe that our two nations can, should, and will live in peace. But a new and inventive leadership needs to emerge, and I really hope that the Palestinians will not just come to the table this time but also use their pen.

THE PUSH AND THE PULL

The subject of the settlements is not in any way, shape, or form at the heart of the Israeli consensus. The internal debate is passionate and ongoing. Here is, in very broad strokes, the internal divide within Israel regarding the subject: the "hawkish" right wing of the political spectrum is leaning pro-settlements, the "dovish" left is anti-, and the center, which is the *majority of the country*, is somewhere around "Give us a good deal and let's talk."[8] The support for the settlements is not mainstream and the internal debate is directly affected by the level of trust Israelis have in the Palestinians.

As of 2020, the Palestinian population in the West Bank stood at around 2.9 million, and the Jewish population was 463,901. When people around the world criticize Israel for the settlements, they should keep in mind that we are arguing over approximately 5 percent of the entire population of Israel. This is not to justify anything, just to give a sense of proportion.

In the West Bank, the Jewish settlers can be divided into three main demographics: religious nationalists who are driven by ideology, secular Israelis who are motivated by government incentives and space to raise families close to nature, and ultra-orthodox Jews (Charedim) who are looking for affordable living and the ability to live in an observant environment. Out of these groups, only the religious nationals are the hard-core ideologues.

The nationalists' "mission" is to return to "Eretz Israel Hashlema," the entire biblical land of Israel. They also like to point to a 1929 poem by Revisionist leader Ze'ev Jabotinsky, "The East Bank of the Jordan," a yearning for both banks of the Jordan River. In his poem Jabotinsky writes: "two borders for the Jordan River, this one is ours, that one as well." This idea had obviously been abandoned years ago, as even the most zealous of Jews understand that they need *a* land, not *all* of it. The same needs to happen on the Palestinian side.

The argument has two passionate sides on its extremes (the majority, again, is open for the right deal)—the left thinking the settlements are a disaster and the right thinking if Israel *leaves* the settlements it'll be a disaster—and both sides are armed with ample arguments. When Ayelet Shaked and I were in Hebron as young soldiers, we managed to form the exact opposite opinion after spending time at the exact same place. We discussed this recently when I came to her house to light Shabbat candles, as two culturally Jewish and secular gals do. We both agree on the same three points—that Israel should be Jewish, democratic, and strong—we just disagree on how to get there. But we are able to have a cordial and friendly debate, jabbing at each other when presenting our respective "proof," which is exactly how politics should be debated.

However, despite Ayelet's burning conviction, even the political right, stemming from Jabotinsky's Revisionist movement, which always advocated for expanding Israel's borders for security and ideological reasons, never executed a full annexation when they were in power. "Nobody," as Ayelet told me recently, "wants to annex the whole West Bank and control the Palestinians." In fact, historically, the right wing made territorial concessions in exchange for peace or in the hope of peace. This was true when Menachem Begin (former Etzel leader) returned the Sinai Peninsula to Egypt and evacuated all the settlements including the large and well-established town of Yamit. This was also true when Ariel Sharon (former settlements evangelist and a darling of the right) unilaterally pulled Israel out of the Gaza Strip in 2005 and evacuated settlements around Gaza and Gush Katif. And this was true in 2020 when Prime Minister Benjamin Netanyahu was considering annexing some of the West Bank (more of a token annexation, which would have still been extremely unhelpful) but abandoned the idea in exchange for a peace treaty with the United Arab Emirates and Bahrain.

Unfortunately, the sad reality is that until Israel and Palestine reach a final peace agreement, millions of Palestinians will continue to live under oppressive conditions, suffering from poverty and lack of opportunity. The reasons vary, from Israeli policies to the Palestinian leadership's inadequacy, but the reality is unsustainable for either the Israelis or the Palestinians.

After the surprising victory of the Six Day War, in addition to the understanding that Israel needs to defend the country's borders, a messianic wave of returning to the biblical "watering holes" took over parts of the population. (These biblical watering holes were described in one of Israel's most iconic songs, "Jerusalem of Gold" by Naomi Shemer.) Religious nationalists adopted valid security concerns and added a zealous fervor. And now when dealing with the West Bank (or Judea and Samaria, depending on your political views), we don't just need to address security. Now we need to also deal with God.

MAYBE IN THE PROBLEM LIES A SOLUTION

In the Middle East, religion is a nugget we cannot ignore. Yes, Israel was formed and is governed as a secular, Western democracy; however, the entire region floats on the tides of religion—Judaism, Christianity, and Islam. As liberal Westerners, we sometimes tend to brush religion off, but in the Middle East, not taking religion into account is a big mistake. Whether it is on the Jewish side when young men pitch a tent on a barren hill in the middle of nowhere and vow to take revenge on Palestinians, or on the Arab side when young men vow to kill all Jews and never give an inch of land to the infidels, both do it on behalf of God.

In the West Bank, a military conflict led to the expansion of borders, and a military need for some fat on Israel's borders became intertwined with a religious cause. Both sides bring proof of their claims as a divine decree, and peace initiatives constantly hit a holy roadblock.

This is what happens when the tail wags the dog. The majority of Israeli and Palestinian voices, those who want to find a way to live side by side in prosperity, are getting drowned out by loud nationalistic, radical, or religious voices on both sides. And since the divine is currently, unfortunately, exacerbating the problem, we may want to consider going to the source to find a solution.

In homeopathic and holistic medical practices there is a cardinal concept that goes like this: *Like cures like*. This means that sometimes the cure for a disease is the disease itself. In Western medicine this practice is called virotherapy. It's a field in its infancy, and tests are being conducted to harness the power of various viruses and infected cells in order to break new ground in the science of healing. We may want to take a page out of the medical world in order to create a Middle East peace reset.

This answer may have been right in front of our eyes all along. Religion is a part of the problem in the region, but there may be a divine point of view that could be used in order to unlock this stalemate. I didn't make this up, of course—as a secular Jew, how could I? I found the suggestion for a possible solution in the life and teachings of the late Rabbi Menachem Froman.

Rabbi Froman was one of a kind. A settler, he was the head rabbi of the Tekoa settlement in the Judean Mountains. He was a student of the late Rabbi Kook (the spiritual leader of the settlement movement Gush Emunim) but also a fierce peace activist. Beloved and admired by the left, the right, the Jews, and the Arabs, Rabbi Froman dedicated his life to making peace between Arabs and Jews, and he wasn't afraid to take a bold stand and controversial actions in order to change people's hearts and minds.

Rabbi Froman believed that the seed of the conflict between the nations is ultimately based in religion. Therefore the end of the conflict and true peace can come only when religious leaders on both sides come to the table and help find an agreeable solution.

Rabbi Froman was relentless. He constantly met with Arab religious leaders and left-wing peace activists. He condemned Jewish attacks on people, on property, and on olive trees. He was fiercely against the Jewish extremist movement Hilltop Youth and would visit mosques that got vandalized by them or other extremists; he maintained a peaceful coexistence and friendship with his neighbors in the Arab village Jubbet ad-Dib.

His grassroots movement, Land of Peace, initiated meetings all over the country between settlers, left-wing activists, and Palestinians. He also met with highly controversial figures, even ones who were considered terrorists by Israel, the US, and the rest of Western civilization, like the spiritual leader of Hamas, Sheikh Ahmed Yassin.

Apparently these two leaders got along like a house on fire. Rabbi Froman used to quote Sheikh Yassin as saying: "Your infidels and our infidels have partnered up to suppress religions."[9] Wow.

I know, I know. As a liberal secular humanistic person, this last line makes the hair on my back stand up. Yassin is a vicious, vile man who deserves to be in hell for eternity. But as Rabbi Froman said: "We've tried to get this car started for 44 years and it's not going anywhere; maybe we should change the engine?" And he's right on that. We *have* tried everything else; why not try another way?

The rabbi and the sheikh knew that only people who believe in God, *any* God, could accept a reality in which their human earthly desires are not being fully realized; that a divine hand is at work and it is responsible for what shows up in life, even if you don't love it.

Religion, interestingly, has always found a way to make concessions and adapt to the changing of times; otherwise it wouldn't have survived. One recent and extreme example of how religion finds unorthodox solutions to modern world problems may be found in, of all places, the Islamic Republic of Iran. In 1986 the Ayatollah Khomeini issued a religious fatwa in *favor* of transgender surgeries, gender-confirmation therapy, and hormone-replacement therapy. Yes, you are reading this correctly. They found a religious basis to issue a fatwa, explaining that if God made "them" that way, then it is God's government's responsibility to take care of this issue. This is obviously not to say that Iran treats its LGBTQ+ community properly. *It does not.* However, the government of Iran does pay for transgender surgeries and hormone therapy. If a religious justification to (very rightfully!!!) support and assist transgender people can be found in Iran of all places, why not a similar solution in Palestine?

It is, after all, written in the Quran that *the Jews will return to the Promised Land*. (I KNOW! Crazy, isn't it?), so maybe in the next peace negotiations, religious leaders can decide to toss aside where it says to kill the swine-y Jews and focus on making the Surah of the Children of Israel, Quran, *Surah Bani Isra'il* 17:104, more popular: "And thereafter We [God] said to the Children of Israel: 'Dwell securely in the Promised Land.'"[10] Maybe this'll help some radical Islamists at least accept Israel's *existence*, which could be a pretty good place to start.

Let me make myself clear yet again. I am not advocating in any way, shape, or form to insert religion into politics. Ever. Israel was established as a secular, culturally Jewish, and democratic state, which means the government respects Jewish traditions while granting complete freedom of religion to everyone—the only country in the region to do so. However, I am willing to start practicing a bit more of my said liberalism and tolerance toward religion as well, instead of canceling it all outright. And who knows: maybe a new approach can be found hidden somewhere in those ancient texts.

Late in his life Rabbi Froman was diagnosed with cancer. He changed his last name to Chai-Shalom, which translated from Hebrew means "Peace is alive." He explained this by saying: "We must understand that in the Middle East, we cannot sweep religion under the rug." His funeral was a reflection of how he lived. Rabbi Froman was carried to his final resting place by Jews and by Arabs jointly mourning this dreamer—their friend. His powerhouse of a widow, his partner in life and in activism, Hadassah Froman, picked up her husband's baton and she continues fighting for peace, initiating meetings between Arabs and Jews and participating in peace demonstrations, some of them in front of Bibi's house. Like many Israeli women before her, she is another Wonder Woman.

The West Bank is a small piece of land where religion in the region is having terrible real-life consequences. So next time we have a peace talk, let's consider bringing a rabbi and an imam to the table to help us find a way out, and not as the beginning of a joke. They are, after all, the people of the book.

CHAPTER NINE

ARABS

LIFE, HUMMUS, AND AN (ALMOST) SEAMLESS COEXISTENCE

My dad loved hummus. Eating in general was a pastime he adored, but growing up in Jerusalem he developed a special affinity for hummus. People in Israel are extremely passionate about their hummus and will forge alliances based on where they think the best hummus in the country is served. Short of team jerseys, it is a national sport. There is one place, however, that is universally agreed upon as the number one spot. That place is Abu Hassan in Jaffa. The establishment is what one would call "a hole in the wall." Tucked on an uphill side street by the old port, it is simple and spartan, with only about ten tables and supremely uncomfortable metal chairs. The Abu Hassan family has owned the place for decades, and they serve hummus. Let me correct that: they serve *masabacha* (or "breakfast" in Arabic), which is not just hummus; it is the divine manifestation, and the most elevated incarnation, of chickpeas available to humanity. It doesn't come close to the dip you may have encountered in supermarkets in the States. *Masabacha* is its own divine meal.

In a spacious soup bowl, nestled in a generous serving of warm and creamy hummus, lies a zesty and lemonish tahini sauce. Both dips include a spoonful of warm whole chickpeas bathed in fresh olive oil. Fresh green parsley and dark red paprika are generously sprinkled from above, and the entire dish is accompanied by a side dip made of lemons, garlic, and hot peppers to spice up your life. Yes, the dish is indeed poetic—as is the look on the face of people while eating it. Cutlery is for amateurs in Abu Hassan. We locals use straight-up pita bread to stuff this heavenly concoction directly into our mouths, or just raw onions if you're as brave as my dad, my sister, and me.

The three of us would go to Abu Hassan often on Fridays around lunchtime, wait patiently in line (there is always a line), and be ready with our orders as soon as our butts hit the chairs. Waiters and cooks bustle around, rushing from helping in the kitchen to serving the tables and back as they yell orders to one another. The place is noisy, busy as can be, and freaking delicious. We'd walk in, order, eat, and get out. As my dad used to say: "Here you don't chew, you swallow."

I'm telling you this story for a couple of reasons. The first is that you really must go to Abu Hassan when you make your way to Israel. The second is to illustrate the reality on the ground in Israel. As the name implies, Abu Hassan is an Arab family-owned business, but the clientele is completely mixed. Arabs and Jews eat together, chat, and laugh without giving a damn about sensationalist international media headlines.

Of course, one anecdote doesn't prove a rule, but the point is that Arab Israelis are a natural part of the fabric of society in Israel. This is such an obvious observation for every Israeli citizen that it feels intensely un-woke to even mention it this way. But when you *do* turn on the news, it seems like the animosity, aggression, and hatred between the two peoples is constant and uniform. It's not.

For this chapter I will discuss the Palestinian people in and around Israel through three separate geographical locations:

- The Palestinians living inside Israel—the Arab Israelis
- The Palestinians living in the West Bank
- The Palestinians living in Gaza

The Arab-Israeli Palestinians, the West Bank Palestinians, and the population of the Independent Republic of Gaza (okay, it's not *really* called that, but you'll see later why I just did that) are sometimes lumped together as one people, and yet they are totally different in terms of their freedoms, rights, governance systems, national standing, international standing, political alliances, and foreseeable future. And also in terms of their relationships with Israel as a state and with the Israeli people.

But few activists in America talk about this. They talk, instead, about a unified Palestine that doesn't actually exist.

THE GENESIS OF PALESTINIAN IDENTITY, OR THIS IS WHERE I *REALLY* GET IN TROUBLE

The first time the Palestinian people were referred to as a nation, by themselves or officially by the international community, was in 1964, despite what they might want you to believe. Let me explain.

The word *Palestine* was first used by the Romans to name the region after the suppression of the Jewish rebellion of Shimon Bar Kokhba in the year AD 135. When they reestablished their rule over the area, Caesar Hadrian changed its name from Judea to Syria Palaestina, which was later changed to Palaestina. The name was based on a non–Middle Eastern (of European origins, according to archaeological DNA testing) tribe that populated the area at the time, and was used in order to subvert the Jewish origins of the land and probably also to annoy the Jews, which I'm sure it did.[2]

"But hey," you might be saying if you know your Scriptures, "what about the ancient Philistines from the Bible? The Hebrews took *their* land first, right?" Well, yes, but the Philistines from the Bible no longer exist, and there is no relation between the biblical Philistines and today's Palestinians. Archaeological DNA testing of the remains of the Philistines indicates that they migrated from Europe,[1] and archaeological writings from that time point to an indecipherable non-Syro-Arabian language (meaning not regional, not Arabic, Amharic, Hebrew, Aramaic, or Assyrian). Furthermore, in terms of religion, Islam wasn't around until centuries later.[3] The argument that the Palestinians are the same nation as the biblical Philistines is convenient, but it is simply wrong. I know this is an utterly un-woke truth, but this doesn't make it less true. Some, like Mahmoud Abbas, have tried to connect the Palestinians of today with the ancient Canaanites, but this beautiful mythology cannot be corroborated anywhere, neither in historical documents nor in archaeological findings.

Them pesky Jews, on the other hand, are traditionally, philosophically, and religiously the exact same people. Even two thousand years ago, Passover was celebrated, kashrut was kept, Shabbat was observed, and the divine was One. The language was also the same, as I can personally read the letters left on pieces of clay on top of the fortress of Masada from two thousand years ago—and, of course, there's the Bible. Today's Palestinians are a proud nation, but the conflict does not go all the way back *there*, as some have tried to argue. This is not a judgment call, nor is it a statement on which nation is better, so please spare me your tweets. This is just about which one is older. (And since I live in LA, older isn't necessarily better.)

The point is, throughout history, there has never been a coherent Palestinian national, religious, or political identity. *Palestine* was used in reference to a *geographical* location, and the people who were born in that region were referred to as Arabs of Palestine, Jews of Palestine, Christians of Palestine, Druze of Palestine, etc. In a 1922 British Mandate census, the Brits divided the occupants of the land into Muhammadans, Jews, Christians, Druze, Samaritans, Bahais, Hindus, and Sikhs—all of them Palestinians. The UN Partition Plan was for a Jewish state and an *Arab state*, not a *Palestinian* state. And even when Professor Zureiq wrote his infamous *nakba* pamphlet, he called the local residents Arabs: no mention of Palestinians anywhere. The term *Palestinians* as we relate to it today is nowhere to be found.

This is because, before the establishment of Israel, the Arab residents of the land did not have one unified identity and were divided among themselves on various issues, ranging from family and tribal loyalties to demands to be annexed to Syria, Jordan, and the like. It was a pan-Arab identity and not a particular nationalistic attachment to Palestine per se. The only thing that was agreed upon among these local Arab groups was the resistance to the Jews and the Zionist movement. They took that agenda so far, in fact, that the Jerusalemite Arab nationalist and Muslim leader Haj Amin Al-Husseini went to Germany in World War II, met with Hitler, and issued a fatwa against the Western Allies prior to fighting side by side with Nazi Germany.

A coherent Palestinian identity was introduced in the first Palestinian National Council conference in Jerusalem on May 28, 1964, and the following June, the Palestine Liberation Organization, or PLO, was created. For the first time a Palestinian national charter was created, and it was extreme, calling for the liberation of all the land and resisting Israel by armed force (this was later changed, though not to everyone's satisfaction). A Palestinian flag was adopted at the conference—black, white, red, and green, a slight adjustment to the Arab flag raised at the Arab Revolt by the tribes of the Hejaz desert and Lawrence of Arabia in World War I. The PLO defined as a Palestinian every person who was born on the land or to a Palestinian father (later changed to both parents), and a somewhat united front was created to work for Palestinian people's rights and nationalistic demands and needs.

It took the older generation a hot minute to catch up to this new reality of a Palestinian nationality, both on the Arab side and on the Israeli side. The world's third female prime minister and a lefty if ever there was one, Golda Meir, famously said on US TV:

"When were Palestinians born? What was all that area before the First World War? When Britain got the mandate over Palestine, what was Palestine then? Palestine was then the area between the Mediterranean and the Iraqi border."

The interviewer insisted: "Are you saying there is no such thing as Palestinians?" Gulp.

"No!" she said. "East and West Bank were Palestine. I'm a Palestinian. . . . There was no such thing in this area as Jews, Arabs, *and* Palestinians. There were Jews and Arabs. I don't say there are no Palestinians, but I say there is no such thing as a distinct Palestinian people of all the Palestinians who live in Jordan. Why have the Palestinians in the West Bank become more Palestinian since the 5th of June 1967 [the start of the Six Day War] than they were before? Why didn't they set up a *Palestinian* country in *addition* to Jordan?"[4]

The Palestinian national entity is, as hard as it may sound to my well-wishing lefty friends, a new identity. It was created for the first time in 1964 as a *political* issue, not an *indigenous* issue. The Palestinian identity was formed as an answer to Israel, in order to deal with a changing world.

Let's be clear on that again: a Palestinian identity is now self-evident and intuitive. If you were born in Palestine, you do and should feel like a Palestinian. The de facto Israeli rule and unfortunate continued land disputes only serve to emphasize that intuitive Palestinian identity. However, as a political and national entity, the concept is new and should not be weaponized to create alternative facts. The region is dramatic enough as it is.

THE WORST APARTHEID STATE EVER

Here is a story of an Israeli named George Karra. He received his law degree from Tel Aviv University and, upon graduation, opened his own firm and later became a judge. In 2011, he was the presiding judge who sentenced a former Israeli president to jail. *New York Times* columnist Thomas Friedman wrote that in his opinion this conviction was one of the things that sparked the Arab Spring. Neighboring Arab citizens saw how in Israel even the highest members of society pay a price when the rule of law is properly practiced. Friedman wrote that "an Israeli court recently convicted Israel's former President."[5] What he didn't mention was that George Karra is an Arab Israeli citizen. The honorable Karra now serves as a justice on the Supreme Court of Israel.

At the end of the War of Independence in 1949 approximately 150,000 Arabs did not get pushed out or displaced, nor did they heed the calls of their Arab leaders to flee. Instead, they stayed inside the borders of the new country. These Arab residents became Israeli citizens, with full rights and obligations. So when well-meaning Americans and Europeans say things like "Israel needs to give rights to the Arabs," I'm not entirely sure what they're talking about.

Protestors like to yell into their bullhorns that Israel is an apartheid state, just like South Africa. This idea is complete bunk.

In many circles, apartheid is understood to mean a minority ruling over a majority for the benefits of the minority population, with legal segregation and discriminatory laws. Let's start with the numbers. At the end of 2020, Israel, a Jewish democratic state, had a total of 9,246,000 people. This broke down into 74 percent Jews, 21 percent Arabs, and 5 percent self-defining as Other[6]—all having equal rights. In comparison, in 1990, South Africa, run by a white government, had around 76 percent blacks and 13 percent whites—with barely any rights for the blacks at all. Only one of these cases shows a minority controlling a majority.

Okay, you can put away your TI-89 calculator. Now that we can agree that Israel isn't a minority subjugating a majority, let's ask how that majority uses its power. Pretty well, actually. The simple fact is this: true to the country's Declaration of Independence, all Arab Israelis who stayed in the newly formed Jewish state are full Israeli citizens. Whether in Jerusalem, Acre, Nazareth, or Jaffa, Arab Israelis vote and get elected to the Israeli parliament. In fact, the participation of Arab Israelis in the Israeli government started on day one. In the first Israeli elections, which took place in January 1949, three Arab Israelis—Amin-Salim Jarjora, Seif el-Din el-Zoubi, and Tawfik Toubi—were elected as members of the first Israeli legislative body, the parliament known as the Knesset. They have been a part of the political fabric in Israel ever since, even when feathers get ruffled.

In 2014, Knesset member Ms. Haneen Zoabi defended the kidnapping of three Israeli teenage boys and claimed that the Israeli military were a murderous group worse than ISIS (all before it was discovered that these three boys were brutally murdered by members of Hamas). In 2015 Knesset member Ms. Heba Yazbak posted her support online for Samir Kuntar (a terrorist who killed, among others, a father and his four-year-old daughter, Einat) and Dalal Mughrabi (a terrorist responsible for killing thirty-eight Israelis, among them thirteen children). Some of her Knesset colleagues tried to prevent Ms. Yazbak from running in the 2020 Israeli elections; however, their petition was overturned by the Israeli Supreme Court. The court concluded that while her posts were an abomination, she was protected by her right to freedom of speech. Just imagine a House or Senate member expressing support for terrorist attacks against American citizens or calling *all US military soldiers* murderers. Ms. Yazbak did get elected and is currently serving as a Knesset member. As resentful as one may feel about this (and I do), *This is what democracy looks like.*

Arab Israelis enjoy equal rights for men and women and protection for the LGBTQ+ community. None of these freedoms are granted *anywhere else in the entire Middle East*. Same-sex marriage is fully recognized under the law in Israel (not by the clergy: much like in America, the religious system is not there—yet!), and regardless of religion or ethnicity, same-sex couples are entitled to pretty much the same rights as heterosexual couples, including all financial benefits (excluding only surrogacy and adoption, which is being highly protested and may even have become law by the time this book comes out). The reason this is important is because, unarguably, an Arab LGBTQ+ living in Israel has a better life than anywhere else in the region, where a member of the LGBTQ+ community can literally be stoned to death. I would also venture to say that, considering the oppressive ways women are treated in most Arab countries in the region, Ms. Zoabi and Ms. Yazbak wouldn't have been as free to speak ill of their governments had they lived anywhere else in the Middle East.

Arabs visiting Israel are sometimes surprised to see that every single street sign and every single product, from a box of diapers to a label on a pack of cigarettes, is written both in Hebrew and in Arabic. Arabs are fundamental to Israeli culture and society—from the abovementioned Honorable George Karra to the chairman of the board of the biggest bank in Israel, Samer Haj Yehia; from IDF colonel and member of the Druze community Hisham Ibrahim, who was asked to light a torch on behalf of the IDF in Israel's Independence Day celebration in 2020, to TV personalities such as the rock star reporter and social commentator Lucy Aharish, to Eurovision Song Contest host Lucy Ayoub. Of doctors and nurses in Israeli hospitals 20.8 percent are Arab; a majority of pharmacists are Arab; my friend Yaeli's daughter's favorite preschool teacher, Rim, is Arab. You get it. I feel like such a racist for having to make that list, but this is not tokenizing; this is the reality on the ground, with all its challenges and complexities, it is a powerful fabric of existence. In addition, as of Israel's third election in one year, in 2020 the third largest party in the Israeli electoral system was an Arab party. How is this apartheid again??

Today Arab Israeli citizens number approximately 1,916,000. Eighty-five percent of them are Muslims, and the rest are Christians and Druze (a unique religious and ethnic group that grew out of Shia Islam and developed their own rules and traditions). As is the case with minorities across the world, their situation is not perfect. Budgets are unevenly divided, resources are fought over, and self-segregation is alive and well, from housing to education. In a multicultural democracy like Israel, the Arab Israeli Palestinians have full rights while also struggling to properly integrate and be heard, much like minorities elsewhere in the world. This is why Arab Israelis vote, get elected, protest, and participate in the democratic system, working alongside their fellow citizens to make a change. And, yes, racism is also still alive and kicking in Israel, as it is all over the world, and it needs to be condemned and rooted out. But even so, in a recent survey done by professor Sammy Smooha from the University of Haifa, 77.4 percent of Arab Israeli citizens living in Israel said they *do not* wish to move to a Palestinian state should one be formed,[7] which should tell you that trying to brand Israel an apartheid state is an exercise in mental gymnastics. Or worse.

When I visited Israel a few months ago, I had a meeting with my friend, current opposition leader Yair Lapid. We met at his favorite café in Tel Aviv, and as I was walking in, I noticed a family of Orthodox Jews having lunch next to a table of lively, hijab-wearing girls. Each group was doing their thing, catching up over a cup of coffee and a salad. The only reason I even clocked that scene was the fact that I was already knee-deep in writing this book. I was observing the scene as an American, not as an Israeli. As an Israeli, I wouldn't have even noticed it, and no one around was blinking an eye. It's just life. At a table next to us sat Knesset speaker and Likud member Yuli Edelstein, and he and Yair were catching up, exchanging laughs.

And just to drive my point a tad further, I later learned that that café is owned by an Arab guy, Faras Kaaba, from the village of Umm al-Qutuf in the Galilee. It is also the only kosher café in the entire neighborhood.

This is Israel. Arabs and Jews, left and right, chilling out on a sunny Tel Aviv afternoon over an espresso. So next time you hear about the Jews and the Arabs warring in Israel, just remember: reality is way more nuanced and sometimes a lot better.

This is the reality for people within the borders of the State of Israel, but there is another reality for approximately 1.9 million Palestinians. A harsh, poverty-stricken, theocratic, violent, oppressive, and hopeless reality. You may have heard of this open prison, also known as Gaza.

FREE GAZA INDEED

To understand what is going on in Gaza, we must first understand Hamas, and for that, we need to understand the Muslim Brotherhood. The Muslim Brotherhood is a Sunni Islamist movement that originated in Egypt in 1928 and aims to implement Islamic law, known as Sharia, all over the world, starting with the Middle East. Sharia law, just so we are clear, is not a preferred way of living if you like democracy, freedom, equality, or human rights of any kind, let alone if you're a woman or a member of the LGBTQ+ community. Under Sharia law, for instance, a woman who is raped cannot testify against her rapist. If she wants to complain, she needs to produce four male witnesses in order for a "court" to believe she was actually raped. If she doesn't produce these four male witnesses, she will be convicted of adultery, which is punishable by death. The rapist, on the other hand, can have his conviction dismissed if he chooses to do the noble thing and wed his victim. Other pillars include: a husband can beat his wife, for she is his property, as clearly stated in the Quran, chapter 4 verse 34;[8] homosexuality is punishable with death by stoning; petty theft is punishable by the literal amputation of the hand; and anyone who apostatizes or speaks ill of, criticizes, or denies Islam, Muhammad as the only true prophet, or of course Allah can be put to death. One can safely say that Sharia, in its original and strictest form, is not conducive to human thriving.

In the sixties and seventies, after the Six Day War, a few scholars in Gaza concluded that Israel's victory was a punishment for the breakdown of a godly society. As a result, they turned to Sharia. A young, idealistic, wheelchair-bound man named Ahmed Yassin joined the Muslim Brotherhood and started organizing the community in Gaza around mosques and schools, preaching for Sharia living. These activities didn't worry Israel at first, as the Muslim Brotherhood had no outright political aspirations.

Around 1979 everything changed, as explained by Ronen Bergman:

> At the time, the Muslim Brotherhood in Gaza was seen mainly as a social movement, devoid of political ambitions. Throughout the 1960s and '70s, that was largely accurate. But then Ayatollah Khomeini overthrew the shah in Iran. A religious scholar, pious and holy, had led a revolution, raised an army, and instituted a functioning government. He demonstrated to Muslims everywhere, not only to Shiites like him, that Islam was not only a religion, constrained to sermons in mosques and charity in the streets, but also an instrument of political and military power—that Islam could be a governing ideology, that Islam was the solution for everything.[9]

An organization that was at first based around social welfare services, *dawah*, now added political ambitions and *jihad*, a holy war. A military wing, the Izz ad-Din al-Qassam Brigades, named after an

Islamic revivalist and terrorist of the twentieth century, was created to carry out this holy mission.

In December 1987, Yassin announced that jihad was upon us and created a new movement: the Islamic Resistance Movement, which, in Arabic, forms the acronym HAMAS. In addition to instating Sharia law, the movement was created with the specific goal of establishing an Islamist theocracy in place of what is now Israel, and to do it by bloodshed. Hamas sees Israel as an Islamic *wakf*, a holy land, that needs to be cleaned out. They announced war on the PLO for not being religious enough, and they wrote a charter, which is a highly recommended read for anyone who wishes to be entertained and horrified at the same time. As a liberal who believes in freedom of religion, I was very much in the Ben Affleck camp of "all religions are cool, let them be."[10] Until I met Hamas. Their charter is quite poetic, and in an impressive lyrical cadence speaks of such wonders as Jewish trees and lost jihadi souls.

Here are a few chosen quotes:

"Tempestuous ocean of creeds and hopes. For our struggle against the Jews is extremely wide-ranging and grave, its ultimate goal is Islam, the Prophet its model the Quran its Constitution. . . . The Islamic Resistance Movement is a distinct Palestinian . . . Movement which owes its loyalty to Allah, derives from Islam its way of life and strives to raise the banner of Allah over every inch of Palestine."

"The time (16) will not come until Muslims will fight the Jews (and kill them); until the Jews hide behind rocks and trees, which will cry: O Muslim! there is a Jew hiding behind me, come on and kill him! This will not apply to the Gharqad (17), which is a Jewish tree (cited by Bukhari and Muslim) (18)."

You thought I was kidding with the Jewish tree, didn't you? I wasn't. It's actually in there. And, of course, there is this one:

"Allah is its goal, the Prophet its model, the Quran its Constitution, Jihad its path and death for the case of Allah its most sublime belief."

All of this is out there in public, written explicitly in the Hamas Charter and found via a quick Google search.[11] The Hamas doctrine is very clear: no land for peace, no Israel, Sharia law, and death as the only way to accomplish this most noble of causes.

By the time the Israeli authorities wrapped their heads around this new threat and threw Yassin in prison, Israel was riddled with suicide attacks on its civilian population. Yassin continued to control his army of jihadists from jail, executing terrorist attacks on Israelis, including one about half a mile from my apartment in Tel Aviv, on Dizengoff Street, where the number 5 bus exploded and twenty-two innocent people lost their lives. The pictures on the news from my neighborhood were horrifying. Mangled pieces of torn-up human bodies splattered on the road, blood everywhere. We lived through hell in those days. For eleven months in 1993, over one hundred civilians were killed by bombs on buses, in markets, in clubs. Nowhere was safe. If a bus would stop at a red light next to me, I would recoil and cross the street. Remember the size of Israel from chapter one? Approximately eight thousand square miles and the size of New Jersey? Gaza is about thirty miles from my apartment in Tel Aviv. We had thousands of Islamist zealots preaching a holy war right outside our door, and as this enemy was driven by a divine commitment to jihad, death was not a deterrent but a holy aim. As Ronen Bergman describes:

> Prison had not lessened Yassin's influence, nor broken his will. "There will never be peace," he told Ben-Zur [his interrogator], after the interviews were over and the cameras were switched off. "We'll take what you give, but we will never give up our armed struggle. As long as I, Sheikh Yassin, am alive, I shall make sure that there will be no peace talks with Israel. I do not have a time problem: Ten more years, a hundred more years—in the end you will be wiped off the face of the earth."[12]

Even though the Gaza Strip was already a part of the Palestinian Authority, as agreed upon in the Oslo Accords, Israel was still controlling security and other elements and keeping an eye over about nine thousand settlers in twenty-six settlements and villages in the area. But in 2005, Prime Minister Ariel Sharon, the hawkish right-wing general, decided that Israel should get out of Gaza, and he pulled out unilaterally. The plan was supported by about 60 percent of the Israeli population at the time, me among them. In the Gaza disengagement, Israeli soldiers dismantled settlers' homes and uprooted their livelihoods in attempting to hand over Gaza for the future Palestinian state.

Within twelve months, everything fell apart. In January of 2006, after much resistance, Hamas ran against the PLO in the first Palestinian legislative elections. Despite polling that suggested the PLO would win by a small margin, Hamas won the elections. Palestinian postmortem research showed that only about 10 percent of Gazans voted Hamas for their deadly political agenda, and the majority did so as a protest vote against the corruption in the Palestinian Authority. Either way, Hamas did win. Naturally the United States, the European Union, the United Nations, Israel, and the rest of normal civilization freaked right out and demanded Hamas renounce their Jihadi doctrine. Hamas refused, as their spokesman Islam Shahawan stated for anyone who still wasn't clear on what had just happened: "The era of justice and Islamic rule have arrived."[13]

Head of the PA Mahmoud Abbas tried to bring about reconciliation between the PA and Hamas, to no avail, and Hamas started attacking and attempting assassinations of heads of the PLO. Inner fighting erupted and lasted for about a year, and in June 2007, Hamas took Gaza by force, launching a military operation against the PLO. The same brigades mentioned earlier, the Izz ad-Din al-Qassam Brigades, burst into Palestinian Authority headquarters and took no prisoners. They looted the offices, lynched people in front of their families, and threw PA members off of rooftops or shot them dead, and at the end of this coup they had killed approximately 160 PA members. Egypt, which also borders Gaza, quickly caught on and, alongside Israel, enacted a blockade on the Strip, trying to stop ammunition supply from reaching Hamas.

The bloody takeover of Gaza by Hamas happened only two short years after Israel withdrew, bringing every Israeli's biggest nightmare to life and handing a perfect "We told you so" to the right-wing Israeli hawks. What Israel got in exchange for unilateral disengagement was not a thriving Palestine in the making but an Islamist, radical, oppressive, and violent regime that promptly started launching rockets and mortar shells into towns and villages in the south of the country and as far as they could reach, sometimes all the way to Tel Aviv. The results of Israel pulling out of Gaza became a huge warning sign for what could happen in our region when Israel offers a helping hand, makes a peace gesture, dismantles settlements, or leaves altogether—you get smacked with Islamist radicals, who literally want to kill you and would kill their own people as well, thirty miles from your house. The Gaza disengagement and the takeover by Hamas serves as the greatest deterrence of the Israeli public against any future land concessions.

As you can imagine, Israel and Egypt have continued the on-and-off blockade on Gaza, trying to control the thousands of rockets launched from the Gaza Strip into Israel. Remember the Turkish flotilla from chapter one, the event that got me into this advocacy business? That boatload-full of activists was sailing to break a "blockade," but what they were actually doing was helping a terrorist organization. Israel may take the majority of the PR flack for the situation in Gaza, but the ones who pay the biggest price are the nearly two million Palestinian citizens living under this horrific, kleptocratic, Islamist, and oppressive regime. This is the tail that wags the whole Palestinian nation. Instead of using the billions of dollars provided by the international community through the years to build schools or hospitals or a better life for their people, Hamas uses the money to build fancy tunnels in order to carry out attacks on Israel. To buy ammunition and drones. They use civilians as human shields, and set up military command bases adjacent to and under apartment buildings and UN hospitals. And in recent years they have perfected another way to terrorize the citizens of southern Israel. They use helium balloons and a, shall we say, popular rubber contraceptive to send bombs into Israel. I mean, can one get more cynical than a bomb hidden inside a floating condom?

And of course, there are the suicide bombers, the *shaheeds*. A suicide bomber is the most vile embodiment of a victim/oppressor complex. He claims to be a victim, therefore he will oppress you by killing himself in the middle of your city. The narrative has been warped into a David-and-Goliath battle to justify this form of guerilla warfare. But as we've seen time and time again, even though Israel may have the bigger and more advanced army, Gaza is armed and funded by even deeper pockets across the Middle East, mainly the oh-so-benevolent Islamist regime of Iran.

So, yes, Gaza is indeed under siege. It is under siege by a terrorist Islamist organization that in its charter speaks of Jewish trees and aspirations for martyrdom, and whose religious doctrine is the earthly manifestation of rape culture and the legalization of violence against women, infidels, and members of the LGBTQ+ community. The people of Gaza do live in an open-air prison, and they deserve better. However, next time you meet a well-wishing activist who's sailing on a boat to break a blockade put on Gaza by its two bordering nations, try to explain that their anger should be pointed in the exact opposite direction. From college campuses to political rallies, there are hundreds of do-gooders protesting against Israel, but where are the protests against Hamas, a group that is the real-life embodiment of exactly what they are protesting?

Free Gaza indeed, I say, but free Gaza from its actual oppressor, not the perceived one. Free Gaza from Hamas.

WEST BANK STORY

There is another reality for Palestinians in the region, the reality of living in the West Bank, which is, again, very different from living in Israel or in Gaza.

As a quick reminder: for four hundred years, until 1917, the entire region was a small part of the huge Ottoman Empire. After World War I, Britain received a mandate from the League of Nations (the precursor to the UN) to control the region all the way to Iraq in the east, the mandate for Palestine. In 1922, the Brits divided their mandate by using the Jordan River as a border and created Transjordan out of all the land east of the river, which eventually became Jordan. The British named what is now Israel, the West Bank, and the Gaza Strip "Palestina EY" (initials for *Eretz Israel*, the land of Israel). In 1948, in the War of Independence (in which Israel was attacked; did I mention that already?), the Jordanians took over the territories on the West Bank of the Jordan River (the West Bank). They attempted to annex these territories, but the move was not accepted by the international community (excluding Iraq, Pakistan, and Britain). In 1967, after Israel was attacked by its neighbors, including Jordan, Israel took the West Bank territories in the swift Six Day War.

When Israel took control over the land in 1967, there were approximately six hundred thousand Jordanian citizens living there, and they were divided between those self-identifying as Jordanians and those identifying as Palestinians. From the get-go, Israel knew full well that this was going to become an issue. In fact, on June 3, 1967, on the eve of the Six Day War, Israel sent a clandestine message to Jordan's King Hussain offering to recognize the Green Line as the official border between the countries—so long as Jordan didn't join the Arab countries' war efforts. Sadly for everyone, the king refused, joined the war, lost the war, and lost the land (that he never *officially* had in the first place).

And then there are the Palestinian people, living in the West Bank for generations, tossed from one side to another between wars. Living under that "belligerent occupation" is living under military control. Despite Israel partly accepting and applying the Fourth Geneva Convention to the territory, it is highly problematic and indeed oppressive. This means checkpoints, restrictions on movement, building permits, water rights, and having no say in your own governance system. As "enlightened" as the IDF has tried to make this (and they did and they do), seeing soldiers roaming your streets every day is awful. This was the reality for the Palestinians until 1995, when the PA got control over lands A (full) and B (PA social control and Israeli security) within the West Bank in what was supposed to be a gradual process that would end in a peace agreement and a Palestinian state. But let's go back a few years.

The tensions between the local Arab population, the IDF, and the settlers exploded in December 1987. On the Gaza-Israel border, an Israeli vehicle hit a Palestinian car and killed four men. Rumors spread that this was an Israeli attack, likely in response to the stabbing of an Israeli man in the Gaza Strip. An authentic and spontaneous uprising exploded in the West Bank, exacerbated by existing financial hardship, frustration over the Israeli military presence, and weak Palestinian leadership. Palestinians threw rocks and bricks at the Israeli military, and the military responded with military force. Less than a year after the Intifada broke out, in July 1988, King Hussain of Jordan unilaterally disengaged from the West Bank and renounced all claims to the land, stripping the Palestinians of Jordanian citizenship and freezing financial and other assistance. He did this to (1) cement the PLO (Arafat's organization) as the sole representative of the Palestinian people and (2) drop a super-hot potato before it compromised his own kingdom's safety and security.

The First Intifada lasted from 1987 to 1993, when a memorandum was signed between Israel and the PLO with mutual acknowledgment and acceptance that the PLO was the political representative of the Palestinian people. It created a framework for future talks, agreed to a system for free and democratic elections for the Palestinians, and brought to life the legal entity called the Palestinian Authority, or the PA. The intention was to resolve all issues within five years. That was in 1993. Sigh.

From 1993 to 2000 the peace process moved one step forward and two steps back, until that final collapse in 2000. That collapse brought on the Second Intifada, in which around three thousand Palestinians and one thousand Israelis died, and over one hundred suicide attacks occurred in bars, in clubs, in restaurants, and on buses in major cities around Israel.

In June 2002, after the terror and bloodshed of the Second Intifada, Israel began to build a wall around the West Bank. In previous years, Israel's peace camp and Labor Party had called for the building of a wall separating Israel from the West Bank, to achieve security for Israel and "separation from the Palestinians" (which could also take us closer to a Palestinian state!). But Israel's right-wing hawks were not having any of it. The *right*, you say? Yep. Remember the right historically didn't want to commit to smaller borders unless pushed against a wall (pardon the pun), but it was getting way too dangerous and the right-wing government gave in to the public's demands for security. Israel built what it called a security barrier more or less around the Green Line. Since then, it's been called many things: border, security fence, segregation wall, apartheid wall, defensive barrier, and on and on.

There is no argument that the wall was built for security reasons, but innocent Palestinian families who never wanted anything to do with those suicide bombers walking through their villages are, as always, paying the price. The wall was erected fast, and as a result it restricted West Bank residents' movements even more. It also cut through farmland, preventing families from working those lands freely and hurting their livelihoods. Israeli human rights organizations and Palestinian families are fighting this wall and constantly appealing to the courts to change its route or rid them of it altogether. An example is the residents of the Arab village Beit Surik, who found themselves enclaved outside the Green Line, while their farmlands stayed on the Israeli side. Unable to work their lands, they sued the state in Israel's Supreme Court, won in 2004, and in 2005 the wall was adjusted accordingly.

This wall is a lightning rod around the world and inside Israel for numerous reasons. It cut through Palestinian lands; it left Jews who had settled in the West Bank "out" of the "official" State of Israel; and for the Palestinians it is restrictive AF. In short, no one is happy. But suicide bombings in the cities stopped. And this is what is so frustrating about being a liberal in that neighborhood. We hate that this is happening to Palestinian families, but what are our options? What are we supposed to do? The violence had to stop.

The reality in the West Bank now is a temporary, blurred-line life. In some cities, like Ramallah, Jericho, and Rawabi, life is pretty normal, and this is where some 90 percent of the Palestinian people live. Fully under PA control, they have their own economy, TV and radio, police, and social services, and people can have normal lives and work to strengthen their state-to-be. But what is the long-term plan? The West Bank lands have shrunk due to a combination of settlements, the security wall, and the Palestinians' refusal to accept a peace deal for decades. The territory is run by a weak and corrupt PA, headed by Mahmoud Abbas, who, as moderate as he is (and he is! which is great!), is now serving his sixteenth year of a four-year term.*
As usual, everyday Palestinians are the ones who suffer most.

* At the start of 2021, Abbas had finally called for an election.

Since the West Bank was not annexed by Israel, and since the Palestinians have not accepted a peace deal to establish their own independent country, this territory is in legal, political, and social limbo. The Palestinian Authority controls area A and partly B, but despite the fact that Palestinians living in, for example, Ramallah or Nablus are fully under Palestinian control, life in the West Bank is tough and undesirable, and their grievances are justifiable. Israel still controls building rights, water rights, and travel rights, which are heavily restricted. Interestingly, the Israeli security forces and the Palestinian Authority security forces work very well together, since neither is interested in Sharia-minded extremists arriving in the West Bank the same way Hamas took over Gaza. Still, in the West Bank, there are indeed different rights for different people, and the settlers get the upper hand.

The separation wall is a highly visual aspect of the region, and it looks real bad if you don't know the context of why it was put there. The incredible street artist Banksy went there, was moved, and started gracing the wall with his sharp political criticism. He opened a hotel in Bethlehem with "the worst view in the world," smack in front of the separation wall, which he named "The Walled Off Hotel." As political activism goes, this is probably one of the most clever episodes out there.

The situation in the West Bank is working for no one, due, in part, to Israeli policies and due, in part, to Palestinian leadership and a refusal to come to the table for peace talks. But the more time passes, the more land the settlers develop, and the less land there is for the Palestinians to call their own.

Israel should constantly aim to perfect herself and live up to Jewish and Zionist values, but despite the fact that there are very real security concerns in the West Bank, it's critical to remember that innocent people who only want a better life for themselves and their children are suffering every day.

To forever remind me of this, I got a Banksy print from the Walled Off Hotel's hotel store, "Wall Mart." It's a small print of a security tower with children's swings hanging from it, and a piece of the wall tucked in at the bottom. It's been hanging in my living room ever since.

A CITY ON A HILL CAN'T BE HIDDEN

As I researched and wrote this book, a gnawing sense of liberal guilt crept over me. In essence it went something like this: "Okay, I am clear about what the Israelis did wrong. . . . But . . . what did the Palestinians do *right*?"

I kept reading both in public records and in my family's history about the actions taken by the Jewish pioneers, immigrants, refugees—the Yishuv—toward building a country. I read through my great-grandfather Nachum Tishby's writings, in which he went against the British Mandate's opinions and created a thriving Jewish industry. I read in my grandmother safta Fania's letters how she physically broke stones into gravel for roads. I read how my grandfather Hanan moved to a kibbutz to become a part of a collective. And how the rest of the Yishuv got busy forming a political system, unions, an agriculture system, a health-care system, an education system. A foundation for a state!

My great-grandparents and my grandparents were forced to leave their homes, and when they came over, they were not happy with the British Mandate, that's for sure. But they didn't just resist the situation; they took their future in their own hands and got to work. They had one focus, one intention: survival. The Arabs had a similar goal—so what went wrong?

Historian Benny Morris describes this in depressing words:

> By late January 1948 . . . in effect, in most areas, the Palestinians remained dependent on the Mandate administration. Consequently, when the administration folded over winter and

> spring 1947–1948, and the towns, villages and roads were engulfed by hostilities, Arab Palestine—especially the towns—slid into chaos. Confusion and even anarchy characterized the distribution and sale of food, the delivery of health care and the operation of public transport and communications. Law and order collapsed. Palestine Arab society fell apart. By contrast, the Yishuv, under the same conditions of warfare and siege, and with far less manpower and no hinterland of friendly states, proved able to cope.[14]

Gulp. This was uncomfortable to read. It felt condescending, judgmental, or just plain old racist. I kept looking, and only then did I start to notice a pattern. There was a ton of fierce, firm, and bloody resistance on behalf of the local Arabs: they resisted the Turks, the Brits, the Zionists. Then there were the refusals of peace deals and a Palestinian state. Resisting is important, but one has to also offer hope and possibility that paints a picture of a better, future society. Prospects for your family, something to aspire to, an economy—jobs! Not just the stuff you don't want, but a vision for the future of your people, the stuff you build a nation toward. . . .

Enter: A City on the Hill.

Bashar Masri was born in Nablus in 1961 to Fatima and Faiq Masri; a surgeon and the director of the National Hospital in Nablus, they were a wealthy and well-connected Palestinian family. When he was a young boy, Masri participated in demonstrations against the Israeli occupation, and was arrested and put in prison several times for throwing stones at Israeli soldiers. In the seventies, the Masri family migrated to the United States and Bashar graduated from Virginia Tech with a degree in chemical engineering. He became a successful businessman, accumulating wealth and influence.

Around 1994, Masri started hearing murmurs about A New Middle East, the vision imagined for us by the late Shimon Peres and

Itzhak Rabin. He understood that it was time for him to return to his homeland and help build that dream. And he did.

The Masri family moved to Ramallah and became a powerful part of the Palestinian economy, but Masri still felt unfulfilled. "I wasn't making enough of a dent," he told me in our conversation. So, as the saying goes, he decided to go big, since he was already home. And he went big. Bashar Masri is the entrepreneur, founder, and executor of one of the most impressive projects the region has ever seen. He imagined, funded, and built an entirely new city, from the ground up, in the West Bank: Rawabi. *Rawabi* in Arabic means "hills," and, true to its name, the city was built on the hills just outside Ramallah, north of Jerusalem. This is the first city that has been built entirely by and for Palestinians. It is a planned community, aimed at the middle class, with affordable apartments, large office spaces for the tech community, and a high-end retail area.

Mr. Masri is a sharp and eloquent man, charismatic even on a transatlantic phone call. I wanted to know when the lightbulb went off, what was the moment that made him come up with this seemingly insane idea.

"It's all about the economy, and I knew I needed to do a 'wow' project. I wanted a way to hire ten thousand people or more, but I didn't know exactly what that was. In May of 2007, I was in Morocco visiting a real estate project I have invested in, and I stood on a hill overlooking that development. I saw thousands of people walking around, like ants, so many of them, and it clicked—real estate! I wasn't thinking of a city at the time, just a real estate development. I came back to the West Bank and started looking into building in Ramallah, but we quickly realized that such a huge project would turn the city upside down, and within weeks we were working on building a whole new city from scratch."

It wasn't easy. While Masri found Israeli companies and businessmen extremely collaborative and helpful, he found the Israeli government to be extremely frustrating and difficult. "I knew they would give me a hard time," he said. (They did, making it a bureaucratic nightmare to get building permits, water, etc.) "But I went hard anyway and at the end we got what we needed." Today, many Israeli entrepreneurs and private companies are doing business in Rawabi for the benefit of everyone. As always, people find common ground even if governments need to strike a pose for the benefit of their bases.

Masri is fired up about building his state. "Most countries," he said, "are built through a war or a coup. We the Palestinians are in a unique position. We have a chance to build a state which evolves over time, a model state, ironically in a place where nations are falling apart all over the region around us. We can build a model state, and in order to do so we have to build a model city and a model government."

In order to do that, he models his companies on what he thinks a model state should look like: equal engagement of men and women. Mr. Masri is adamant on this point: "Some of my staff told me that we have the highest percentage of women in our workplace. It's twenty-eight percent! I said that's not enough. Fifty percent is the population of women, and this is where we should be."

This is not something to take lightly in a region where Islamist groups around the corner, in Gaza and other countries in the Middle East, still see a woman as her husband's property. This is something to inspire not only the region but the world.

Rawabi is a shiny city on a hill, complete with brand-new buildings made out of white stones cut from a nearby quarry. Many believe that this project is the beginning of the Palestinian people's pivot toward taking charge of their own future, a future of industry, equality, liberalism, and empowerment.

Masri understood a very simple thing: if you build it, they will come. He is not your token Palestinian friend. Rawabi is not your token Palestinian city. They are both what the future of the Palestinian people and the Palestinian state can be.

THE CLOSER YOU LOOK, THE MORE COMPLICATED IT GETS

To understand the region and the issues facing the Palestinian people, I had to clarify the very different obstacles they are dealing with, dictated by geographic location, history of conflict, political affiliations, and religious agenda. You can't blanket-criticize Israel about the Palestinians' state of being, and the state of their future state, without differentiating between these three very different factions:

- The Arab Israeli Palestinians with full legal rights (albeit with legitimate racial and socioeconomic concerns): human rights, the right to vote, to speak, and to love whomever they want;
- The Palestinians in the West Bank living under a weak Palestinian Authority and/or the constant presence of the Israeli military;
- The Palestinians under siege in Gaza who are under blockade both by Israel and Egypt and ruled by the terrorist organization Hamas under horrific Islamist Sharia law; a violent regime, without safety, prosperity, or basic human rights.

A coherent Palestinian identity, and the ability of the Palestinian people to clearly define *for themselves* who they are, what they want, and what values they stand for, is of course crucial for the security of Israel, the region, and the rest of the world, but it is mostly crucial for the future of the Palestinians themselves. The Palestinians must no longer define themselves by what they *resist* (the Ottomans, the British Mandate, the Zionists, etc.) but instead by what they want to create. And they need to get real with a very basic question: What is the Palestinian national ambition *really* about? Is it about having a state and living side by side with Israel? Or is it about wiping Israel off the map and creating a Sharia state?

I can tell you that as a centrist/lefty Israeli, I keep looking for the Bashar Masris of the region. But so far the Arab nations and then the Palestinian people have refused each and every offer. From 1922, 1947, 1948, 1967, 1973, 1994, 2000, 2008, and 2019. It has just been one big fat "Nope."

We get what you don't want, but what is it that you *do* want? There are a lot of us in Israel—a majority of us, in fact—who are anxiously waiting for the answer that will allow for a peaceful Middle East to arise.

PART III

BE

CHAPTER TEN

BDS

WTF IS BDS?

BDS is a three-letter acronym that's tossed around more than pita bread on an Israeli barbecue (which, by the way, we call *mangal*). But what is this movement, *really*? If you haven't been on a college campus in the last fifteen years or don't follow the region closely, you may have missed this revived movement altogether. But if you're somewhere in the zone of millennial to Gen Z, and/or associated with the liberal left or social justice movements on any level, you've probably come across the name. Maybe you even found the cause admirable! In this chapter we are going to discuss the BDS movement, what it *says* that it is, and what it's *actually* about. We'll also explore the lies it has spread and the damage it has done, and why it needs to be ousted from any liberal society.

Let's start with a quick rundown of what BDS claims to be and why it attracted so many young Americans. And Pink Floyd bassist Roger Waters.

BDS is the acronym for Boycott, Divestment, Sanctions, and it acts to do just that: to wage economic warfare on Israel. It advocates for divesting investments away from Israel, boycotting Israeli products and academia, not doing business with Israeli companies, and placing economic sanctions on Israel, like the ones imposed on apartheid South Africa. BDS claims to be a "citizen-led" organization and the great hope of the Palestinian people. At face value, BDS presents itself as a left-leaning movement that only wants to do good in the world, and who can argue with that? On its website, it's official statement is this:

> Boycott, Divestment, Sanctions (BDS) is a Palestinian-led movement for freedom, justice and equality. BDS upholds the simple principle that Palestinians are entitled to the same rights as the rest of humanity.

So far, so good. I fully stand for the above as well. The popular narrative is that BDS pushes for a boycott of Israel only in *reaction* to Israeli policies in the occupied territories and only in order to press the Israeli government to do the right thing and give the Palestinians a state so they can live side by side with Israel. At first glance, this looks good, too. It's a politically correct, highly sympathetic message, which is likely why the movement has gained support from some members of the US House of Representatives, including Representative Rashida Tlaib (D-MI), Representative Ilhan Omar (D-MN), and Representative Alexandria Ocasio-Cortez (D-NY). Not to mention former British Labor leader Jeremy Corbyn.

In only about fifteen years or so, BDS managed to become pretty successful in altering the conversation about Israel, infiltrating liberal circles, and becoming a hip extracurricular activity for my friends in the woke crowd. BDS has had incredible success reaching young

Americans, who then become extremely active on college campuses and later on, in all walks of life, convincing those young Americans (and Roger Waters) that they are only after justice for all.

This couldn't be further from reality. A dive into the movement reveals a well-coordinated manipulation of American public opinion. BDS is not what it appears to be, and many people behind the BDS movement are working hard to make sure unsuspecting and well-meaning people stay in the dark.

Here is how.

WHAT ARE YOU HIDING BACK THERE?

Let me be clear: BDS is not a movement for justice *or* for peace. The movement doesn't offer *any* solutions for peace *anywhere*. BDS leaders try not to say it out loud this way, of course, but it's very easy to see, once you take a look. Here are the BDS movement's three stated goals, and the issues they conveniently choose to ignore.

Goal #1. *Ending Israel's occupation and colonization of all Arab lands.* In this seemingly innocuous statement, the devil is in the details. What, exactly, do they mean by "all Arab Lands"? The BDS movement is intentionally opaque, but its leaders clear things up when directly asked. The movement isn't interested in Palestine peacefully coexisting next to Israel; they simply want Israel to not exist. As stated by the founder of the (recent! We'll get to that, too) Boycott movement, Omar Barghouti: "Definitely, most definitely we oppose a Jewish state in *any* part of Palestine."[1] Pretty clear words, I would say.

Goal #2. *Getting Arab-Palestinian citizens of Israel full equality.* We covered this as well in chapter nine. Palestinians in Israel *have* full rights. And what a great thing that is! How does Hamas treat Palestinians living under its rule in Gaza? They beat unarmed protestors, fire live ammunition, and randomly arrest and torture journalists. Not to mention killing their PLO brothers, honor killing women, and arresting and torturing people in the LGBTQ+ community. Whose rights is the BDS movement fighting for, exactly?

Goal #3. *Promoting the rights of Palestinian refugees to return to their homes and properties*. As you remember, this is one of the biggest sticking points in the Israeli-Palestinian peace negotiations. Let's start again with a reminder that the wars of 1948 and 1967 (defensive and preemptive/defensive) were started not by Israel but by its neighbors, hoping to destroy Israel.

We've touched on this before, but let's drive home the point again, since BDS is using it—*a lot*. From 700,000 to 750,000 Palestinians lost their homes after the 1948 war; today 5.6 million "refugees" are registered with UNRWA due to the organization's twisted concept of inherited refugee status. Automatic "heritability" of a refugee status doesn't exist in any other group of refugees in the world, and Palestinians should be held to the same standards. You should not be able to inherit your refugee status and then blame Israel for this problem.

Of course, this is not how BDS frames things on its website. Instead, they speak of Israeli atrocities, murder, apartheid, genocide, and systematic ethnic cleansing. The only problem is that it's a giant pile of crap—misinformation, disinformation, manipulation, elimination of history, and flat-out lies.

Here are a few examples of how critical factual historical information is left off of the official BDS website in order to achieve this magnificent manipulation upon unsuspecting, well-intentioned, and ill-informed Americans (and Roger Waters):

Regarding the establishment of Israel. "Israel was established in 1948 through the brutal displacement of nearly 800,000 Palestinians. . . . This premeditated cleansing is known as al-Nakba." ← This conveniently leaves out the fact that the United Nations granted the Jews a return to their ancestral homeland after the Jewish people were nearly destroyed in the Holocaust; that Israel agreed to the UN Partition Plan for Statehood; that the Arabs refused it and *attacked the new Jewish state in order to destroy it*. There was literally zero systematic ethnic cleansing, then or now, as proven by the fact that Israeli Arabs constitute 21 percent of Israel's population (and hold high levels of employment in public service, the IDF, government, etc.).

Regarding refugees. "The majority of Palestinians are the 7.25m refugees who have been forced from their homes to make way for Jewish Israelis and are denied their right to return to their homes." ← This makes it sound as if the Jews invaded a highly developed, heavily populated country and *forced out* 7.5 million people (where did they get *this* number from, anyway?). We've been through this in chapter three; it's absurd.

Regarding Gaza. "Israel carried out horrific massacres of Palestinians in Gaza in 2008–09, 2012 and 2014. . . . Israel deliberately attacked Palestinian civilians, schools, hospitals and other civilian infrastructure." ← This conveniently fails to mention that these attacks were in response to military aggression started by Hamas, a terrorist organization that *actually* massacred their internal opposition and imposed Sharia law on their people. Israel, a democracy, and Gaza, ruled by terrorist organization Hamas, are effectively *in a state of war*. Between the year 2005 and June 2014, 9,062 rockets and 5,099 mortars were fired at Israeli civilians by Hamas. In 2018, 1,119 rockets were shot on Israeli civilians. Yes, the IDF responded and there were very regrettable Palestinian civilian deaths and casualties, but this is in part *because* Hamas places military headquarters and ammunition under hospitals and schools. Knowing that Hamas puts its citizens at risk, Israel has a "roof knock policy," a policy that is far above and beyond what any other military conducts. This practice seeks to prevent civilian casualties by dropping a non-explosive device as a warning shot in advance of firing an explosive. Israel goes to extensive lengths to warn civilians of forthcoming military action by air-dropping leaflets, placing phone calls to homes, and broadcasting the details on future attacks with megaphones and on the radio airwaves. Hamas, however, wants as many Palestinian casualties as possible, so they order their citizens to stay put. This works with their jihadi agenda; it gaslights the international media against Israel, and innocent people pay with their lives.

Another pearl on Gaza. "Since 2006, Israel has imposed a siege on Gaza that makes it virtually impossible for the vast majority of Palestinians to leave and severely restricts the movement of goods into and out of Gaza." ← Not a single word here about the fact that Israel pulled out of Gaza in 2005 and got rockets in return—which is why Israel *and* Egypt set up the siege to begin with. Naturally, BDS also "forgets" to mention Egypt. It also "forgets" to mention Hamas importing ammunition, launching rockets and mortars at civilians, building attack tunnels, enacting Sharia law, forcing civilians to act as human shields, and murdering members of the PLO.

And yet another. "Israel used alleged 'security concerns' to justify its siege on Gaza." ← The quotation marks around

> "security concerns" are actually there. Like these "security concerns" are fake! Like the thousands of rockets launched into Israeli cities never existed or the bus that exploded half a mile from my house was invented. Like I dreamed it.

On its entire website, throughout their entire impassioned plea for human rights, BDS never mentions the radical Islamist organization that is now controlling, oppressing, and terrorizing almost half of the Palestinian population of the West Bank and Gaza. They talk about mass Jewish colonialization and naturally fail to speak of the Jewish roots in the land or the fact that the United Nations granted the Jews the right to return to their land. They talk about millions of displaced Palestinians but not the Arab nations responsible for the wars that led to their displacement, or the millions of Jews who were killed and displaced from their homes in Europe and in Arab countries. They show pictures of Palestinian children flying kites in Gaza but not the balloons (and condoms!) that have bombs attached to them. They talk about apartheid and unequal legal rights, but they fail to mention that the majority of Israeli Arabs would prefer to live in Israel than a future State of Palestine, or that some of them were "ethnically cleansed" straight into parliament.

Of course BDS doesn't mention any of this, because the truth would completely dismantle their agenda and would turn off those young liberal Americans they are trying to recruit. They present themselves as a movement that is only about justice, and they try to claim that they are only against Israel's *policies*, not specifically Jews in Israel. This is a lie. The truth is that the concept of boycotting Jews goes way back, way before Israel was even created.

ANTI-ISRAEL OR ANTISEMITIC?

Though you won't get this from your shiny BDS leaflets, the boycott movement preceded the State of Israel. In fact, the movement has nothing to do with any recent land disputes in the West Bank or anywhere else.

The Arab global boycott movement actually started back in 1945, with the formation of the Arab League—an organization that was basically created to prevent the Arab nations from fighting directly with one another (which I guess is working, if you squint your eyes at Yemen and Libya, or the numerous other proxy wars between nonmember Iran and Saudi Arabia). In December 1945, five months after the end of World War II, the Arab League took its first collective action: a formal boycott of the Palestinian Jewish community's products. Let me repeat—in December 1945, five short months *after* the mass extermination of European Jewry had ended and three years *before* the creation of Israel, the Arab League's first collective action was a refusal to do business with the Jews in Mandatory Palestine. In a feat of misdirection worthy of David Copperfield, member states—Egypt, Iraq, Saudi Arabia, Syria, Jordan, Lebanon, and Yemen—some of which weren't countries with the most democratic governance systems you can find, found a moral excuse to discriminate against Jews.

This movement to boycott Jewish goods continued after the creation of Israel, when the Arabs decided that the best use of their time would not be working toward a Palestinian state to call their own or making peace but instead boycotting Jews. In 1947–48 the Arab Higher Committee (a political organ that came and went around the establishment of Israel) had an *actual political arm* called the "Boycott Committee" (headed by Rashid al-Khatib), which oversaw the boycott of Jewish goods and services"[2]

Later on, the Arab League put financial pressure on countries and international companies to not do business with Israel, which slowly worked. At its peak in 1951, over eighty-five hundred companies were under the Boycott Committee's thumb.

Around the time of the 1967 and 1973 wars, the boycott movement lost some of its stamina, but the idea stuck around, and in 2005 it resurfaced again. BDS, in its current incarnation, was founded in 2005 by Omar Barghouti, a Qatari-born Palestinian with an MA and in the process of receiving a PhD from Tel Aviv University. If you haven't caught the irony, allow me to hand it to you: Barghouti became an advocate for the academic boycott of Israel while holding a degree from an Israeli university.

The BDS movement now has a professional US headquarters, yet it still presents itself as a "grassroots" Palestinian movement. We will get to this soon, too, I promise. So, given the antisemitic history of boycott movements against Israel, is BDS antisemitic or "just" anti-Israel? Let's use the criteria created by Natan Sharansky, a world-renowned human rights activist who spent nine years in a Soviet prison and was only the fourth non-American to receive the US Presidential Medal of Freedom. He created a standard to separate legitimate criticism of Israeli policies from antisemitism, and this framework was adopted by the US Department of State in 2010. It is called the 3D test: Delegitimize, Demonize, Double Standard. If a person or an organization criticizes Israel (which is totally a valid and a legitimate thing to do!) but expresses any or all of the above Ds, we have an antisemitic winner. BDS is a winner indeed.[3] Here we go:

- **Delegitimize.** BDS flat-out delegitimizes and denies Israel's right to exist. Not only does it reject the legal basis for the creation of the state by the UN, but it also denies that Israel is the historic homeland of the Jewish people. When asked, BDS leaders expressly state that Israel indeed should not exist in its current iteration as exemplified yet again by Tel Aviv University graduate and current PhD student Omar Barghouti: "I am completely and categorically against bi-nationalism because it assumes that there are two nations with equal moral claims to the land."[4]

- **Demonize.** BDS demonizes Israel and the Jews with constant descriptions of Israel as "brutal," "murderous," and guilty of "premeditated ethnic cleansing," generally presenting the country as a warmongering monster. Again, what an irony when the Arab world has historically tried to eliminate Israel and Israel is presently combating a terrorist organization aligned with Sharia law. Add to this the antisemitic slur posts and tweets expressed by its leaders and supporters, and BDS wins this one hands down.

- **Double Standard.** BDS proudly displays the mother of all double standards. As mentioned above, there is not a single word in all their well-manicured literature about Hamas, Sharia law, suicide attacks, elaborate attack tunnels, bombs attached to balloons and condoms, placing civilians under military bases, ammunition factories in Gaza, and so on. And don't even get me started on the BDS double standard toward the only consistent democracy in the Middle East (Israel) versus *every single other country in the region*. Israel is surrounded by some of the most vicious, theocratic, autocratic, dictatorial, oppressive Islamist regimes and a bunch of failed states, yet BDS singles *only* Israel out. BDS leadership doesn't care at all about the plight or human rights of Palestinians anywhere else in the world—if they did, they might work toward improving the horrifying conditions in overstuffed refugee camps in places like Lebanon or on reforming UNRWA, which enables Palestinians to stay "refugees" for three generations and counting.

I highly doubt that all this smoke-and-mirror action is by accident and not by design. BDS is literally cloaking their dagger. They know that they won't be able to attract as many liberals to their ranks if they put their real agenda front and center. They have concluded, very wisely, that in order to win a long game they must slowly infiltrate the hearts and minds of young people, and they understand that in order to do so they must change their language from "Jews" and "death to Israel" to "justice" and "human rights." But the ideas and the people behind them are the same.

If you have ever been approached by BDS activists or considered contributing your time or money to a movement that claims to support freedom and justice for all, know this: BDS is a movement that is actively working to eliminate the State of Israel. Their catchy chant "From the river to the sea, Palestine will be free" is literal. BDS supporters would like a country that *exists* to *not* exist. As simple as that.

How much bloodshed exactly will they be willing to accept in order for this to happen? No one knows, but in the meantime the movement is causing some real financial damage.

But not to Israel.

The real damage is to the lives and livelihoods of the Palestinian people themselves.

THE PRICE IS NOT RIGHT

Israel is not a perfect country; it has a lot to learn and many improvements to make. However, citizens on both the Israeli and the Palestinian sides are trying to make all their lives better, one entrepreneurial endeavor at a time. The only way to allow peace to exist between the two nations is to actually coexist: through day-to-day experiences, shared objectives, shared businesses, projects, meals—life! And this is what many private sector leaders are trying to accomplish. Throughout the years, private companies and NGOs have tried to facilitate more opportunities for both nations by forming personal and professional relationships. But this time the roadblocks are not being erected by the Israelis but by international activists, and the Palestinian people are the ones who, as always, suffer the most.

As we have established, BDS wants to put Israel under a total financial freeze. It aims to stop the collaboration between Israelis and Palestinians and pressures businesses around the world, including the Palestinian Authority, to not work with Israelis and demand for all companies to leave the West Bank. As we've established, the West Bank has about 2.9 million Palestinians and approximately 464,000 Jews—so who do you think suffers most from the lack of opportunity? Yes, the same Palestinians BDS claims to try and "save." As Palestinian Israeli journalist Khaled Abu Toameh puts it:

> The current Palestinian political economy, influenced far too greatly by the BDS and anti-normalization campaigns, amounts to a corrupt, unsustainable, terror-supporting regime that is disinterested in the economic well-being of its own people and the development of a new state.[5]

There are many examples of people and companies being pushed out, sanctioned, harassed, and threatened for doing business with Israelis. Israeli supermarket owner Rami Levy is one; peace activist Professor Mohammed Dajani Daoudi is another. Levy was harassed by BDS for the audacity to simply open supermarkets in the West Bank (and hire Palestinians for double the pay offered by the PA and full benefits), and Professor Daoudi for taking his Palestinian Al-Quds University students to visit the Auschwitz concentration camp, and his Israeli students to visit Palestinian refugee camps. Both the Israeli businessman and the Palestinian professor have tried to promote mutual understanding between the people and create financial opportunities specifically for the Palestinians, and both have been subjected to on- and offline threats and harassment by BDS activists.

However, the best example of the movement backfiring is the stunning story of the Israeli company SodaStream, which began operating in the West Bank in 2007. SodaStream is a classic old British company that was bought by an Israeli businessman in 2007. The Israeli entrepreneur revamped the brand and started manufacturing a slick carbonation machine for home use. Basically, it enabled you to make your own sparkling water or flavored sparkling drinks in your kitchen. Pretty cool.

SodaStream CEO Daniel Birnbaum is all about the big picture. He is an avid peace advocate and environmentalist (SodaStream is promoting eliminating single-use plastics). "Each one working in the company will tell you that at SodaStream we manufacture peace, and along the way, we also make soda,"[6] he brags, but he also puts his money where his mouth is, and his company's policies are perfectly aligned.

In 2007 he opened a factory in Mishor Adumim in the West Bank, which employed 1,100 workers—850 Palestinians and 250 Jews—a beautiful tapestry of the region working together every day. The social justice keyboard warriors of BDS got a whiff of this blasphemous coexistence, and their manic base was activated.

Nabil Bashrat, a Palestinian living in the village of Jaba near Ramallah, wrote: "The BDS movement is causing the most amount of damage to the Palestinian workers." He continued, "The BDS movement is pressuring SodaStream. They are saying that the company treats us like slaves. This is a lie. We work here together, Arabs and Jews, Israelis and Palestinians. My salary is three times higher than the one I had before, and I get health benefits for me and my family. BDS has no interest in Palestinian workers."[7]

He pled with BDS to let go of SodaStream, which of course they ignored. In 2015 the factory closed and moved to the Negev desert, consequently eliminating hundreds of good-paying jobs for local Palestinians. Great work, BDS. (Mr. Bashrat was one of the lucky ones, and he kept his job in the new SodaStream factory in the Negev.)

BDS did not stop SodaStream's political and social agenda from carrying on, and they continue to work toward peace and coexistence. One hundred and ten Palestinians now work in the new factory in the Negev desert, and the company proudly displays a sticker on its product that reads: "This product is made by Arabs and Jews working side by side in peace and harmony."

This is not lip service from a cozy US college dorm. This is real-life damage BDS is inflicting on the people who are on the front lines, trying to coexist, provide for their families, and live a normal and peaceful life.

It's hard to put an accurate dollar amount on the cost of the boycott movement, however by all accounts it is high and painful. In 2015, RAND Corporation published research in which it created a projected calculation of the cost of various scenarios of the Palestinian-Israeli conflict. It estimated that the growth of this so-called nonviolent resistance (BDS doesn't denounce violence, actually) will cost the Palestinian economy approximately $2 billion annually.[8] In each and every scenario for a two-state solution, both nations' GDP grows when the Palestinian economy grows. The lack of collaboration and coexistence between the two peoples is terrible for everyone. After all, an enemy you get to know cannot stay an enemy for long.

The goal for every liberal should be peace, and to achieve that peace even *more* normalization and collaboration is required, not less. BDS goes as far as boycotting *peace itself*. The breakthrough normalization and peace agreements between Israel, the UAE, and Bahrain are now also a target of the movement, as BDS founder Omar Barghouti is vowing to boycott Arab companies doing business in Israel.[9]

Creating agreements and joint ventures in various fields is crucial to help cultivate personal relationships between people, which will eventually grow to better understanding, empathy, and love and can only help establish a foundation for peace. But BDS doesn't care about all this. "Don't talk to them!" they yell at their brothers struggling on the ground, from their comfy living rooms in America.

This much-hyped socio-political-economic movement has had a major impact on the Palestinian economy and its people's well-being, but no major effect on the Israeli economy. GDP and international investments have been rising steadily in recent years, and the military and economic collaborations between Israel and the Palestinian Authority are continuing consistently.

So why is BDS still such a big deal?

PR. And good PR can cost a lot of money.

FOLLOW THE MONEY

There is nothing a social justice warrior loves more than being heard. It's a unique new human breed created and amplified by social media, where everyone has an opinion and facts aren't as important as adopting a seemingly noble cause—an admirable cause, one that makes you look like you actually care about humanity. This is what the PR arm of BDS is after.

Imagine you are a freshman, excitedly arriving on your campus, where you are welcomed by an extracurricular fair, filled with many awesome tables vying for your attention and your precious time. You'll weave your way through the Greek life groups, the Democratic and Republican Parties, and groups promoting health, pets, or veganism. Among them, you'll also find a harmless-looking table that calls for "Justice for Palestinians." What a noble cause indeed! The fresh-faced young activists at the table will invite you to an introductory session, which will sound fascinating, especially if you're interested in justice, peace, or politics. And so, BDS will get you on the hook.

Here is what is less known. These innocent-looking tables don't simply represent a student-led, organic, grassroots movement that is spreading on its own because of the authentic interest of college attendees. BDS on college campuses is a savvy, well-funded political operation whose sponsors and organizers include groups and individuals with ties to Islamist agendas.

I didn't make this up. A much smarter person than me said this in his sworn testimony in front of the United States Congress. Here is Dr. Jonathan Schanzer, former terrorism finance analyst for the United States Department of the Treasury:

> The overlap of former employees of organizations that provided support to Hamas who now play important roles [in the BDS movement] . . . speaks volumes about the real agenda of key components of the BDS campaign.[10]

Schanzer, now senior vice president at the Washington, DC–based think tank the Foundation for Defense of Democracies, is an expert in uncovering financial ties that are *designed* to be hidden. In his testimony, Dr. Schanzer describes a head-spinning web of financial and personal connections between BDS and supporters of terrorism.

The BDS US campus operation represents a savvy rebranding of the Palestinian cause to make it more palatable—and, you know, less terror-y—for the American people. Key figures in the BDS movement come from a particularly uncompromising strain of Palestinian nationalism that calls for a State of Palestine to stretch from the river to the sea (yes, without Israel). Apparently, when they saw that their message was not resonating with Western society (not surprisingly, I would say), they decided to pivot and started pouring their resources into American colleges in order to influence future leaders and voters in America and Europe. "Investing in the future they are," as Yoda would say.

The BDS on campus operation works in two primary ways. The first is meetings, or "training and educational" sessions. BDS distributes flyers or Facebook invites for pro-Palestine or anti-Israel events in which a speaker will present their standard talking points—misinformation, disinformation, a skewed reality, and the convenient elimination of history or facts. They will share a rough personal story to create a one-sided narrative that would rightfully infuriate anyone with a beating heart. The second critical operation is political. When campus voting season comes around, representatives descend on college students in order to push anti-Israel resolutions or referendums at the university. In the weeks and days leading up to a vote, the BDS movement will flood the university with those "educational" sessions, social media posts, and campus ad campaigns, which will make any anti-Israel vote seem like a legitimate cause, creating major divides in student bodies on campuses.

As it turns out, it is very easy to drown a campus with propaganda if you can afford it. Of course, you could argue that Jewish or pro-Israel organizations can also afford it. They may be, but while these organizations promote understanding or support of Israel, not a single one of them is aimed toward *eliminating* another country or people. What makes BDS so different?

The BDS on campus operation is organized by, among others, a group in Chicago, Illinois, called American Muslims for Palestine, or AMP. For years, AMP, through its sponsorship of Students for Justice in Palestine (SJP), has been sending strategists, digital and communications experts, graphic designers, video editors, and legal advisors to colleges all over America and running flashy events in expensive hotels for the purpose of delegitimizing Israel, minimizing pro-Israel voices on campus, and harassing Jewish and pro-Israel students in order to deter them from supporting Israel. The embodiment of Cancel Culture. Managing such a sophisticated network of political operatives, extensive marketing, and (pre-COVID) ritzy gatherings at nice hotels is extremely expensive.[11] So where is the money coming from?

I tried to follow the money at AMP and failed miserably. It seems like they keep the source of their funding extremely murky. Here is what we do know:

> AMP is incorporated in the State of Illinois, but is not a 501 (c) (3) tax-exempt organization. In order to receive tax-exempt donations, it uses an organization known as "Americans for Justice in Palestine Educational Foundation (AJP)," located at the same address, as its "fiscal sponsor." It appears that AJP does not sponsor any other projects.[12]

Now let's break this down, and please bear with me, as I believe they keep this complicated *on purpose*. AMP's legal structure allows them to avoid federal fillings that would make their finances more transparent, and they are funded by AJP, which has the exact same address and does not seem to finance anyone else; for now, let's relate to them as the same organization. So who are you, AMP/AJP? And what does this tell us about BDS?

Can you handle the truth? Here is the truth: Some of BDS's most significant supporters (through AMP/AJP, and others!—but we don't have time for everyone now) are also supporters of Hamas. Yep, the terrorist organization, the arm of the Muslim Brotherhood, the one that aims to enact Sharia law. Some of the people who support that organization are also supporting your innocent-looking grassroots campus movement. I know this sounds horrific, but again, I didn't make this up. Let's hand it over to the terrorism finance expert again:

> The corporate structure of AMP is cause for concern, but it pales in comparison to the significant overlap between AMP

> and people who worked for or on behalf of organizations that were designated, dissolved, or held civilly liable by federal authorities for supporting Hamas.[13]

Dr. Schanzer is referring to, among others, an organization called the Holy Land Foundation (HLF), which, in 2001, was exposed by the FBI and found guilty of funneling approximately $12.4 million to Hamas. Seven of its leaders were sentenced to fifteen to sixty-five years of jail time, two of them fled the country, and five are in federal prison. Some of those involved in HLF and other organizations changed course and essentially turned their efforts to a slow-moving terror attack: delegitimizing Israel's right to exist. They pivoted to a tactical focus on BDS, as well as to a strategic effort through AMP and SJP. AMP and SJP are now funding political campaigns in plain sight on your college campuses. Schanzer's testimony is obviously complex, but his conclusions are pretty awful. Here is one of them:

> In short, at least seven individuals who work for or on behalf of AMP have worked for or on behalf of organizations previously shut down or held civilly liable in the United States for providing financial support to Hamas: The Holy Land Foundation, the Islamic Association for Palestine, and KindHearts.[14]

I won't confuse you with all the details; you can read the full testimony for yourself. But what's beyond clear is that BDS operatives at AMP have hidden and not-so-hidden ties (including crossover of leadership, board members, speakers, etc.) and a highly similar agenda as the late HLF and other organizations that supported Hamas. They are now polished and rebranded and spiced up with words that appeal to a liberal ear like "justice" and "peace." The BDS movement—usually through their legal arm, Palestine Legal—has frequently threatened to sue people for defamation, so I won't be surprised if my lawyers receive a call from them. But if I do get that call, I am asking them to please focus! Not on what I am suggesting (or what was suggested by other people)—that their sources of funding should be properly looked into!—but on the core issue: please tell me how the BDS movement is okay with the existence of Israel as the one and only Jewish state in the world.

I am not—let me repeat, I am not—saying that BDS and Hamas are *directly* connected. What I am saying, however, is that this super suspicious overlapping relationship needs to be, at the very least, thoroughly investigated, and it certainly needs to be made fully known. And our favorite terrorism finance expert, Dr. Schanzer, is pointing to exactly that.

A CORRUPT CULTURE CLUB

I am going to give the majority of college students and activists who've signed up for BDS a clean pass. I believe that they don't know that they are being used as pawns to promote the annihilation of Israel. I believe they'd prefer democracy over Sharia any day of the week. And I'm pretty sure they are unaware that BDS offers no solutions for peace in the region other than to end Israel, or that its calls for justice do not include justice for Palestinians anywhere else in the world. I believe that they don't know that among the sponsors of BDS activity are supporters of terrorism.

But what about the intellectuals and policy makers such as Alice Walker, AOC, Rashida Tlaib, Ilhan Omar, and my favorite punching bag, Mr. Roger Waters?

In 2006, former Pink Floyd bassist Roger Waters was invited to perform in Tel Aviv. He went to Israel, but instead of touring the whole country to educate himself about its history, he went only to the West Bank and was probably shown some horrible realities and possibly some well-managed propaganda. Only the Lord above knows why, but this talented musician decided to put his public relations capital behind BDS. Did he investigate who is behind BDS? Did he investigate what it is that the BDS movement really wants? Did he ever fact-check to find out the full history of what had happened in 1948? I am pretty sure the answer to all of the above is a "Nope." Of course, I don't really know the answer to these questions, but I do know that Waters became the Energizer Bunny of the boycott movement: ranting and raving about "justice for all" on every outlet that would have him, completely ignoring how we got to this obviously unacceptable point. History doesn't mean much when one can get some free press, I guess.

Here is how he works. Every time an international music act announces an upcoming tour in Israel, Mr. Waters immediately sends off a self-righteous open letter (of course it's open; what's the point if no one can see it?). The letter is usually followed by massive interwebs troll attacks that often freak the artist in question right out, resulting in them canceling their gigs to the disappointment of their fans and the financial hardship of local organizers. (Lorde and Lana Del Rey, I'm looking at you.)

I don't blame these artists; interwebs troll attacks can be a scary thing. And indeed, since BDS was somehow able to brand itself as the hip new WokeCause, it's had some success with smaller artists who can't take the heat and succumb to what Mr. Waters calls the "BDS Picket Line."

The biggest chutzpah that he and BDS exhibit is their demand that even *Arab* artists refuse to perform in Israel for their *Arab* fans. BDS targeted Jordanian singer Aziz Maraka, pressuring him to not perform a show at the Christmas Market celebrations in the Arab village of Kfar Yasif in the Galilee. Maraka ignored the trolls and played a show to five thousand excited fans, later saying: "I am unwilling to shut up anymore. I am unwilling to be dictated what to believe and who to talk to, not even by BDS. . . . I can now say BDS will think twice before targeting an Arab artist again."[15]

The absurdity in demanding that Arabs living in Israel should also suffer cultural isolation is infuriating. Each one of these concerts is not just a music event but a financial engine and job-creating machine that BDS wants to eliminate. This would inflict more, not less, financial damage on the Palestinians. What hypocrisy from the keyboard activists enjoying their comfy lives abroad while riding their liberal high horses and damaging the lives and livelihoods of Palestinians in Israel!

Luckily, Mr. Waters is having only lukewarm success in his crusade against Israel, the only democracy in the Middle East. Big acts like Radiohead, Paul McCartney, the legend that is Jennifer Lopez, and almost every single successful international DJ have ignored Mr. Waters. But that doesn't stop him from trying. In the summer of 2015, the Rolling Stones announced a show in Tel Aviv. As always, they were met with the inevitable Waters letter. So I picked up the phone and called my friend Mick (Sorry, I believe I just dropped a name there. Want to pick it up?) and passionately explained to him why he should ignore the letter and the entire BDS movement and should not cancel the show. I won't share exactly what he said on that call, only that it was hilarious and clever, that it completely calmed me down, and that the story ended with the Stones traveling to Tel Aviv that summer and playing their show. It was beyond epic.

THE SORROWS OF A YOUNG(*ISH*) LIBERAL

I am a Zionist and I am also pro-Palestinian, so there is nothing I and my friends want more than to find a way to kumbaya. Boycotting Israel and restricting Palestinian people's livelihood—BDS-style—*is not the way.* There are many constructive ways out there for liberals to actually strengthen the Palestinian people while making sure Israel is safe and secure and neither Hamas nor ISIS (nor worse!) jumps in to take over. I'm in no way an expert on this, but I am going to throw a few out there:

- Start by encouraging private capital and investments in the Palestinian economy. The Palestinians should not be reliant on international aid and support; economic resiliency should be goal number one.
- Find ways to "shrink the conflict," a concept flushed out by Micah Goodman in his book *Catch-67: The Left, the Right, and the Legacy of the Six-Day War*, in which he identified a few concrete steps to make life better for everyone (encouraging international and local trade, land reallocation, easing travel abroad, expanding employment in Israel, etc.).
- And lastly: everyone should demand a responsible Palestinian leadership.

  Like, *everyone*.

All these can immediately replace the absurdity and futility of the BDS movement's tactics and should be researched and implemented by any liberal who wants to make a real difference, off or on any campus anywhere in the world. But in the meantime BDS is continuing to run amok, causing damage in the most surprising of places.

The most impressive and dangerous thing BDS has been able to achieve is its insertion into mainstream social and liberal conversations in America, slowly eroding the legitimacy of only one country on earth. Again, this is not by mistake. The boycott movement uses intersectionality as a tactic to co-opt legitimate social grievances and win public legitimization by association.

Following the horrific shooting of Trayvon Martin and the acquittal of his killer, George Zimmerman, an incredible grassroots movement emerged: Black Lives Matter. After another shooting shocked the nation, that of Michael Brown Jr. in Ferguson, Missouri, BDS activists reached out to the BLM leaders and offered to lend their support. After all, they said, Palestinian Lives Matter as well. BLM welcomed those BDS activists, to the shock and disappointment of people in the know, not to mention the American Jewish community, which by and large is a huge supporter of BLM. The same thing happened with the Women's March. The majority of American Jews are liberals; Zionism was founded on liberal and progressive ideals, and I don't need to harp again on the oppression of Jews throughout the last, well, few thousand years. Jews have always been at the forefront of the fight for human rights and social justice, like Rabbi Abraham Joshua Heschel, who was literally on the *front line* of the march from Selma to Montgomery, hand in hand with Ralph Bunche (the same UN diplomat who helped shape the Partition Plan in 1947!) and, of course, Dr. King.

Through delegitimizing Israel, BDS was able to put a wedge between the Jewish community and these extremely crucial social justice movements, intentionally confusing every American who supports democracy and human rights, Republican or Democrat, and is also a supporter of Israel, into thinking that these two aren't aligned. This couldn't be further from the truth. Israel is the *only country in the region* with the same values as Western democracies, no matter on which side of the political map you position yourself. (Remember we're dealing with an imperfect yet single democracy, and forces on the other side that are the exact opposite of liberalism *or* democracy.) BDS activists brand every pro-Israel liberal as a PEP, "Progressive Except for Palestine," which is just another example of invoking identity politics instead of trying to win their point through a thoughtful discussion about liberal values. This breaks my heart, and it needs to stop.

Here is the thing. I am a fierce advocate of freedom of speech, even hate speech, so BDS activists certainly have the right to speak and even to lie! But since BDS is *intentionally* hiding its agenda, I also have the right to expose that agenda for what it is: a nefarious intent to destroy only one democracy on earth (which also happens to be Jewish, but maybe that's just a coincidence?) while masquerading under pretentious PC woke lingo. As usual, Dr. Jonathan Schanzer said it best:

"Americans have a right to know who is behind the BDS campaign. And so do those members of the BDS campaign who may not fully understand its history."[16]

Most Americans don't know who these people are, and for the sake of our democracy, this needs to stop. BDS is a movement where way too often the ones with bad faith prey on the ones with bad knowledge. BDS cleverly aligned itself with various human and civil rights movements and with an anti-apartheid agenda, yet it is nothing but a false cognate.

To conflate these movements is an insult to human rights movements, to the anti-apartheid movement, and to black Americans.

CHAPTER ELEVEN

MAY THE MELTING POT NOT MELT US ALL

AN ISRAELI FISH IN SAN FRANCISCO

I was nineteen years old when I traveled to the US for the first time. I was still on active military duty, but I convinced my commanders to allow me to leave the country so I could travel to the US and check out drama schools (leaving the country while in active service isn't an issue these days, but it was not allowed at the time). My father and I landed in San Francisco, and the next morning I dragged him to the Gap so I could get me some Americana. I was browsing through the shelves when a lovely woman approached me. "Hi! How are you doing today?" she asked cheerfully. I turned my head and stared at her suspiciously. "Do I know you?" "Not at all, I just wanted to see how you're doing! If you need any help, let me know!" I paused, truly puzzled. "I'm fine," I said finally, and the lady walked away, surely convinced that this young girl was the rudest person she'd ever met in her life. I, of course, didn't think I was being rude at all. I seriously had no idea why that woman was talking to me. She didn't know me, so why was she trying so hard to be nice?

A couple of years later I moved to Los Angeles and shortly after was invited to go on my first date. The guy came to pick me up, and as we walked to his car, he beelined for the passenger side and opened my door. I gave him that same suspicious stare. "What are you doing?" I asked. The dude was confused. "I'm . . . getting the door for you?" I got irritated. "I know how to open a door on my own." He smiled and probably thought it was adorable, because we ended up dating for a bit after that. But I wasn't playing a mind game. I was truly offended by this gentlemanly gesture. How dare you suggest that I can't get a car door for myself??

A fish in water does not know it is in water, and I had no idea that my demeanor was . . . unique. I thought I was just being "real." Almost everyone else thought of me as impolite, rude, aggressive, or everyone's favorite: "Noa, you're so *intense*!" I spoke with my hands a lot; I started way too many sentences with the word "Listen"; and I generally felt like if I didn't push my "truth" on people, I was doing them wrong. I also used this one specific hand gesture that in Israel means "Wait a minute" and in other cultures means "F#@k you." After a few years living in the US I learned that my behavior could generally be described as being "Israeli."

Up until now in this book, I've moved across history chronologically, like a sassy Ken Burns. But I am going to use this chapter to touch upon the lesser-known internal issues within the country, like "Who is an Israeli?"

In his documentary *Remember My Name*, David Crosby gives a very simple definition for *synthesis*: "when you take widely separated things and put them together to create something new." This is a great way to describe Israelis. We are a bunch of refugee mutts living side by side while creating an entirely new breed. Israel is like a worldwide experience in refugee assimilation and migration, blending cultures while constantly on the defensive, which is probably why I come across as "aggressive." Old habits die hard.

Israel is also a casual society that doesn't waste time on unnecessary ceremonial decorum. My brother-in-law got married in jeans, and no one batted an eye. Almost every politician has a nickname, and that nickname is not used to condescend but to relate. One Prime Minister Benjamin is Bibi, the Alternate Prime Minister Benjamin is Benny. Ziporah is Zipi, Isaac is Bougie, Reuven is Ruvi.

Israelis laugh at themselves more than you can imagine, and *no topic* is off the table. Do you know how many Holocaust jokes we have in Israel? A lot. Do you know how it went when I tried telling one at a dinner party in Los Angeles? Not well. We don't believe in PC in Israel. We believe in being straight up, or, as my dad used to say, the "Tachles department."

Israel today is a modern mosaic, a tightly knit yet divided society. A society that is haunted by old traumas and at the same time is drowning in joie de vivre. Yes, this sounds like a paradox, but so is the entire concept of Israel reemerging.

So. Who *is* an Israeli? Legally that's anyone born in Israel, the child of one or both Israeli parents, or anyone who immigrates to the country or has lived in it for a number of years and gone through the process of naturalization.

Culturally, however—well, culturally, it's complicated. As we've seen in the preceding chapters, Israel is a refugee state and therefore the ultimate melting pot. From Russians to Ethiopians, from kibbutzniks to ultra-Orthodox, from progressives to settlers to Christian Arabs to Muslims and Druze.

Israelis are like a box of chocolates—you don't know exactly what you're gonna get, but you can be sure it's going to be very opinionated.

A SOCIETY MIXED, NOT STIRRED

The population of Israel at the start of 2020 was 9,246,000 people, and the broad divide, give or take, is 74 percent Jewish, 21 percent Arab, and 5 percent who identify as Other.[1] Among the Arab population, 84.8 percent are Muslims, 7.4 percent are Christians and 7.8 percent are Druze. Within the Jewish community, 45 percent describe themselves as secular, 25 percent as traditional, 16 percent as religious, and 14 percent as ultra-Orthodox or Charedi.[2]

Naturally a secular person is a secular person all over the world. This would include atheists and agnostics, but also people who define themselves as culturally Jewish but don't observe the religion. They'll celebrate the big holidays but more as a family thing than anything else.

Someone who defines themselves as traditional is like an American Christian who goes to church on Easter but not each Sunday and aims to keep a life aligned with the teachings of Christ. In Israel they would lean toward keeping mostly kosher (so not so big on pork and shellfish), and while they'll chill on Saturdays to celebrate the Sabbath, they might still drive the family for a hike or to watch a soccer game. They're interested in the "spirit of the law" but aren't observant in a technical way.

The religious follow as many rabbinic laws as they find practical. They skip all work and driving on Shabbat, keep kosher, likely wear a yarmulke, and follow the Jewish traditions. All of the above are full contributors and active members of Israel's society, economy, workforce, military, culture, etc.

The 14 percent Charedim are a different story, and they mostly keep to themselves. They wear those distinct black outfits and furry hats, and they're some of the most religiously observant of the Jewish people. More on them later.

The Arab citizens of Israel number about 1,946,000, which is 21 percent of the Israeli population, among them Muslims, Christians, Bedouins, and Druze, self-defined as Arab Israelis or Palestinian Israelis. Among those, 12.1 percent define themselves as secular, 55.2 percent as traditional, and 29.5 percent as religious or very religious, including approximately 145,000 Druze.[3] In 1957 the Druze were recognized as a distinct religious community in Israel—the only country to grant their leaders this wish. Druze are incredible soldiers and are overrepresented both in Israeli politics and in the highest ranks of the IDF, and many describe themselves as Arab Druze Zionists.

There is nothing cohesive, Eurocentric, or even "white" about Israeli society. In addition to the religious groups listed above, there are Samaritans, Bahai, Circassians, Armenians, and of course the occasional Scientologist. From the Bedouin tribes that have roamed the Middle East for centuries, to the Spanish Jews living in Jerusalem for generations, to the Arabs who stayed after the war in 1948, to the millions of new immigrants and refugees who've found a safe haven in Israel, each culture has brought with it its distinct characteristics and cultural traditions, food, music, history, and art.

However, for the first ten years of the new state, instead of organically allowing that pot to melt, the original leadership almost burned the dish.

The "Melting Pot Policy" was a term used to describe the need to blend this mishmash of refugees into one nation. It wasn't an official governmental policy but an idealistic agenda instigated and enacted by Prime Minister Ben-Gurion and his long-governing Labor Party. The intention was to completely negate the diaspora, blend the different cultures the immigrants brought with them, and create one unified ethos for the nation. As we know from the results of this policy today, a great way to describe it would be "The road to hell is paved with good intentions."

Ben-Gurion was the voice of the nation, and his party was the executor of his ideas. Inspired by the American melting pot ethos, Ben-Gurion knew that cultural assimilation usually took decades if not centuries. Without the luxury of time, he decided Israel must do it yesterday. The country just barely won the 1948 war; it had constant threats from the outside and from within, it was under a massive Arab boycott, and the place was flooded with millions of refugees from all over the world. The country doubled its population in two years and tripled it in less than ten, an unparalleled event in world history. The situation was dire: there was no housing for the new arrivals; there were years of austerity and governmental stipends; and people were fighting for survival. Ben-Gurion was a pragmatist, and he knew he needed a story that could unite all the refugees, displaced people, Holocaust survivors, and war-torn, poverty-stricken people. Here are his words:

> ״אנו מעלים לארץ עם יחיד במינו.... ומוטל עלינו להתיך מחדש כל הציבור הרב והמנומר הזה ולצקת אותו בדפוס של אומה מחודשת. עלינו לעקור המחיצות הגאוגרפיות, התרבותיות, החברתיות והלשוניות המפרידות בין החלקים השונים ולהנחיל להם לשון אחת, תרבות אחת, אזרחות אחת, נאמנות אחת, חוקים חדשים ומשפטים חדשים״

And here they are loosely translated by me:

> We are bringing to this land a unique people. . . . And it is our duty to melt anew this massive and speckled public and cast it in the shape of the new nation. We must uproot all geographical, cultural, social, and linguistic boundaries separating the people and endow in them one language, one culture, one citizenship, one loyalty, with new rules and a new legal system.

Makes sense, right? In a nutshell, the Labor narrative at the time sounded something like this: "We are hereby creating the new Jew! S/he is amazing! Strong! Not a lamb carried to the slaughter! None of this shtetl or darabukka-drumming business! We are secular! We work the land and we shun the old ways of our fathers, old traditions, old religions, and old family rituals! We work hard and also—money sucks! The collective is *the best*! Yes we can!"

Okay, you see where I'm going with this. The Labor government wanted to create one collective identity for the new nation, so they modeled that identity on the only one they knew: that of the pioneers and Zionists who had been there before a state was created. On themselves. What they didn't take into account was that the demographics were shifting, and they'd failed to adapt their story to these changes. The Labor Party of the time ignored and dismissed thousands of years of *other* traditions, mainly North African ones. Their vision was idealistic, but the implementation was god-awful.

Zohar Yakobson is my manager and sister at heart. She migrated from Morocco to Israel in 1967, right after the Six Day War. Back in Morocco, her father was a successful haute couture tailor, meticulously creating three-piece suits for the local elites from fabrics he personally sourced each season in Paris. They lived in the liberal city of Fez, where her mother managed the house, surrounded by help, and took care of the huge family like a roaring lioness. Life was full of love, music, food, and celebrations. Things became rough for them when sentiment started changing and their neighbors, once close friends, turned against the Jews. Zohar remembers a time when her father was measuring an old client and friend for another suit, when his sons burst into the store and violently dragged their dad away, ordering him to never return to this "dirty Jew." "We started feeling the animosity everywhere," she says. "Antisemitism exploded around us. It became dangerous to walk outside. We had to leave." They were getting pushed out.

The family decided that their best chance at survival was to fulfill their dream of returning to Jerusalem, and so they did. The magnificent family left their life, their house, and all their valuables behind and hurriedly emigrated to Israel. "And it was hell." Zohar's family was placed by the government immigration department in the southern town of Beersheba in the poverty-stricken D neighborhood. "There were wood beams where stairs should have been," she tells me. The family fell apart. Her father, the grand master of the household, lost sixty-five pounds and his honor, resorting to sewing buttons onto IDF pants, a far cry from his fabulous Parisian past life. The Labor Party, which was pretty good at building kibbutzim and agricultural communities, sucked at building towns, and the city lacked a proper economy, industry, or any sort of a capitalist system, so there was no possibility for upward mobility. It was a dead-end life, and as a tween, Zohar's anger bubbled up. In addition to there being no financial possibilities, the new culture forced upon her was out of whack.

"They put us in school and started teaching us stuff that had nothing to do with us. Why are they teaching us Bialik and Tchernichovsky, poems from the shtetl, without any context? How is that narrative connected to me or my family in any way?" She is right.

The first Israeli narrative that was forced on *everyone* was completely foreign to millions of people who came over with their own stories. Zohar's story was full of love, laughter, and Jewish traditions of its own. The secular, lightly socialist, work-the-land-with-your-hands kibbutz story, my safta Fania's story, was not one size fits all, and it was a big mistake to try to circle that square. Seriously, who decided that a violin is superior to a darbuka drum?

With all due respect to the old guard's dream of a melting pot, multiculturalism cannot be forced, and ancient and splendid cultures don't just disappear, nor should they. Society does not congeal into a homogenous nation in a hurry. Everyone, including my grandparents, was expected to change their name and drop every old cultural tradition they had, whether of a European persecuted diaspora or a Middle Eastern vibe, which sowed the seeds of class imbalance, lack of opportunities, political rifts, and justified frustrations that have manifested in everything from massive riots to fabulous music.

Ben-Gurion and his crew thought they were doing the best thing for the greater good. But they weren't operating out of pure idealism. There was, of course, another reason they tried to force *their* culture on everyone else.

EVERYONE'S A LITTLE BIT RACIST

Wait! I didn't say that! Princeton and Kate Monster did!

These are, of course the two adorable puppets from the 2004 Tony Award–winning musical for Best Book, Best Original Score, and Best Musical—*Avenue Q.* The musical, brilliantly written by Jeff Marx, Robert Lopez, and Jeff Whitty, was ahead of its time in so many ways. In it, a mixed group of puppets and humans live together on a fictional avenue in New York City and, in a spectacularly non-PC way, deal with life's problems: work, love, and, yes, racism. Just imagine these words coming out of the sweet and cheerful puppets Princeton and Kate Monster:

> "Everyone's a little bit / Racist, sometimes
> Doesn't mean we go around committing / Hate crimes.
> Look around and / You will find,
> No one's really / Color-blind.
> Maybe it's a fact / We all should face
> Everyone makes /Judgments . . .
> Based on race."

I learned this the hard way when I was fourteen years old and had my first boyfriend. He was a year older, a good student, nice and respectful—one of the good guys. When I excitedly told my dad, his first question was: "What's his name?"

"Gaby," I answered.

"No," my dad clarified and pointedly repeated. "What is his *name*?"

What my dad was inquiring about was my boyfriend's *last* name, which would indicate to him if he was Ashkenazi, of European origin, or Mizrahi, of North African and Spanish origin.

Racism is one of humanity's least favorable qualities, and low and behold, it exists even among the Jews themselves. So, yeah, we're going to touch upon racism *within* the Israeli Jewish society, and for those who are about to get offended—go clutch some pearls, will ya?

The source of my Ashkenazi father's discriminatory inquiry was the assumption that Ashkenazi is better than Mizrahi. I severely beg to differ for *so* many reasons.

The millions of people who migrated to Israel were not treated the same at the start. The old guard of the Labor Party treated "the ones from *ours*" very differently from the emigrants from North Africa or members of the political right. To be fair, the problems weren't just with the placement of North African emigrants in remote locations. Eastern European emigrants were also placed by the government in forgotten towns and in tents in refugee camps called *ma'abarot*, and if you were not a part of the Labor Party you had a much harder time getting by or moving up (like my great-grandfather Nachum Tishby, who was not a member of Labor and did not become the actual minister of trade and industry despite having started that office). If you weren't a part of the network of power, you had no support system to help you move ahead, causing severe repercussions for generations of immmigrants.

The first time an outcry about this discrimination exploded into the public sphere was eleven years after the establishment of the country, in the 1959 demonstrations in Wadi Salib, a neighborhood in Haifa. Riots clued the rest of the country in on the poor living conditions and desperation of the neighborhood's mostly Moroccan emigrants. The government handled the crisis locally, in the neighborhood itself, relocating the residents and providing them with better living conditions, but it did not address the overall crisis that continued everywhere else.

In 1971, the Israeli Black Panthers movement emerged from the Musrara neighborhood in Jerusalem. It was led by five powerful emigrants from Morocco, and its leader was a charismatic young man named Saadia Marciano, "the Hero from the Atlas Mountains." (I don't want to objectify this important political leader, so I won't go into how handsome he was, but I suggest you google him.)[4] The Panthers demanded an end to discrimination and the start of proper government funding for neglected groups within the new state. They were, of course, spot-on. The old Ashkenazi guard reacted by criticizing the *way* the protestors acted, as Golda Meir condescendingly commented: "They are not nice." I guess they were expecting a polite protest, like all politicians do.

This divide can be traced all the way to present-day internal politics. The inner sectorial rift—or, as it is sometimes called, the "sectorial demon"—is still a hard driver of the voting patterns of Israelis.

The charismatic leader and founder of the Likud Party, Menachem Begin, a Russian born in Belarus, was the first to identify these real grievances as political capital and harness them to his benefit. Begin, as the former leader of the underground organization Etzel, was also discriminated against and dissed in the political game for years. A brilliant orator, Begin was able to speak authentically about his experiences and relate to those who were also left behind, the "forgotten." He toned down his revisionist tendencies and pivoted toward the center of the political map, turning these rightful grievances into the main pillar of the Likud political agenda. He campaigned in those same tent towns and southern cities Labor founded and neglected, and in 1977 he flipped the government for the first time in Israel's short history when the Likud won the elections.

Begin was also a master at harnessing pop culture, and in 1981 he won reelection after cleverly reappropriating a derogatory term used by a late actor. The word *chachtchahim* is virtually impossible to pronounce in English, but it was commonly used to belittle Mizrahi Jews. Awful. When that late actor used it in a political rally to describe the voters of Likud, Begin seized on it and in a spectacular speech tore that actor in pieces and took full ownership over that word. This is not unlike "the Deplorables" from a few years back, a term that came to bite a certain US presidential candidate you know where. Two days after "the *chachtchahim* speech,"[5] Begin won reelection. Since the days of Begin, an almost unbreakable bond has been created between the Likud Party and the periphery of the country, while Labor and the center left continue to play defense.

But despite politicians who still use "origins" to gaslight the media and fire up their base, there has been an astonishing cross-pollination in every other area of the fabric of the country: comedy, art, academia, food, music, fashion, law enforcement—*everywhere*. The result of this mix of cultures is a new, authentic Israeli character, one that melted on its own.

After almost a hundred years of melting cultures while fighting wars of survival, a new breed of Jew emerged—one who grew up surrounded by Polish, Turkish, Arabic, Romanian, Moroccan, or German elders but, unlike them, didn't care about last names. This Jew was no longer a nebbish-y shtetl dweller but a feisty, survival-driven fighter. Aggressive on the outside and sweet on the inside, this Jew is called a *Sabra*.

Sabra is the Hebrew word for the fruit of a cactus tree. Yes, a cactus has a fruit called the prickly pear, which, as indicated by the name, is indeed prickly. But once you've maneuvered your way through the spikes and rough peel, the pulp inside is surprisingly soft and sweet.

This is the magnificently on-the-nose metaphor for the new Israeli. (Sabra hummus, which you may know from your local grocer, is named after the people, not the fruit!)

If you've ever dealt with an Israeli in business or personally, or even if you've just met one of us in an elevator or in a hotel lobby, you're probably smiling (or sighing). You know what I'm talking about. There is a *thing* about Israelis. We have a certain reputation and it's not always the greatest. A Sabra is rough around the edges until you get to know her, and then she's your bestie for life, as loyal as a Labrador retriever. A Sabra is someone who will fight with a date who dares to get the door for her or who will stare down a saleslady at the Gap.

GOD IS IN THE DETAILS OF POLITICAL POWER

In his book *Flexigidity*, Gidi Grinstein hypothesizes that the most fundamental aspect of Judaism is its ability to adapt, to be rigid and flexible at the same time. As he explains it: "Jews are not powerful, they're just very resilient," and he goes on a quest to understand the reasons behind this resiliency. From the days of the First Temple in Jerusalem thousands of years ago to each corner of the world today, some Jewish rituals stayed the same, some evolved, and some were thrown out. The Charedi people have done their best to keep the old traditions in vogue.

The Charedis are the ultra-Orthodox, super-observant people of the Jewish world. You know them as the ones who sport the big beards, wear black suits and big fluffy hats, and often have huge families. You know them better if you've watched the American show *Unorthodox* or the Israeli show *Shtisel*. However, while the Charedi communities *seem* ancient, they're actually a relatively new phenomenon.

The Charedi movement developed in Europe in the eighteenth

and nineteenth centuries as a resistance to the Enlightenment Period, which spread across Europe and also penetrated the Jewish communities. Around the year 1782, a few countries in Europe emancipated their Jews and started granting them civil rights, allowing them to join schools and academia, own land, etc. This process, along with the winds of intellectual transformation, allowed the Jews to finally leave their closed-off shtetls and start merging into European societies. Fearing that the trends of modernization might cause an exodus from Judaism, the old-guard rabbis created the Charedi courts.

Charedi in Hebrew comes from the word *chared*, which literally means "afraid,"[6] and when people are afraid, they push back hard. The Charedi system follows the strictest version of Judaism, a puritanical take on the law that aims to follow all traditions to a T, including but not limited to prayers, eating habits, personal relationships, culture, education, and even sex. The Charedis live in closed-off communities in neighborhoods and towns around Israel (and elsewhere in the world, like Brooklyn) and maintain an Old World way of living. There are many different courts with different traditions around Israel and the world, but broadly speaking, their agenda in life is God and the Bible, with an emphasis on family unions and Jewish tradition. Which is all great so far as everyone is entitled to live however they want. However, there is a problem with how this way of life manifests itself in Israeli society.

Israel was created as the homeland of the Jewish people—a culturally Jewish, secular state filled with people who speak Hebrew and chill on Shabbat but aren't necessarily particularly religious. However, after the Holocaust, the numbers of the old-school Orthodox were at an all-time low, and though Israel's first prime minister, David Ben-Gurion, was secular, he understood that respect and attention needed to be given to those OG traditionalists. A little after the establishment of the country, the new secular government and the old-school rabbinate agreed to give the boys who wanted to go study some

Torah a pass from their military service. There were about four hundred yeshiva boys back in 1951, and they got to skip the military to go deep into the Scriptures. That was then.

In the years since, the Charedi community has grown faster by percentage than the secular community, and they've joined the Israeli political game to establish their own political parties. Israel is a parliamentary democracy, with 120 seats in the Knesset. Because it is a vibrant democracy, anyone can start a party, and any party can run the government: all they need is a coalition with a majority of the 120 seats. The Charedi now have two major ultra-Orthodox parties—the Ashkenazi Yahadut Ha'Torah and the Sephardi Shas—and as they have about sixteen seats between them, they are a critical part of the governing system. In recent elections, the Charedi parties were the ones with the political power to tip the balance in order to create a majority coalition. This gives the ultra-Orthodox parties outsized importance, which in and of itself isn't an issue. The problem is what these parties request and often receive for their constituencies in exchange for that political support. There may have been four hundred yeshiva boys back when Ben-Gurion made the deal to exempt them from military service; now tens of thousands of young boys are automatically exempt (unless they volunteer) from military service and receive other benefits like tax relief and child support.

Just think about that for a second. According to the Bureau of Statistics, 14 percent of the Israeli population are self-described as ultra-Orthodox, or Charedim. Both the Charedi community (14 percent) and the Arab community (21 percent) of Israel are automatically exempt from mandatory military service unless they choose otherwise. This leaves 35 percent of the Israeli population out on the bench! That is a staggering number of civil duty exemptions for a country as small as Israel. If you were the rest of the country, how would you feel? Yeah. Not great.

Let me be clear: I have nothing against the Charedi people whatsoever, and I make sure to say this, since every attempt to discuss the community, especially in the political sphere, can be interpreted as a threat to their lifestyle. There are many inspiring elements of their culture, like the closeness of the family unit, the depth of debate on questions of philosophy and ethics, and, of course, their passion for Judaism. But, understandably, the rest of Israeli society is bubbling with resentment about having to serve in the military and pay taxes for a population that insists on seclusion. This population is also growing at rapid speed. Despite an increasing number of young Orthodox adults leaving the Charedi world and becoming traditional or secular, the birth rate among the Charedim is leading to a demographic shift. The average Charedi family has 7.1 children, and the average secular family has 2.2.[7] Some projections by demographers claim that by 2065 the Charedi population will reach 32 percent of Israel's population.

The problem, as always, starts and ends with education, and this is where I do have a real issue. One of the political deals that's been cut with the Orthodox parties over the years allows the Charedi community to create its own education system, which is sponsored by the rest of Israeli taxpayers. That system is based on studying the Torah and its trillion interpretations, which is indeed fantastic; however, many schools that fall within this system also do *not* allow for *any* secular studies, not even the most basic of them. Unlike the rest of the Israeli education system, which is similar to the education systems of other Western countries, the Charedi school system precludes its students from international core curriculum subjects such as math, English, science, and computer science.

This issue is a delicate political football within Israel, with potentially grave consequences for the country's future. How can a Charedi boy or girl join the workforce, support their family, and contribute to the country's GDP if they have no basic knowledge in math, science, and English? How are they prepared for life if they don't know how to work a computer? The Charedi education system is preventing its students from acquiring the basic tools needed to merge into any other society, and, at least from an outside perspective, it seems designed to keep its population paralyzed and its voting base uneducated. The result of this lack of basic education creates a built-in dependency on the state for financial support. When children are not given a proper education, they grow up, marry young, have 7.1 children, and stay dependent on meager governmental allowances to survive. It causes the majority of the Charedi community to stay in a cycle of extreme poverty, which leads to a slew of other social and domestic issues.

There's also the issue of archaic gender dynamics. Similar to other religions, Charedi tradition often justifies the repression of women as respect for women. The Charedi community leaders argue that even though the *roles* of men and women are different, one is no less than the other. Thus, the men should go to yeshivas to study Torah and the women should raise the family and financially support their husbands' studies through domestic work. This is not a judgment; this is the reality, and it is imposed on the entire community by the Charedi political leadership.

A pivot, and a massive one, needs to occur *within* the Charedi community, and pockets of resistance are indeed springing up. Feeling like their voices were not being heard in the Ashkenazi Charedi political system, a group of Mizrahi ultra-Orthodox formed their own political party called the Shas in 1982. Their spiritual leader was the charismatic Rabbi Ovadia Yosef, a highly regarded Egyptian-born mega leader. He had eleven children; his eldest is a passionate woman named Adina Bar Shalom. I can't speak for her childhood, but I imagine she was a rebellious kid, since she dedicated her entire adult life to fighting for access to higher education for Charedi people. Bar Shalom founded the Charedi Academy in Jerusalem and formed many organizations to build understanding between the Israeli secular and Orthodox communities (a recent Pew Research poll found that 93 percent of secular Israelis and 95 percent of ultra-Orthodox would feel "extremely uncomfortable" if a member of their family were to marry someone from the other community,[8] so understanding is indeed needed). She is also a peace activist and a recipient of the Israel Award, and speaks publicly against the discrimination of women in the Charedi sphere while still keeping her Charedi lifestyle.

Though she's paid a personal price, her work seems to be gaining traction, as there are loud voices from within the community, both men and women, who are demanding change. Women of the Charedi sector are better represented in the higher education system than men, and they are pushing themselves into the public sphere, understanding full well a change is needed. There are trailblazers like Racheli Ibenbuim, who started an organization to help Charedi women join the Israeli workforce; community leader and politician Omer Yankelevich; and Charedi feminists Estee Ryder Indursky and Estie Shoshan, who founded Elect, an organization committed to forcing Charedi politicians to allow their women to get elected in the Charedi parties.

All of these activists are sacrificing their own personal comfort and reputations to improve a community that's highly resistant to change. These are super–close-knit communities that adhere to rabbis above anyone else. Since most Charedis do not watch TV or read mainstream news outlets, most of the communication is done by *pashkevils*, which are messages posted on the walls in Charedi neighborhoods explaining to the population what is virtuous behavior and what isn't, and even *who* behaved virtuously and who did not. It's a powerful shaming practice that can leave families ostracized, children rejected from "good schools," and young adults without a good match in marriage (yes, there are still arranged marriages in the Charedi community).

The Charedi population boom and the community's resistance to proper modern education is a problem in and of itself, but there is another political aspect of the rabbinate system that is counter to Israel's founding principles, and possibly to Judaism itself. The rabbinate system in Israel is aiming to become the one and only authority on Judaism. As a general rule, one top-down authority on any religion isn't great. Gidi Grinstein described this best when he explored that elusive quality known as Jewish resiliency. One of the sources of that resiliency, in his opinion, is the fact that Judaism is decentralized and encourages dissent. Jewish law and Jewish ways of living have developed over thousands of years through intellectual meritocracy and constant debate. Rabbis of yore competed on the validity of their judgment, and over time, one view would become dominant over another. What's more, Jewish legacy is such that all dissenting views were and are systematically documented! As such, each one of us can go back to this scholar or that scholar, hundreds or thousands of years back, and develop and grow our own understanding of Judaism accordingly. This is a magical aspect of Judaism in my opinion. It explicitly tells you *not* to just read the Bible, take it on, believe every word, and shut up. It highly encourages questioning one's faith. Maybe this is why Jews always answer a question with a question. (I don't know, why do they?)

The Charedi political machine is attempting to undo all this history by centralizing Judaism and cementing one right way to be Jewish, even if it goes against thousands of years of Jewish adaptability and culture of debate. The Israeli rabbinate system controls many domestic issues, from marriage and divorce to conversion and burials, and is actively resisting, for example, stores and buses from being in business on Shabbat. And the irony is that this very group was only created in the late 1700s! By virtue of their black coats, and hats, and traditions, they're harkening back to the shtetl Judaism of Eastern Europe—*not* the Judaism of Moses and the Israelites (who probably wore robes and sandals and most definitely did not wear furry hats during their forty-year trek through the desert). This relatively new group is trying to decide for everyone what is the right way to practice

Judaism or be Jewish, and even *who* is a Jew to begin with. This is so un-Jewish of them!

In a thriving democracy, there is room for everyone as long as you don't infringe on anyone else's human rights, safety, or security. And for the most part, there has been a healthy push and pull of religious influence through the years, resulting in a general equilibrium. But there were a handful of times in Israel's history when religious disagreements turned violent, such as in 1995, when a Jewish extremist (*not* from the Charedi community but still using God as his commander) used religion to justify the assassination of Prime Minister Yitzhak Rabin.

The fear is that this latest bud of fundamentalism will bloom into a massive inner conflict that prioritizes one form of Judaism over another. While this sounds crazy given Israel's super-diverse and modern society, there is a precedent. There was, after all, a time in Israel's past when religious zealots tried to force their ways on the rest of the population, and when it happened, it ended in two thousand years of exile.

JERUSALEM'S TRAITOR

Yosef Ben Matityahu Ha'Kohen was an elitist. Born around AD 37 or 38 to a high-society and well-to-do family in Jerusalem, he was educated, multilingual, and worldly. Jerusalem, much like the rest of the region, was under Roman rule and part of a vassal state called Provincia Judea. Despite being effectively under Roman occupation, the Jews were allowed to worship as they chose, were not forced to convert to paganism, and the Second Temple was active, hosting pilgrims, holding ceremonies, and burning tons of farm animals as gifts to God. Hey, times were different back then.

Yosef grew up in an era in which the Jewish population in Judea was already extremely divided, particularly over how to behave under the Romans and how to worship God. Even though the Romans did allow the Jews to practice their Judaism freely, they were still oppressive and, well, Roman. There was a growing class divide, in which the upper-echelon and mostly secular intelligentsia enjoyed preferential living conditions. Naturally, they leaned toward maintaining the status quo, even though the rest of the population suffered high taxation and varying degrees of poverty and oppression.

On the other end of the spectrum were the Zealots. A hard-core, ultra-nationalistic, and religious group, the Zealots pledged their loyalty to God only, and pushed for a rebellion against Rome. Their subsect, the Sicarii, named after a curved knife they hid under their robes, were particularly deadly. The Zealots and, in particular, the Sicarii fought for control of the country and killed anyone who didn't follow their lead.

When Yosef was twenty-six years old, he was sent to Rome to advocate for the release of a bunch of his rabbi buddies. He went to the royal court, which was home to the flamboyant Roman emperor Nero. Yosef, a gifted diplomat, befriended Nero's wife Poppaea Sabina, who showered him with gifts and eventually assisted him in releasing the clergymen. The young Yosef had a grand ol' time in Rome, and the two years he spent there shaped the young man's point of view in ways that would prove to be detrimental to the future of the Jewish people.

When he returned to Judea, the internal unrest was at a boiling point, and a rebellion against the Romans was on its way. Yosef was freaked out. In his time in Rome, he'd seen firsthand the unimaginable might of the Roman military. He wrote terrifying details of their modern weaponry, organizational skills, obedience to a command chain, and physical strength. These guys were beasts, training day in and day out; it wasn't for nothing that the Roman military had dominated the world for centuries. Yosef apparently tried to convince his people to ditch the crazy thoughts of rebellion, but he failed. Thus, the First Jewish Roman War started, and Yosef reluctantly joined the Jews in their fight.

Despite having no military experience, Yosef was sent by the rebellion committee to serve as the commander of the Galilee. The problem was, the locals didn't trust him. He wasn't one of them; his heart was not in the fight; and he had just returned from Rome, so they were suspicious, and for very good reasons.

Vespasian, the Roman commander who was sent by Nero to Judea to quash the Jewish uprising, started military attacks on towns and villages up north, decimating everything in his path. They killed the men, sent the women and children to be sold as slaves, and burned everything to the ground when they were finished with the killing and looting. The level of violence the Romans exhibited was excruciating. After severe losses on the Jewish side, Yosef retreated to the relatively secure town of Yodfat (Jotapata), and the Romans started one of their notorious sieges against the city. In July of AD 67, after forty-seven days of siege, the Romans took over the town, and Yosef along with forty other men went down into a cave to hide. This is where his life took a mind-boggling turn.

Knowing their days were numbered and unsure what to do, Yosef convinced his group not to surrender to the Romans but rather to kill each other until there was only one man standing, who would then kill himself. Miraculously, Yosef was the last man standing. He was a cunning, clever mathematician, and this story is known today in computer science and mathematics as the Josephus Permutation. It is a theoretical problem in which, with advanced planning, a known number of people, a set starting point, and a predictable counting direction, one can choose the right position in a circle to avoid execution. Well done Yosef! As the last man standing, he gave himself up to the army of Vespasian.

He was taken captive, but a man like Yosef would not spend his years as a prisoner of war. In another cunning move, he prophesized to Vespasian that the Roman commander would eventually become the Roman emperor and that he would release him from his chains at that time. Needless to say, the ambitious military leader loved what he heard, and instead of putting his prisoner to death for treason against Nero, he kept the sycophant by his side.

Yosef became an observer and a narrator of the events that would change the fate of the Jewish people forever. A prolific writer and a gifted historian, he witnessed (or claimed to witness) everything he wrote about, and his four massive books have lasted in full until today. His work is one of the main sources of information used by researchers and historians in the last two thousand years, and they provide phenomenal insights into a world long gone (even if some scholars have questioned the veracity of some of his accounts).

In his book *The Jewish Wars*, he tells us that Judea had disintegrated into a horrific and bloody civil war with two sparring sides—those who were against rebelling and fighting the Romans and those who were for it. The Zealots were running wild, murdering men, women, and children, including the high priest Ananus, which, in retrospect, he theorizes was the moment that initiated "the total ruin of the Jewish state." As he describes it, Jerusalem was taken over by two extremist leaders who were fighting each other: John of Giscala (Yohanan of Gush Halav) and Simon Bar Giora, both nationalist, religious, and claiming to be the Messiah. Both cray.

By AD 68, there were rivers of blood in the streets of Jerusalem, so instead of Vespasian attacking Jerusalem, he told his men to hold off.

> If we wait for a little bit longer, however, we shall have a lot less of them to fight, as it looks as if a fair number are going to be killed in the faction fighting. . . . Since our enemies are busy dying by their own hands and suffering from the worst handicap imaginable—civil war—the best thing that we can do in the circumstances is stay as spectators instead of taking on

fanatics who welcome death and are already busy murdering each other.[9]

Wait, said Vespasian. Let's let the Jews kill themselves. They'll do our work for us. This speech punched me straight in the gut. There is nothing holier in Judaism than human life, and these madmen who were calling themselves righteous were slaughtering each other. For what, again? This would cost the Jewish people greatly.

Meanwhile, Rome was going through infighting of its own. AD 69 became "the Year of the Four Emperors," and by the end of the year Yosef's prophecy came to be. Vespasian indeed became the Roman emperor, and he did indeed free Yosef, who changed his name to Josephus and his last name to Flavius, honoring the emperor's family name.

The pause in Rome's attacks on Judea was not used by the rebels to unite, rebuild, stock up on supplies, or come to their senses; on the contrary—it made the civil war worse. Team Johan and Team Simon barricaded themselves in various areas of the temple, killing priests and pilgrims who happened to be in their path. They also set fire to the town's food storage, burning down wheat, salt, and oil, which could have fed the city for years, sentencing the people to starvation.

On April 14, AD 70, Titus, the new emperor's son, returned to finish his father's work and led an army of tens of thousands of soldiers to place a massive siege on Jerusalem. Josephus was right there by his side. Josephus was both an observer to these events and a participant. Always a pragmatist, he knew this was not going to end well for his people, and he describes in excruciating detail the five-month siege of Jerusalem, the horrific famine, suicide missions, and heroic small victories that came along with it.

He also describes how Titus sent him to speak to his people in Hebrew to try and convince them to cut a deal and at least save Jerusalem. He says that for these speeches he found a safe spot by the walls where he tried to speak to the rebels' hearts but mostly their common sense.

"You would be wise to change the way you have chosen to behave before total disaster becomes unavoidable and to take some helpful advice while there is still a chance of doing so. The Romans are not going to bear a grudge against you because of what had happened, so long as you stop being stupid.

"Men with iron hearts! Why don't you drop your weapons and take pity on a country already on the brink of destruction? Turn around and look at the beauty you are betraying—what a city! What a Temple!"[10]

The rebels, in return, threw stones and javelins at him.

On the ninth day of the month of Av (August), the walls of Jerusalem fell, and Titus's army took over the holy city. The Romans saw dead bodies piled on the streets and inside homes, and they killed whoever else they found alive. They destroyed the city and burned down the temple.

The rebel leaders Simon Bar Giora and John of Giscala were captured by Titus. Simon was immediately executed; John was sent to Rome to be presented as a prisoner at the parade thrown for Titus upon his victorious return. On display in that parade were a plethora of treasures and artifacts of worship looted from the temple, including the gold candelabrum, the holy menorah. The scenes from that parade were literally cemented in stone ten years later by Titus's brother, Emperor Domitian. You can go check it out; it's still standing, carved onto the Arch of Titus at Via Sacra, Rome, Italy.

In his breathtaking book *Jerusalem's Traitor*,[11] author Desmond Seward takes the reader through the horror show that was the First Jewish-Roman War and inside the questionable character of Josephus Flavius. Was he a traitor? Was he a rationalist? Is he even trustworthy? Josephus as a historian is not without blemishes: he was vain and conflicted, and his disdain for the rebels probably tainted his writing. He was a grandstander, wrote in hyperbole, and most likely exaggerated details and numbers for effect. But, based on scholarly consensus, it seems that the main details of the war are undisputable and can be corroborated in other writings of the era or ones written shortly thereafter. So I guess some degree of thanks is owed to Yosef for coming out of that cave in Yodfat and joining the Romans, bearing witness to history, writing these elaborate masterpieces, and giving us a firsthand account of ancient history. A priceless act.

So why, exactly, did Jerusalem fall? Was it inevitable, or was it avoidable?

Chazal, the Jewish sages of the Mishna and Talmud who established the Talmudic tradition after the fall of Jerusalem, claimed that Jerusalem fell because of "*Sinat Hinam*": baseless hatred within and between the Jewish people. In Hebrew the word for *zealots* is *ḳanaim*: "jealous" or "fanatics." We should all be concerned when the spiritual practice of *any* religion becomes fanatical and overzealous.

Excavations done in the Old City of Jerusalem exposed the huge white stones that still lay as they fell on the day Titus demolished the temple two thousand years ago. It's chilling. You can almost hear the screams and feel the pain. But we should only feel that pain in order to listen to the past and learn from it. Jerusalem today is a flourishing town, where believers and nonbelievers, secular and Orthodox, Jews and Arabs, live peacefully and collaboratively side by side. But even one political or religion-based murder is one too many. The entire world is experiencing some form or another of zealotry these days, and we cannot allow fanaticism, from *any* religion, nation, or political group, to infect *any* country *ever* again.

We have a very well-documented past to learn from.

CHAPTER TWELVE

UP UP NATION

DOUBLE BOTTOM LINE

Let me take you from one civil war, two thousand years ago, to another, happening right now, smack on Israel's northern border. The Arab Spring of 2011 ignited one of the bloodiest and most prolonged conflicts of our time: the ongoing civil war in Syria. This war is characterized by atrocities caused by conventional and nonconventional weapons alike. By most accounts, Syrian President Bashar al-Assad has killed over four hundred thousand of his own people, many of them children, through vicious and internationally illegal methods. It's abominable.

A short time after the war started, wounded Syrian people started showing up on the northern border of Israel. A trickle turned into a flood. Fighters, refugees, mothers, and many children desperately needed medical treatment—enough so that they were willing to cross into an "enemy" country. At first, these Syrians were afraid of Israel. After years of conflict between the countries and systematic propaganda campaigns on behalf of the Assad regime, Israel was, understandably, a terrifying idea. But the word of Israeli hospitals had traveled through the population over the years, and patients gradually changed their minds. In the words of Galilee Hospital's Dr. Eyal Sela: "If I treat one man, 50, 1,500, and they go back to Syria, their families will be grateful. At some stage the child or grandchild will ask about their scar, and they'll explain that the Zionist enemy treated them and saved their lives."[1]

As the war raged on and Syria's healthcare system collapsed, Israeli hospitals Galilee Medical Center in Nahariya, Ziv Medical Center in Safed, and Poriya Medical Center outside of Tiberias became the ones responsible for those Syrians fleeing from Assad. In 2013, the Israeli military created a designated unit called Shchenoot Tova, translated as "good neighboring," to coordinate treatment and aid for the Syrian people. To date, over two hundred thousand Syrians have been treated in Israel, a fifth of them children.

All wars are horrific, but it seems like in this civil war the world has completely abandoned the children of Syria, who have been given little to no protection by the warring sides, contrary to international agreements. According to Smadar Okampo, the head nurse in pediatric surgery in the Galilee Medical Center: "Children arrive with missing limbs and shattered faces, and many are severely neglected and carry lice. The first order of the day is cleanup, many arrive without parents. Some arrive unconscious and don't realize where they are when they wake up."[2]

Doctors in Israel are treating these refugees daily, as an obligation to their Hippocratic Oath and their commitment to humanity. In addition to creating these human bridges, this horrific war has familiarized Israeli doctors with a gruesome array of war injuries. Dr. Masad Barhoum is the general manager of the Galilee Medical Center in

Nahariya (and, yes, another incredibly inspiring Arab Israeli citizen). "Treating Syrians is one of Israel's decisions that I appreciate the most, obviously first of all for humanitarian reasons, but that's not the only thing. . . . We may be the only Western hospital in the world with experience in accepting and treating such serious wounds. . . . Today, we reconstruct wounded people's faces, implant jaws, and print everything on a 3D printer. . . . We have become a leading hospital in trauma."[3]

Unfortunately, Israel has a lot of experience in times of disaster, and it is sharing that experience with the rest of the world, making sure that the children of Syria, at least the ones closest to the Israeli border, have a place to go to get treated and healed. Small islands of trust are emerging on the Israeli-Syrian border, but Israel's goodwill did not start there.

The first initiative to create a governmental arm to assist other nations came in 1957 with the establishment of MASHAV—Israel's Agency for International Development Cooperation. Golda Meir understood that Israel had experience that could be relevant to other developing countries and decided that the government should share its know-how in fields such as education, agriculture, and medicine—and, in recent years, climate change and food security. MASHAV believes in "training the trainers": in addition to sending teams around the world, they bring educators to Israel to share valuable knowledge. Some of MASHAV's recent projects include providing courses on early childhood education in Kumasi, Ghana; beekeeping courses in Rwanda; drip irrigation in Kenya; the Center for Agricultural Excellence in Haryana, India; generating income and women's empowerment in Guatemala; establishing neonatal units in Ghana; establishing trauma units in Haiti and in Kisumu, Kenya; and building an eye surgery hospital in Nepal.[4]

But it's not just technology and infrastructure. Whenever there's a major international disaster, Israel seems to be on the scene. Remember the soccer team stuck in a cave in Thailand? A group of Israeli divers assisted in the rescue. Remember the major earthquake that hit Haiti in 2010? Israel was one of the first countries to send aid. And that aid was not just in the shape of water or blankets. Israel sent over a crew of nurses and doctors. It was the first country to set up a field hospital on the ground and the only country that was able to perform complicated operations throughout the recovery process. The first baby who was delivered in the wreckage was delivered by Israeli doctors, and his mother decided to name her newborn child Israel.[5]

One of the main forces behind Israeli aid is the NGO IsraAID. The organization was founded in order to coordinate and support various other humanitarian NGOs and is now active in seventeen countries around the world, with a mission to support people affected by humanitarian crises.[6] IsraAID provides physical and psychological support to 160,000 refugees in Kakuma Camp in Kenya; it created the HoneyAID project for female empowerment in Nepal, where they train local women to support their families and communities through beekeeping. They also provide support in countries like Japan. Four days after the Fukushima nuclear disaster, IsraAID was on the ground. Japan does not allow NGOs to assist in natural disaster recovery, but IsraAID identified where they could uniquely contribute: post-trauma psychological support. IsraAID brought over sixty Israeli experts to train over three thousand Japanese healthcare professionals in "non-verbal therapy" methods to help treat survivors.[7]

Psychological help to overcome trauma is a highly developed field in Israel, and IsraAID, along with three professors from Bar-Ilan University, created a program to help Yazidi women who were enslaved by ISIS (the training is called STAIR narrative therapy for trauma-related disorders, developed by Dr. Marylene Cloitre). In May 2019, Lamiya Haji Bashar, Yazidi survivor, human rights activist, and recipient of the European Union Sakharov Prize, along with fourteen other Yazidi survivors, went through this program in Israel before returning to Iraq to treat other survivors and help them overcome the unimaginable atrocities inflicted upon them by ISIS.[8] (Lamiya lives in Germany, which is why she was the only woman who could use her full name. The rest of the survivors could not disclose that they'd visited Israel.) IsraAID also helped establish the unbelievably inspiring School for Peace for refugee children on the Greek island of Lesbos. The school is yet another collaboration between Jewish and Arab Israelis. In addition to IsraAID, it was run by the Jewish youth movement Hashomer Hatzair and the Arab youth movement Ajyal. Together, this "mishmash of Israelis, Syrians, Iranians, Iraqis, Greeks, Afghans, and Congolese" helped over five thousand refugee children, mostly from Syria, Iran, and Afghanistan. This is H (who did not want to be identified by his full name), twenty, who lives on Lesbos:

"My whole life, all through my childhood in Syrian schools, I was taught that the Israelis are the enemy, and then the first thing I see when I approach the Greek coast is the Star of David on the shirts of Israelis who reach out and place me on the ground."[9]

The School for Peace ran programs from 2011 to March 2020, when it was burned down. The perpetrators were never found, and the light that school was giving these kids is dimmed—for the moment. But the volunteers who built that school are committed to rebuilding it.

The unbelievably inspiring School for Peace in Lesbos, the Yazidi woman who goes back to Iraq with tools to heal, and the hundreds of thousands of men, women, and children who go back to Syria after being treated in Israeli hospitals may carry a key to regional transformation. After decades of violence and propaganda, I see a glimmer of possibility. A possibility carried in the heart of a wounded child, who was taught to be fearful but is now returning to Syria after seeing Israel in a whole different way.

This is Israel. This is what we give. And if not for boycott movements and animosity from regional powers, this could be a win-win for the entire Middle East.

This chapter is about what is possible.

THIS IS US

Israel is not only helping the world's humanitarian efforts. True to its capitalist nature and the chutzpah-full energy of the people, Israelis are now contributing to almost every field of the world's economy. Israel gives to the world in a way astonishingly disproportionate to her size, and no one has made this point better than Dan Senor and Saul Singer in their 2009 international bestseller *Start-Up Nation*. They asked the question "How is it that Israel—a country of 7.1 million people, only sixty years old, surrounded by enemies, in a constant state of war since its founding, with no natural resources—produces more start-up companies than large, peaceful, and stable nations like Japan, China, India, Korea, Canada, and the United Kingdom?"[10]

They attributed this phenomenon to:

- A structurally egalitarian and classless society (though not without its problems, as we've established). Israel's socialist roots created a free public education system and universities that are subsidized and affordable for everyone. This is as close as you can get to merit-based upward mobility.
- A society that encourages dissent, debate, and taking initiative.
- A society that is under constant threat, thereby forcing young people to take responsibility and follow through on their goals.
- A society wherein most people are required to perform at least two years of national service, which creates social bonds that last a lifetime.
- A society that uses elite military units to train future talent, giving them the opportunity to practice and achieve high-level tasks at a young age. Where else could a young kid develop and deploy computer viruses to infect, let's just imagine, Iran's

nuclear power plant? (I have no inside knowledge of any of this. I just know how to read newspapers.)

- A society based on constant waves of immigration that infuses the population with new ideas and inspiration.

The book *Start-Up Nation* became not only a commercial success but also a must read for the tech community and world leaders. In short, get the book to get the full story.

Israel is now a major player not just in start-ups, but in the entertainment world as well, and *In Treatment* paved the way. I first learned about *In Treatment* from the newspaper, and in true Israeli fashion told the creator I was going to sell the show to HBO, not knowing, of course, how one sells a show to an American network. It worked out well, and I managed to sell many more shows to many other networks, including HBO, ABC, CBS, Comedy Central, MTV, and Showtime, but none of them was as successful as my first. What did happen, though, was incredible to watch. Israeli creators started selling so many shows overseas that Israel became a content powerhouse, often without anyone around the world knowing that their favorite TV show actually came from that controversial tiny sliver of land somewhere in the Middle East.

A new industry was born.

I don't have enough space to credit each and every creator, writer, producer, network, and actor who's been a part of this revolution, but I'll mention just a few shows you may know and love. There are the shows adapted from Hebrew to English, such as the hit HBO show *Euphoria*; the reality TV music competition *The Four: Battle for Stardom*; and the comedy *Beauty and the Baker*. And the shows streaming in their original Hebrew, such as *Shtisel*, *Srugim*, *Teheran*, and the crown jewel of original Israeli content, *Fauda*. Also the shows created by or about Israel or Israelis, such as *Unorthodox*, *Dig*, *The Spy*, and *Tyrant* (the last three by the genius Gideon Raff). And then, of course, there is President Obama's television obsession, the international smash hit *Homeland*. Yes, *Homeland* is based on an Israeli show by the name of *Hatufim*, or *Prisoners of War*. *Homeland* became a cultural phenomenon, was nominated for a whopping 172 awards, and won 60, including Golden Globes for Best Drama and Best Actress. Arguably, the original show may have been even better. *Prisoners of War* is streaming in America and is considered a masterpiece. As 2019 came to a close, the *New York Times* chose it as the best international show of the decade.[11] Considering that the creator, Gideon Raff, is one of my best friends on the planet, I am nothing short of a proud momma goose when I read things like that.

TECH TALK

As you may have noticed, this is the chapter in which I describe all the goodness Israel contributes to the world, and there is no other field in which that contribution has been more apparent than technological innovation. It's super-logical to argue that Israel's technological innovation was born from security concerns, and many smarter people than me (Hello again, Dan and Saul!) have done just that. When Israel was established, David Ben-Gurion understood that in order to overcome the numerical disadvantage of a tiny Jewish state surrounded by hostile Arab nations, the country must have a scientific and technological advantage. He sent scientists to study abroad and advance every field from industry to agriculture. This encouragement from the top down continued, and over twenty years ago the Israeli government identified tech start-ups as essential businesses, offering support and incentives for private innovators and investors.

The success of Israeli innovation is breathtaking. It is virtually impossible to mention all the technological companies, inventions, and solutions that Israel has contributed to the world. But I'll mention just a few, just so you can get the scope.

An Israeli company invented the first DiskOnKey, a flash drive with an integrated USB interface that served as a portable data storage device, as well as the first viral "social network" technology, a free instant messaging software called ICQ that was developed in Israel in 1996 and sold to AOL in 1998. In 1993, when the World Wide Web was only two years old, Israelis founded the security software company Checkpoint and developed Firewall-1 software, which is now in ninety countries with seventy registered patents. Gilat telecom satellite technology is helping connect people in remote areas in over thirty countries, and ReWalk Robotics is helping amputees walk again by reading their centers of gravity. If you need to build a website, you're probably using Wix, and if you need to get anywhere, you should really use Waze, like one hundred million other users around the world. Mobileye created a camera technology for safety and autonomous driving that is now installed in more than twenty million vehicles around the world.

In agriculture, Israel is responsible for drip irrigation technology. The company Netafim invented a watering solution that produces 70 percent more crops with 50 percent less water. This was in 1959; today fifteen billion of these drip systems are manufactured each year, saving water and helping agriculture worldwide. Israelis invented a new way to net hay! CoverEdge is now wrapping 50 percent of the world's bales of hay and is considered the most advanced product in the field (no pun intended). Israelis invented a new type of biological pest control, automized milk farms, and developed a new way to monitor a cow's health and well-being with a smart collar.

In medicine and health, Alpha Omega became the world leader of technology in the field of neuroscience and functional neurosurgery with a brain stimulus and recording device. Medinol created the revolutionary heart stent for coronary arteries, a small metal device that is inserted into a blocked heart artery to keep your blood flowing. My father thanked them daily, as he had a few inside of him. Given Imaging transformed the endoscopy world when, in 2001, they introduced PillCam, a twenty-six-millimeter camera tucked inside a pill you swallow with a glass of water, which takes a video of your insides while you live your life. Way better than the other option.

Israel is a leader in water desalination, with forty countries using its IDE reverse osmosis technology. It also developed an advanced fighter pilot helmet that is used by thirty air forces around the world, and the Iron Dome missile defense system.[12]

In 2019, nine Israeli inventions made it onto *Time* magazine's Top 100 inventions of the year, among them: OrCam, an AI-powered device to be clipped onto glasses to assist the visually impaired; ECONcrete, which developed sustainable, ecofriendly marine concrete to "encourage growth of diverse plants and animals such as corals and oysters"; a migraine-zapping wearable device; the first all-electric commuter aircraft; and . . . a device that turns air into water. For real. Watergen makes water out of thin air, and their device is now being used in natural disaster areas around the world.[13]

Israelis are now gaining international success in other fields that are somewhat but not entirely related to tech or science. Food is one of them. Moshik Roth is a world-renowned chef with his Michelin two-star restaurant, &moshik, in Amsterdam, and Tal Ronnen built the celebrity favorite Crossroads in Los Angeles. Eyal Shani brought his lovemaking to tomatoes (I know how this sounds, but this is literally how he describes it) to Miznon in Vienna, New York, Melbourne, and Paris. Assaf Granit's Palomar and Barbary made it on *GQ* and London *Time Out*'s lists of best restaurants of the city. And culinary stars Yotam Ottolenghi (with his Palestinian partner Sami Tamimi), Einat Admony, Ori Menashe, and the amazing New Orleans Shaya from Alon Shaya are also feeding people all over.

Considering the utilitarian nature of the pioneers' outfits and Israel's years of austerity, you might not think of Israel as a leader in fashion, but you'd be wrong. From Princess Diana's favorite swimsuit line of the eighties (Gottex) to Lady Gaga and Beyoncé favorite Alon Livné, Israeli fashion designers are quietly rocking it around the world: Dodo Bar Or with her must-have Ibiza attires; the head designer of French fashion house Lanvin, Alber Elbaz; and Kobi Halperin, Nili Lotan, Yigal Azrouël, and Elie Tahari. Serena Williams and her entire wedding party wore Galia Lahav, as did Beyoncé for her vow renewal with Jay-Z. Lahav is also a favorite of Katy Perry, Emma Stone, and Jennifer Lopez. For their big days, Meghan Trainor and Kacey Musgraves chose Berta, an Israeli designer also loved by Carrie Underwood, Ariana Grande, and Kylie Jenner. And let us not forget celebrity children, who are all decked out in my friends Iris Adler and Tali Milchberg's high-end kids' clothing line, nununu. A very partial list of their young clients includes the offspring of: Gwen Stefani, Chrissy Teigen, Fergie, Victoria Beckham, Halle Berry, Jessica Alba, and the entire Kardashian clan,[14] not to mention my little guy, Ari.

Israeli innovation, technology, and science are also being used to build bridges with other countries in the Middle East, and not just the friendly ones. It was alleged to me by a former intelligence officer friend that citizens of nations that do not have official diplomatic relationships with Israel use Israeli technology and even invest privately in Israeli start-ups. Those technological bridges between the nations are active in the private sector as well, specifically in Rawabi. Israeli, American, and other international tech companies outsource their programmers through Asal Technologies and Jaffa Net, based in the city. Companies such as Mellanox (now Nvidia), Wix, Microsoft, Alcatel-Lucent, Western Digital (SanDisk), Intel, Cadence, Synopsys, Nuvoton, and CEVA hire local programmers, and Israeli venture funds such as Jerusalem Venture Partners (JVP) are working to connect American companies with Palestinian programmers and companies based in Rawabi. Private citizens also use tech as a peace-building bridge, creating programs such as MEET (Middle East Entrepreneurs of Tomorrow), which brings together Israeli and Palestinian kids for three-year tech camps in Jerusalem and Nazareth.

Israeli *stuff* is everywhere, whether you know it or not. If you have Quartz Caesarstone slab in your kitchen, it came from Israel. If you have a newborn and use the Donna car seat/stroller, if your baby monitor is Babysense or Nanit, if you play Rummikub, wear Shoresh sandals, or eat Bamba from Trader Joe's—they all come from Israel. Israelis also invented the world's first electric home hair removal device, Epilady, in 1985. Oh, and do you like cherry tomatoes? You know, the tiny ones? That's also an Israeli invention.[15]

Phew! I know, this was a lot, but trust me, it's nothing compared to what's out there. Israel has more companies registered on the NASDAQ and the New York Stock Exchange than any other country in the world per capita, more start-ups per capita, more academic papers in the field of medicine per capita, and more venture capital funds per capita.

Israel contributes to the world disproportionately to its size in every walk of life. It's enhancing health, culture, science, and lifestyle and assisting in humanitarian endeavors around the globe—even in places that officially refuse to have political ties with Israel. If you're not knowingly using Israeli technology, you may be watching something from Israel, wearing something from Israel, or eating something from Israel.

And this is the *real* story. Not the stereotypes you've been fed from sensationalist news media or hidden international agendas on your college campus. This is who Israel is, *right now*. This is what we have to share.

A WRONG CONCLUSION

Now let's get this straight—many countries around the world participate in humanitarian efforts and contribute to the world in various fields—as all countries should. So please don't take the above shameless horn-tooting as some state-sponsored propaganda. It is not. Everything I have stated above, in the bluntest of manners, is what Israel can not only give to the world but can give to the entire Middle East.

If only the Middle East would be willing to take it.

We've already established that on a very basic level, every human, and as such every country, wants to be loved (or respected), so it's obvious that Israelis are highly invested in both effecting change in the world and letting the world know that Israel is not such a bad place. We are proud of what we've achieved in such a short time and against all odds, and it is infuriating when the good stuff about Israel is drowned in the flood of negative stuff. Israel has so much to share with its neighbors, why are they not willing to be partners with us, or only willing to do so in secrecy? Why can't more Yazidi women come to Israel to be *helped*, without being afraid of being *killed* when they go back to Iraq?

And not only is the help not being received by our neighbors, the "boycott Israel" movements have become legitimate, and Israel of all places has become in some circles the regional Death Star. Activists from Baghdad to Berkeley to Brandeis are crying for sanctions and boycotts, effectively trying to stop Israel from helping the world and her neighbors advance in technology, healthcare, and agriculture, to stop Israelis from hiring Palestinians in Rawabi, and from helping traumatized Yazidi women.

How is this helping anyone? Wouldn't you be pissed?

When you weigh the entire region and look at Israel's unique freedoms (of religion, speech, gender, LGBTQ+ rights, etc.) and add to those what Israel gives the world *and can also give to the entire the Middle East* in tech, arts, sciences, and humanitarian aid and knowledge, it is really hard to understand why it sometimes feels like everyone wants to drag us down.

And if you thought I was pissed up to now, just wait until we get to the last chapter, in which we try to understand how the hell we got here.

CHAPTER THIRTEEN

WHAT'S WITH THE OBSESSION, WORLD?

HERE'S WHAT'S UP

As I'm writing this book from the coziness of my West Hollywood apartment, I can't help but wonder: Who are you, my reader? Who are you to have found this book and stuck with it all the way to chapter thirteen? What was *your* perception of Israel, and what was your reaction when the topic came up? I'd like to think that if I've done my job sorta well up to now, you may be asking yourself "How did I not know all (or some) of this?" Ha! Great question: this is what we're here to do. But first, let's do the numbers.

The hard numbers show that, within the general worldwide population, Israel as a "brand" is actually positioned just outside the top third. According to Best Countries Report—a ranking done by *U.S. News & World Report*, Y&R's BAV Group, and the Wharton School of Business[1]—Israel moved up from the thirtieth place in 2018 to twenty-ninth in 2019 out of eighty countries worldwide, while Americans ranked Israel at number sixteen. Not too bad in general, but when looking at the numbers closely, some problems become clear. The first issue is how badly Israel is perceived among millennials; the second issue is that Israel is perceived as a religious country that uses "banks and tanks" too often.

Millennials around the world rank Israel forty-sixth overall; they place it at number nine in the world in terms of power, and they think it is the second most religious country in the world, smack in between Saudi Arabia and Iran! This level of misinformation is shocking, considering that Israel is the only country in the Middle East in which you can practice any religion you want freely while making out with your same-sex partner on the beach.

In addition to Israel's perception issue, the people who *do* hate Israel hate her with passion and are extremely vocal about it. In the realm of the interwebs, if you post anything even slightly positive about Israel, you'll be trolled to oblivion, attacked with millions of "Free Palestine" comments and insanely vicious slurs. You may also become a target of the puritanical left, which has been permeated by the lingo of BDS. As a result, Israel is a "hands off" zone for a lot of high-level individuals in the US. In my own adopted town of Hollywood, California, people will express their support of Israel privately to me but will almost always shy away from speaking up publicly for fear of the backlash.

Israel is a touchy subject. But why? Why does Israel evoke so many emotions, some of them entirely irrational?

As someone who was raised on the liberal side of the political spectrum, my immediate answer to this question is simple: they hate us because we act badly. This is what I hear from many of my friends in both Israel and America. And the truth is—it's true! We do sometimes act badly!

But it's not like other countries don't act badly, right? Why such passion when Israel comes up? Why aren't the boycott movements, worldwide condemnations, political resolutions, international media headlines, demonstrations, and twitterstorms not equally directed at, say, China, North Korea, Syria, Iran, Venezuela, Yemen, Turkey, Russia, Saudi Arabia, Myanmar, Burundi, Egypt, Algeria, Sierra Leone, Pakistan, Libya, Iraq, and Chad? Israel is misunderstood not only by the people who were intentionally educated to misunderstand her but also by the people who should really know better.

Ironically, the answer might have to do with the very international body that played a central role in creating the State of Israel: the United Nations.

NOT AGAIN, UN

I love what the United Nations stands for. My grandfather Hanan, whom we'll get to shortly, worked in the diplomatic corps and was a member of the Israeli delegation to the United Nations, and I was honored to speak onstage at the General Assembly Hall in 2016 and 2018. I still get the chills every time I walk into that building.

The UN was created as an intergovernmental body aimed to promote international peace and security, harmony, and collaboration between nations around the world. The first iteration of the UN was the League of Nations, which was formed after World War I for the purpose of maintaining world peace. Clearly, it failed, and after World War II, the nations reshuffled the organization and declared, "This time for real! No more fighting!" Thus, the United Nations was created.

From the early days of Zionism, Herzl and the rest of his OG crew knew that Jewish self-determination depended on its acceptance by the international community. They understood the importance of worldwide legitimacy and crisscrossed the globe a few times over to enroll world leaders in the project of Jewish state-building, gaining limited support with a few (Britain and the League of Nations) but failing with most. The world had to wait for the horrors of the Holocaust to realize that after thousands of years of discrimination, pogroms, and persecutions, the Jews should probably have a place to call their own—you know, just in case.

In fact, one of the first major accomplishments of the baby United Nations was indeed the Partition Plan, which granted the Jews their state again. Thirty-three nations voted in favor of the resolution, thirteen opposed, and ten abstained. (As you may remember from chapter six, the Jews agreed to that plan, all members of the Arab League and all Muslim countries voted against it, and the Arabs started a war, but we don't need to get into that again.) When Israel was established in 1948, there were fifty-eight states who were members of the United Nations.

Today, as a result of changing world borders and emergent countries, there are 193 members of the UN, 53 percent of them non-democracies,[2] and herein lies at least one of the problems. The United Nations, which was born out of the atrocities of World War II, understood what could happen if the Jews *didn't* have a place to go should the shit hit the fan again. Their agenda, however, has changed throughout the years, leading to a major headache for Israel and a real security risk.

From its early days, Israel worked hard for international recognition, creating partnerships in hopes of being treated as an equal. Israel jumped on board first to recognize and send ambassadors to new countries and international entities, among them for example the precursor to the European Union—the European Economic Community (EEC). When colonialism was finally winding down and African countries were gaining their independence, Israel saw these countries as its kin and made a massive push to create diplomatic relationships and offer support. It wasn't out of nowhere that the Israeli government pushed for relationships with Africa. This affinity is in the DNA of Zionism from the days of its inception, specified by none other than the father of Zionism, Theodor Herzl.

The Zionists always believed the black communities and the Jewish communities had an unbreakable bond and a divine partnership in the fight against discrimination. This bond is described in one of the most pivotal texts upon which Zionism is built, Herzl's novel *Altneuland*:

> There is still one problem of racial misfortune unsolved. The depths of that problem, in all their horror, only a Jew can fathom. I mean the Negro problem. [An aside: This word horrifies me. Sadly, it was acceptable in 1902.] Don't laugh, Mr. Kingscourt. Think of the hair-raising horrors of the slave trade. Human beings, because their skins are black, are stolen, carried off, and sold. Their descendants grow up in alien surroundings despised and hated because their skin is differently pigmented. I am not ashamed to say, though I be thought ridiculous, now that I have lived to see the restoration of the Jews, I should like to pave the way for the restoration of the Blacks.[3]

In his 1902 book, Herzl condemns the oppressions and discrimination of the African people and expresses a desire for their equality. The new state of Israel was working hard to make Herzl's vision a reality, and for many years was able to do so. However, that special relationship started to erode in April 1955 at the first Afro-Asian conference in Bandung, Indonesia, when an anti-Israel sentiment started emerging. A surprise speaker at that conference was none other than Hitler's buddy Palestinian leader Amin al-Husseini, who spoke against, you guessed it, Israel. Throughout the years to come, Arab countries continued to put financial and political pressure on countries in Africa and around the world while simultaneously working to exclude Israel from key groups in the UN.

In 1957, the UN was divided into regional groups based largely on geographic locations. The people on these "working groups" represented their states day-to-day in the UN; they sit on various steering committees, and they are the ones who decide and control the UN's entire agenda, budgetary allocations, etc.[4] However, because all Arab states unanimously objected to working with Israel, Israel was left out of the region where it is, well, located. This was, of course, part of the Arab nations' systematic attempts to delegitimize Israel as a state. It prevented Israel from participating in committees that tackled all the major regional problems and controlled key decision-making at the UN, including shaping the organization's agenda and priorities. In 2000, Israel was finally accepted as a member of "Western Europe and Other Groups" (WEOG) and, for the first time, was able to participate in the inner workings of the UN.

Unfortunately, between the Arab pressure campaign and years of exclusion, the damage had been done and Israel turned into the UN's supervillain and its favorite target. Here are some facts:

- From 2015 to 2019, the United Nations General Assembly adopted more resolutions against Israel than against Iran, Syria, North Korea, and Russia *combined*.[5] Israel was officially condemned ninety-six times, Syria seven, North Korea five, and Iran five—and China was condemned *zero times*.

- In 2019 alone, the General Assembly of the UN adopted *eighteen* resolutions against Israel, and *seven* for every single other country in the world *combined*.[6] (17 General Assembly +1 at ECOSOC)

- One of the UN's most important committees is the Commission on the Status of Women. Since 2015 this committee has issued only four condemnations, all targeting only one state. You got it. They were against the Israeli treatment of Palestinian women.[7]

(Can we throw back to Ms. Haneen Zoabi and Ms. Heba Yazbak for a sec?)

- Israel is always the hottest topic of conversation at the UN; lucky for us it is all documented. In 2019, for example, Israel was the *third* most discussed topic in speeches of world leaders in the "General Debate" of the General Assembly, right after climate change (#1) and the sustainable development goals of the UN (SDGs) (#2). Israel also made it to the third place of UN leaders' obsession in 2018, right after climate change (#1) and the horrific war in Syria (#2).[8]

- From the time of its creation in mid-2006 to July 2020, the UN Human Rights Council has adopted 217 resolutions criticizing specific states. Nearly half of these resolutions[9] (41.5 percent to be exact, 90 of them!) were against the only democracy in the Middle East; the entire world got to split the rest.

- In that same body (the Human Rights Council), Israel is the *only* country with its own state-specific agenda item. (Agenda item no. 7)

- Since its establishment, the Human Rights Council has initiated thirty-one commissions of inquiry and fact-finding missions to investigate allegations of human rights violations. Twenty-five percent of these investigatory mechanisms (eight of them) have focused exclusively on Israel.[10]

- Various other agencies of the UN, which are designed to focus on specific professional subjects, also tend to single out Israel for criticism. For example, member states of the World Health Organization, which should really be focused on keeping the world healthy (How are we doing on HIV or COVID-19, for example? Are we done with them?), pushed for a resolution that forces the organization to issue only one country-specific report annually. I'll let you guess which country is singled out for criticism by the WHO: Israel, of course.[11] Just so we are clear, Israel is a world leader in *universal healthcare* and medical technologies, not to mention being there for the wounded children of Syria.

- There have been ten Emergency Sessions ("Uniting for Peace") held in the General Assembly. Five out of ten of those Emergency Sessions were dedicated to Israel. The final session was never concluded, BTW, so it is technically still pending.[12]

WHAT??? Is Israel really the biggest, baddest wolf on the block? Heck no. Even if you put every single one of Israel's mistakes under a microscope, they still wouldn't come close to those of *many* other countries around the world. In Saudi Arabia, Chop Square is literally a place for weekly public decapitations. In Dubai, the working class are literal slaves. In China, disappearances are normal and Muslims are being tracked and put into camps. In Turkey, journalists and activists are imprisoned and killed. In Iran, LGBTQ+ people are executed. In Syria, the government uses chemical weapons against its own people. In Russia, there is arbitrary detention, and worse. In Myanmar, the army is massacring the Rohingya Muslim population. In Brunei, Sharia law was just enacted. In North Korea—no description needed.

All over the world, millions of people are dying because of tyrannical leaders, civil wars, and unimaginable atrocities. But you don't see passionate picket lines against Dubai or Turkey or even Russia. The one country that's consistently singled out is . . . Israel.

The UN has stated values of human dignity, equal rights, and economic and social advancement that are indeed fantastic, and they are the values upon which Israel was established and is operating. The sting is that countries that certainly do not adhere to some or any of these values are often the ones who criticize Israel while keeping a straight face. "Look over there!" those leaders say, so the world will not look at their backyards and see their own gross human rights violations. All this led to a disproportionate number of UN resolutions against the only Jewish state and the only democracy in the Middle East. Israel is an easy punching bag, but this obsession over one country only is being used to deflect time and energy away from any real discussion of human rights in the world's *actual* murderous regimes.

And Israelis aren't the only ones who have noticed this disproportionate censorship. The United States uses its veto power to shut down almost every Security Council resolution against Israel, and it does this not because of "powerful lobbies" (sorry to burst your bubble). The reason the US shuts down most of these resolutions is because the US gets it. In a closed-door meeting of the Security Council in 2002, former US ambassador to the UN John Negroponte is said to have stated that the US will oppose every UN resolution against Israel that does not also include: condemnation of terrorism and incitement to terrorism, condemnation of various terrorist groups such as Hamas and the Islamic Jihad, and a demand for improvement of security for Israel as a condition for Israeli withdrawal from territories. If a resolution doesn't include this basic and rational language, the US will veto it. And it did and it does, thank the good Lord, in what we know today as the Negroponte Doctrine.

The UN's hypocrisy has also been noted by many others, including Ban Ki-moon, the long-running eighth UN secretary-general. As he acknowledged on the eve of his departure, December 16, 2016: "Decades of political maneuvering have created a disproportionate volume of resolutions, reports and conferences criticizing Israel."[13]

In the words of this highly respected and decorated South Korean diplomat, the unequal treatment of Israel is the result of "decades of political maneuvering." This constant international "outrage" is not a legitimate criticism of a country's policies; it is political puppetry of the first degree. But it has widespread repercussions. This constant Israel bashing by a respectable international body gives the anti-Israel movements, whether on the left or the right, a false sense of legitimacy, reaching all the way to your college dorm.

In a heated Israeli cabinet meeting in 1955, David Ben-Gurion was quoted as angrily dismissing the UN: "*Um-Shmum!*" he yelled, mixing the Hebrew name for the UN and a clever touch of Yiddish condescension. Kofi Annan, another former UN secretary-general, made a joke about this phrase when he visited Israel. This saying caught on, and it is still used to describe the overwhelming attitude of Israelis: "Whatever we do, they'll always come out against us, so the hell with them anyway."

This is, of course, not true. It's kinda like the nation-state version of a self-protection mechanism: if the boy in school doesn't like me, well, *who needs him, anyway?* But we do. It is extremely important for Israelis to be understood and accepted, and the United Nations is ground zero.

My grandfather Hanan understood that, and he dedicated himself to international diplomacy and service in, among other places, the United Nations. He gave his life to trying to make the world a better place, only to see Israel get dissed by that same institution that was supposed to bring the world together in peace.

THE DIPLOMAT

My grandfather was born as Hans Berkowitz in Cologne, Germany, in 1911. A Zionist, he migrated to the British Mandate for Palestine in 1936, moved to the newly formed kibbutz Kfar Maccabi, and as he had studied economics in Germany, he became the kibbutz's treasurer. On his many travels to the big city of Tel Aviv he met my stunning albeit justifiably broken grandma, Hilda Schorr, and the two got married, had my mother Yael, and a few years later her brother Noam. My grandfather became active in the Labor Party and, per Ben-Gurion's request, changed his name to the Hebrew name Hanan Yavor. (Remember the melting pot? Everyone was expected to change their names back then.)

My grandfather was able to give back, not just to his new tiny country, but to another huge awakening continent. In my research for this book, I found many articles about my grandfather's life and his work, but one moved me the most. It's a story by journalist Nahum (Herbert) Pundik from the *Davar* newspaper, dated September 23, 1960.[14] The article, sub-headed "Israel's One-Man Team," includes an interview with the then minister of foreign affairs, Mrs. Golda Meir, about Israel's extraordinary relationships in Africa and the cross-pollination of knowledge traveling back and forth from the new state in the Middle East to the new states forming in Africa. Golda discusses the importance of the relationship, explaining that, like Israel, African nations were gaining their independence from Great Britain and racing toward state-building.

"The key to understanding these new countries," Golda writes, "is the fact that they are impatient. They do not want to be told by the Europeans that things need to go slowly. . . . They do not think in terms of hundreds or dozens of years, they want to develop quickly. What we tell the African nations is that we did and still do make mistakes and should they choose to learn from us, both our knowledge and our mistakes, they can and will save precious time."

The new countries in Africa (Ghana, Liberia, Nigeria, Ivory Coast, Kenya, Cameroon, and more) were getting their independence one after the other. They needed help, and Israel was there for them. Or, more specifically, my grandfather was there for them. Golda talks about my grandfather extensively, crediting him with this flourishing relationship. My grandfather was the first person to represent Israel on the entire African continent. He showed up in Accra in March 1956, a year before Ghana's independence, and started working, as he told Mr. Pundik: "In my first year . . . I was on my own in Accra. I ran my office on my own out of my hotel room, working all day and typing at night. A few months later my family joined me and my wife started helping me."[15]

It seems that my grandfather was like a little superstar, as the magazine *West Africa* wrote in December of 1957:

> His hard work and the authentic interest he takes in the development of Ghana are clear to all. There aren't many ministers of Ghana who will not mention, sooner rather than later, a meeting or a conversation they had with Hanan Yavor. Here was the man who was willing to seriously work towards an economic development.

An earlier article, from the November 29, 1957, *Haboker* newspaper by Colin Legum, acknowledges my grandfather's success in real time:

> Ghana chose international relations with Israel despite an Arab boycott and severe warnings from Arab countries. Ghana decided to collaborate with Israel on a variety of industries such as communal agriculture, water, roads and electricity, infrastructure, and the navy. It is hard to understand why this affinity to Israel other than the Ghanaian people . . . being surprised and curious by Israel's achievements. This success should be attributed to the young and enthusiastic Hanan Yavor.[16]

In March 1957 Ghana received its independence, and my mother, who was already living there, remembers the day clearly. She was a sixteen-year-old, short-haired kibbutz girl, dancing in the streets of

Accra with the liberated Ghanaian people. Not long after, my grandfather handed the formal ambassadorship to Ehud Avriel and started traveling to Liberia and then Nigeria, initiating a relationship there as he became the representative of one the first five countries to submit a letter of credence to the new Nigerian government, alongside the US, France, Lebanon, and West Germany. He became Israel's official ambassador to Liberia and then Nigeria, and continued to impress his colleagues and the international press.

In a December 2, 1960, article, journalist Abiodun Aloba writes:

> Ambassador Hanan Yavor, a specialist in communal agriculture, stated yet again his country's willingness to assist the new state of Nigeria in agriculture knowledge with the intention of improving Nigerian agriculture efficiency and improving its economy in a similar climate. . . . Up until a few years ago you couldn't have imagined that Israel would have such a stellar reputation in Nigeria especially with the hostile Arab propaganda, and in Nigeria who has a Muslim majority. However the past few years' experience, have proven to the Nigerian people that not only does Israel have the knowledge to offer, but she offers it excitedly and dedicatedly.[17]

Okay, you get it—my grandfather kicked ass. But he kicked that ass on behalf of the State of Israel, on the basis of sharing in the future. The level of cooperation and collaboration between Israel and emerging African nations at the time was unheard-of. Thousands of experts from various fields went back and forth assisting in everything from agriculture, shipping, medicine, military, architecture, education, economics, and more. Liberia didn't have any eye doctors until Hadassah and the Hebrew University established a clinic in Monrovia. The Israeli shipping company Zim was building or advising several African countries on how to establish their fleets. The Africans and Israelis also collaborated on bringing the concept of the kibbutz to Africa, helping to build small communal agriculture youth groups around the continent.

The years 1957 to 1973 were considered the golden age of the relationship between Israel and Africa, and my grandfather spearheaded the effort in the times when the world was willing to receive what Israel had to offer. But he was still alive to see his life's work crumble as Israel's standing in the world—with African nations and others—slowly started taking a turn for the worse.

It breaks my heart to think that my grandfather's work was in vain. We have now come to a point in which Israel-hating is not just a hidden agenda or a secret handshake by high-up diplomats in dark back rooms around the world. It is now a legitimate, popular social and political stance to take. The numerical advantage and years of "political maneuverings" of some of these highly undemocratic countries who also do not want Israel around, combined with the false sense of legitimacy from a manipulated UN, have legitimized an anti-Israel sentiment around the world.

This has created a brand-new political "activism," one that prides itself on being oh-so-righteous, and would have shocked my grandfather.

It's called: *anti-Zionism*.

A NEW, HIP SOCIAL JUSTICE CAUSE

If Zionism is about the Jewish people having the right to a state of their own, how did it become a slur? How did being an *anti-Zionist* become a thing to be proud of, something that even some of my friends carry as a badge of honor? The concept of being an anti-Zionist is bandied about as if it's a legitimate criticism of governmental actions. "I'm not an antisemite! I am not anti-Israel! I'm just an *anti-Zionist*!" Sounds good, but what does this *mean*?

In 1975 the United Nations General Assembly passed resolution number 3379, which declared "Zionism to be a form of racial discrimination."[18] That UN resolution was horribly wrong, and it was rightfully revoked in 1991,[19] but the misconception that Zionism is racism has only strengthened. (Remember, Zionism is about having a Jewish state, not an *exclusively Jewish* state!) Some people claim that being an anti-Zionist has nothing to do with Israelis and has everything to do with the Palestinian people. It's become a popular way for some people to describe how they identify with the underdog while claiming to facilitate change. But being an anti-Zionist has *nothing* to do with a particular Israeli government's policies. Rather, it's a repudiation of Israel's right to exist as a state, period.

The Grand Ayatollah of Iran, Ali Khamenei, is a passionate anti-Zionist, and like many other anti-Zionists he does not believe in Israel's right to exist. In fact, he won't even refer to Israel by its name but calls it "the Zionist Entity." In doing so, he rejects the reality that Jews are a *nation* and the reality that Israel *is* a country in which nine million people are currently living. By insisting on this alternate reality, what is he suggesting? Is it, as journalist Bari Weiss puts so well, a calling for "a country which *exists*, to *not* exist?" This can surely not end well. I would like to think that my self-described anti-Zionist friends are unclear about the term rather than advocating for a massacre.

Anti-Zionism, as benign as some activists would like it to sound, is targeting only one nation on earth. Negating that one nation's right to have a state, and doing so with vigor, flare, and self-righteousness that should probably be saved for North Korea. So why, for the love of the good Lord, do these social justice keyboard warriors target the one and only Jewish state? And the question that naturally follows is: Can anti-Zionism be consciously uncoupled from antisemitism? Can the promotion of the destruction of a country be separated from the promotion of the destruction of the people that live in that country?

LET'S TALK ABOUT ANTISEMITISM

I made a bunch of calls to friends and colleagues for this chapter, asking people to give me the first thing that came to mind when I asked: "Why do you think people hate Israel?" This is clearly not an academic research, but I thought these anecdotal chats might be revealing. One of the people I spoke with was a man named Maajid Nawaz.

Maajid Nawaz was a radical Islamist. Born in England to Pakistani parents, he was arrested in Egypt 2001 and imprisoned for being a member of the fundamentalist Islamist group Hizb-ut-Tahrir, which aims to reestablish the Caliphate and enact Sharia law. While in prison, Maajid was exposed to reading materials about human rights and was helped by Amnesty International, which made him do a one-eighty on his Islamist dogma. When Maajid got released, he committed his life to transforming Islam from within. He wrote a bestselling book about his experience, *Radical*, and coauthored another, *Islam and the Future of Tolerance*, with Sam Harris. He is a lion of human transformation, and I am proud to call him a friend.

After I asked him this question, Maajid didn't skip a beat, and sighed. "Oh, Noa, this is so simple," he said. "People hate Israel because of antisemitism."

I went quiet.

"Hello?" he checked in. "Why did you go quiet?"

I told him this was a bit shocking.

"You will hear other answers, but if you keep asking, 'but why,' you'll end up at the bottom of the pit that is antisemitism."

I was floored by his answer. Every other person I posed this question to elegantly danced around antisemitism. They would at some point say something like: "and maybe some people don't like Jews." No one said it with such clarity or conviction. I was also floored because I really did not want to go there in this book. I grew up in a world that seemed *post*-antisemitism. Remember the conversation I had on that boat in Greece with that hot German dude in chapter four? Until I heard him negate the Holocaust and accuse Israel of systematic hate crimes, I didn't know people were that ill-informed. After moving to America, I met many ignorant or naïve people, but even the most ardent anti-Zionists claimed to support *Jews*; in fact, some *were* Jews. But this of course is just a part of the picture. Antisemitism is old, and old habits die hard.

The sport of Jew hating goes back as far as the Jews themselves. My buddy Josephus from chapter eleven wrote a twenty-volume book called *The Antiquity of the Jews* in order to fight pagan antisemitism and misconceptions about the Jews—and that was in AD 93–94! So, yeah, antisemitism has been around for a while. Sadly, recent years have shown us that antisemitism is not only still around but it also seems to have become acceptable again. In 2019, the Anti-Defamation League found that antisemitic incidents reached an all-time high since it began tracking them in 1979, with a 56 percent increase in assaults.[20] In Charlottesville, white supremacists chanted, "Jews will not replace us," proudly and without even covering their faces, and in the Tree of Life Synagogue in Pittsburgh, eleven people were shot dead. There's been an uptick in killings, harassment, vandalism, assault, and fatalities of Jews in the *US*. In the incredible social justice demonstrations that followed the murder of George Floyd, people spray painted "Jews we're coming for you" at a park by my apartment. And, of course, there are the millions of posts and tweets about how the Jews are the ones who actually created COVID-19. Jews are only 2 percent of the United States population, but they are the target of 50 percent of national religion-based hate crimes.

So, okay, antisemitism is still a thing, but it still seemed too simplistic to connect it to Israel hatred.

Maajid continued: "Why do people judge Jews by one standard and the rest of the world by another? People say Israel is a colonialist country; why not cancel America or Australia as well? People are up in arms about Israel being a Jewish state; why not boycott Pakistan?"

His parents are both from Pakistan, so he knows.

"There is almost no difference between the establishment of Israel and Pakistan. They were both created as a safe haven for persecuted groups: Jews and Muslims. They are both engaged in land disputes. They both control religious sites of other religions. And they were even established only a few months apart."

Maajid proceeded to send me to a piece he wrote that echoed the same sentiment:

> And yet, there are no calls to boycott Pakistan by the far-left and their Islamist fellow-travelers. No fashionable movement exists to shame musicians who choose to perform there, no blockade of speakers at universities and no protests decrying the "historic injustices" of the Punjabis. The truth is, there is absolutely nothing that can be said of Israel, that cannot be said of Pakistan.[21]

"People simply do not feel comfortable with Jewish self-determination," Maajid continued over the phone. "It cost me greatly to come to this conclusion [his family disavowed him], but considering everything else that is going on in the world and if you only use logic, I can't see another explanation to this vicious Israel hating."

Oy.

It killed me to hear this, but I had to admit, he may be onto something. We all carry subconscious biases about various races, nationalities, sexual identities, etc. Usually when confronted with such accusations, we immediately jump to self-defense, lobbying on behalf of the virtues of our character. "*I am not that person!*" I do this as well, but I also recently learned that it is probably best to shut up and listen.

I do think there is an unconscious bias when it comes to Israel, and I'm going to go out on a limb here and suggest that it may have something to do with a hidden conversation people have in their heads about . . . them Jews. Being an overt antisemite is totally out, so few people will walk around owning it. But as Bari Weiss so perfectly described it: "Antisemitism is not just a prejudice, it is a conspiracy theory. . . . It says that there is a secret hand controlling the world, and that secret hand is called the Jew."[22] In other words, it's a subconscious bias. So if you have a conversation in your head about Jews "controlling the world," "the media," "the money," "Benjamins," or even just a loose association of Jews with the word "cabal," I'm *not* saying you are an antisemite, but you might want to check in with your subconscious biases and then reevaluate your positions on Israel based on facts, not feelings.

Anti-Zionism is the politically correct version of antisemitism. It's this new and improved concept—anti-Israelism. That said, some of the most powerful voices speaking against Israel are indeed from within the Jewish community, something anti-Israel groups take pride in. And they should! As Judaism always sides with human rights and encourages dissent, I am all for speaking against the Israeli government's policies when you don't like them. But when students at Brandeis University, a university created for Jews when they weren't accepted into Ivy League colleges, cry in support of BDS, I'm not sure what the goal really is, and I am pretty sure they don't know either. If you vehemently oppose certain actions taken by the Israeli government, make sure you judge other countries by the same parameters. If you support boycott movements, check who's paying for your activities, and what it is that they are after.

And when it comes to the black community and the Jewish community, let's remember Herzl's words. Let's remember Rabbi Abraham Joshua Heschel (google that picture from the Selma march), Michael Schwerner and Andrew Goodman (Mississippi civil rights workers who, along with James Chaney, were murdered in the "Freedom Summer Murders"), and many, many more.

Let's not let the BDS movement and others taint the deep bond between these two communities, and let's remind the world, over and over again, that *no discrimination will ever be okay*. In order to weed this evil out we need to look it straight in the eye—even when it's uncomfortable—and admit that antisemitism does have something to do with the anti-Zionist party after all.

I hate the victim card. And as many detractors point out: Israel is strong. They argue that the Jews are strong (or, as Gidi said: resilient). The Jewish lobbies are strong (which is true, in some ways, and antisemitic in others). However, the powers acting to undermine and delegitimize Israel are also strong, and rooted in deep biases. Succumbing to these powers would be detrimental for the world at large, not to mention for the only democracy in a tumultuous region, a democracy doing the best it can in the most volatile of environments.

A COUNTRY WITHOUT SIN, CAST THE FIRST STONE

Each and every country around the world deals with a constant push and pull between idealism and pragmatism, between the vision for the country and the reality on the ground—especially democracies. This is the reason the Founding Fathers resolved in the US Constitution "to form a *more perfect* Union," indicating that this work will never be done. But the tension between political theory and practice is nowhere more evident than in Israel. It is very easy to be idealistic when you live in San Francisco, London, Paris, Seattle, New York, Sydney, or Los Angeles. Try being as idealistic when a terrorist group is trying to create a Sharia state thirty miles from your doorstep, and twenty-one countries around you (give or take, depending on the year) are conspiring to decimate you. The fact of Israel's existential vulnerability shapes many of its policies and actions, and unfortunately they are all woefully disregarded by social justice warriors spewing anger from their couches.

With that in mind, here are some of their favorite arguments against Israel:

- **Colonialism.** The most popular anti-Israel argument is that it is a colonialist state. It is not. Israel is a *refugee state*, reestablished after the British *left*, as the Jewish homeland following thousands of years of exile and persecution. The Jews did not go back to Israel to "colonize" or to operate on behalf of any European power, but to literally save themselves. The argument of Israel being a European colony is also a dud since only 31 percent of its citizens are European Jews; the rest are of Middle Eastern descent, Arabs and Jews, which makes them locals to the region. (Sorry, I know how this sounds. But I do get this argument a lot, put to me in this exact racist terminology.)

- **Apartheid.** There has been an attempt to brand Israel an apartheid state, similar to South Africa. This is infuriating. South Africa was a horrific regime with fierce segregation and discriminatory laws and no rights for its majority black population. Israel grants equal rights to all its citizens, including, of course, the 21 percent of citizens who are Arab. The third largest political party in the Israeli parliament is an Arab party, Arabs serve in the IDF, and they are a part of the judiciary system, academia, entertainment, and medical fields—all of it. It is not perfect, but it is a powerful democracy. We can and should have a separate discussion about the situation in the West Bank, but when we do, let's also try and be clear about why there isn't a Palestine on these lands yet. To paint the entire state of Israel as an apartheid state is a lazy argument with possible grave consequences for the only consistent democracy in the region. It is also, simply, false.

- **Ethnic Cleansing.** Some people try to allege that the Jews in Israel engaged in systematic and preplanned ethnic cleansing of the Arab population. This is preposterous. In 1948, the UN gave both Jews and Arabs a land. The Jews accepted and the Arabs declined. The Arabs' first act was to declare war. They did, they fought, and they lost. Many Arabs suffered and still suffer greatly, but there was no Israeli desire, systematic or otherwise, to eliminate the Arab people. The ones who stayed are now full citizens in an imperfect yet flourishing democracy. There is certainly racism in Israel, and infringements on human rights of its Arabs citizens occur, should not be tolerated, and should be fought against constantly, but to describe these acts as ethnic cleansing is an intentional slander with an alternate agenda.

- **Unequal Warfare.** There is an argument that Israel has an aggressive and oppressive military, far more advanced than Palestine's, and it has wielded unnecessary force in response to minor attacks. And, yes, it sometimes does. But think about what would happen if Canada launched missiles into Seattle or Mexico threw rockets into El Paso. What is a "proportionate response" to a thousand missiles and a hundred terrorist attacks on *your* hometown?

- **Occupation.** Yes, Israel did take over territories in a defensive war, and then returned them in exchange for peace when that option was available. Israel gave up the entire oil-rich (and stunning) Sinai Peninsula, which is bigger than the State of Israel itself, in exchange for peace with Egypt. The Gaza Strip was handed back to the Palestinians, only for Israel to watch Hamas brutally take it over, killing both Palestinians and Israeli civilians. The West Bank is in limbo, and the living conditions for many Palestinians there are harsh and oppressive. There is enough blame to go around, but people cannot expect Israel to solve the problem without Palestinian leadership.

Israel hasn't been particularly good at addressing these arguments for a few reasons, but I think this may encapsulate them:

- **Forward-Facing Blunt Force.** When Israelis *do* try to explain themselves, their straight-up, in-your-face attitude doesn't always land well. There is an urban legend I like that I was unable to corroborate, but it illustrates my point regardless. The legend goes that when US secretary of state Cyrus Vance visited Israel in 1978, Prime Minister Menachem Begin asked then chief of the military Rafael Eitan (who, BTW, also went by a nickname: Raful) to explain to Vance the challenges Israel was dealing with. Raful wasn't into giving the full rundown, but after a push from Begin, he relented and begrudgingly said: "We go in. We kill. We go out." This encapsulates the Israeli attitude when explaining the complexities of the region: you don't talk, you just do what you gotta do to survive. As a result of this attitude, up until a few years ago Israel didn't invest too much thought or too many resources in good old PR. This left Israel with incredibly strong brand recognition and incredibly bad brand association. After all, how can nine million Israelis compete with billions of anti-Israel trolls? Historically, most Israeli international diplomacy has come from someone who will declare in a rough accent, "Izrael haz ze right to difend itself!" Totally true, but not necessarily convincing when you don't have all the facts.

As I am bringing this book to a close, I'd like to leave you with the following questions:

How would *you* handle a wannabe Sharia state thirty miles from your house? How should Israel retaliate when Hamas fires thousands of rockets into southern Israeli towns? Why haven't the Palestinians agreed to make a final peace deal? Will the PA unite with Hamas, and if so, will Hamas denounce violence, like, ever? Why is Israel singled out? What about other countries that actually do systematically abuse human rights? Why aren't activists focused on their freedoms of religion, speech, and assembly, which Israel grants all her citizens? Where are the boycott movements of neighboring countries that literally kill people for their beliefs, desire for freedoms and democracy, or sexual orientation?

There are so many whataboutisms that deserve serious thought and debate. None of what I'm saying is to excuse human rights abuses, bad policies, or the use of overwhelming force. But the fact is that Israel is not dealing with the same realities the rest of Western society is dealing with—not by a long shot. Judging it by the same criteria, when you don't understand the life-or-death nature of being Israeli, is an intellectual half measure at best.

This is what Israel deals with, and this is what we get in return: crap-talking, shade-throwing, anti-Zionist activists, and boycott movements enjoying a tailwind from respected international bodies. And it doesn't need to be this way! Why, for the love of our mutual God, can't this be a win-win for everyone? The region can flourish, borders can be erased, people can actually get to know each other, connect, grow! But instead a young Syrian man is being fed anti-Israeli propaganda his entire life, is shocked to find a group of kids wearing a Star of David pulling him out of the Mediterranean Sea, and he *still* can't give an interview using his full name, fearing death, for crying out loud!

I don't know where the region will go. My grandfather gave his entire life, both in Africa and at the United Nations, to promote world peace and collaboration and share his and Israel's knowledge with the world. But in recent decades powerful forces are working to undo it all. I don't know what kind of Israel my son, Ari, will grow up knowing, but this current hypocritical dynamic of political maneuvering, biases, and nefarious hidden agendas needs to stop. Now.

The countries of the region have a choice. They can keep feeding their kids "Elders of Zion" bull propaganda, or maybe they can come to the table in peace. Recent events that started with the Abraham Accord are showing signs of a new possibility for the region. Arab nations are finally starting to accept Israel and commit to prosperity, collaboration, and peace. I hope the Palestinian people will not resist these changes (by cuddling up to *other* nations in the region, for example) and will join the moderate voices in the Arab world so we can finally create that "New Middle East" for the future and a new reality for our children.

I said this many times, but as this book is coming to an end I will say it again: Israel is not a perfect country. But if you know of a country that hasn't sinned, please let it cast the first stone.

I can bring a nice one from the shores of the Sea of Galilee.

AFTERWORD

THIS IS A PROMISE

I was probably around seven or eight years old when it dawned on me that my house didn't look like any of my friends' houses. I grew up in a four-bedroom apartment in a nice suburb of Tel Aviv. The apartment was middle-class, simple, and utilitarianly furnished, always clean and with a dog as a family member. All pretty sweet and normal. But our walls were covered, floor to ceiling, with huge, detailed, and stunning African artwork, masks, and ancient weaponry, which caused my friends to gasp when they would walk through the door. A mysterious round wooden *thing* was hanging smack in the middle of our living room, and it was the cause of real mystery. That artifact was an ancient tray used by tribal doctors to mix herbal remedies and poisons. It was given to my mom as a gift by its owner, Obanjo, a chief healer from the Ga-Dangme tribe when she was growing up in Ghana.

While researching this book, I got a call from Professor Lynn Schler from the Negev Department of Politics and Government at Ben-Gurion University. Professor Schler is an Africa specialist and has written many books about the continent. She is currently working on a book about Nigeria and has been, to quote her, "living with your grandfather for a whole year." Lynn was an incredible source of materials and information for this book, and her appreciation for my grandfather's work and personality was contagious. She may be his biggest fan, which makes me so proud and happy.

Professor Schler read through fifty thousand documents from the period that my grandfather was an ambassador in Nigeria and got to know him intimately. "The archive that your grandfather left behind on Nigerian history—it's unfathomable," she said to me.

From the documents you can find a man who was extremely hard-working, committed, and pedantic. He created close and personal relationships with the highest officials in the Nigerian government and would meet regularly with the major political leaders of the era. They all dined at my grandparents' table and would share with my grandfather not only their political insights but also personal stories and gossip, all of which he wrote down in detail.

My grandfather was also extremely sensitive to the language used by the foreign ministry and other Israeli representatives when working with the Nigerian people. In a telegram dated August 3, 1961, he says the following:

> I have an important request from you. Please remove from your lexicon the use of the word "Kushi." A man of Nigeria must be referred to as a Nigerian or an African. The name "Kushi" is long being used in a derogatory manner, as we also were deeply offended when we were called "Jews" in Europe as a derogatory term.

My grandfather sharply scolds his peers about being racially insensitive—in 1961! Professor Schler was in awe of my grandfather's passion and commitment and kept asking me, "Why was he *so* obsessed with helping Nigeria?" I didn't know, so I asked my mom, and she said the answer was very simple. "My father saw the Jews and the Africans as kindred spirits, kindred people, kindred countries," she told me. "He kept saying, 'We must help them, for they are going through what we went through. After years of discrimination, oppression, and persecutions, they are now becoming independent, and as such, we have a responsibility to help.'" And so he did. My grandfather was the embodiment of Jewish and Zionist values. The same values I found on my journey.

As the years have gone by, I've realized that forgetting all about Rosh Hashanah all those years ago was a gift. That dinner at Katsu-Ya led me on to this extraordinary journey, which I hope you found useful.

The legacy of my grandfather's time in Africa filled our walls and was the visual backdrop of my childhood, and that mysterious, ornate wooden tray was the focal point of our living room. Finally, my mom told me the story behind it. There was an art store near her house in Accra, and when she was a teenager in Ghana, she became friends with the local owner. One day, a man walked into the store wearing full traditional garb. He was introduced to my mom as the Ga-Dangme tribe juju-man, a healer and doctor by the name of Obanjo. He was wearing that tray on a chain around his neck, like a breastplate that a high priest might have worn in biblical times. When my mom asked about it, he told her it was highly poisonous from years of being used to mix various healing herbs. My mom and Obanjo became friends, and when her family was leaving Ghana for Nigeria, Obanjo gave my seventeen-year-old mom that breastplate under one condition: she was never allowed to part with it, and it was to be buried with her when she died. My mother took that tray with her from Ghana to Nigeria and then to Israel. She took it to her home with her first husband, Aki, on the air force base where he was killed. She then took it to Tel Aviv, where she married my dad and I was born. When I was growing up, we were forbidden from touching that tray; I never did, and I never will. But one day, the tray will be buried alongside my mom, just like she promised Obanjo.

This book is a fulfillment of my promise to my mom. My mom is a warrior, opinionated to a fault. You do not want to find yourself on her NinJew side when it is activated. My mom, the monstrous safta Yael, stands up, speaks out, and acts against anything that isn't in line with her values. She fought with the IDF when they stopped looking for Aki's sunken airplane in Egypt, and she fought the Israeli government when she thought an anti-missile laser-guided weapons system would be better than the Iron Dome against Hamas and Hezbollah. She crossed the border to Ramallah to shake hands with Yasser Arafat when she thought he was Israel and Palestine's greatest hope for peace, and was quick to condemn him when she found out, like the rest of the world, how vile he was. She is a true social justice warrior, not a keyboard one, an old-school one who doesn't just speak but *yells* truth to power. Her commitment to liberalism, to Israel's founding principles, and to making the world better is a force to be reckoned with. She continues fighting for these values, the values of the country she and her family helped build, despite paying the unimaginable price when she was widowed at twenty-six. My mom did not become jaded, discouraged, or resigned in the face of every obstacle imaginable. Her heart breaks into a million pieces every time Israel screws up, every time a leader doesn't adhere to the original values of Zionism, every time she uncovers corruption, lack of ethics, needless violence, racism, oppression. Just like her father before her, my mom paved a road for us on how to fight for what you think is right, even if you ruffle a million feathers: Arm yourself with facts and go get yourself in good trouble.

My mom never asked me to do anything to follow in her footsteps, but her actions spoke louder. My words are the fulfillment of that promise not asked.

THIS IS A LOVE SONG

Midway through writing this book, the world tipped into the year 2020. It was June, and Los Angeles was under lockdown orders as COVID-19 was making its way through the known universe. I was holed up in our bedroom, trying to make my deadline for this book in the sporadic moments I wasn't homeschooling our 4.5-year-old Ari, or cooking, cleaning, building Lego, cooking, cleaning, baking, cleaning, making art, or trying, like everyone else, to stay sane. Ari was loving COVID days. He had both his parents at home all day and he was super into "mom school," so the times I would hide in the bedroom to escape the dread of a pandemic into lighter topics such as research into Hamas did not go down easily. Ari kept coming in and out of the room, jumping on the bed, trying to play with the keyboard, asking to "write his name," which in our house is his keyword for "pretending to type really fast," like Jimbo does on *Super Wings*, his favorite show. He kept asking many questions, like if I knew what Dinotrux like to eat, and if we were all made of steel would we still feel hugs and kisses. At some point he hopped into bed and curled up next to me. He looked at the screen.

"What are you writing?" he asked.

"I'm writing a book," I said.

"What is it about?" he asked.

"It's a book about Israel," I said, still clicking away.

He gasped and his eyes lit up: "A book about Israel! I love it! *Is it for me???*"

I froze. My eyes welled up. I closed my computer, wiped my face, and turned to face him. "Yes, monkey," I said. "I'm writing a book for you. Now let's go take a bath."

APPENDIX

A MUCH QUICKER GUIDE

By now you've stumbled through a megillah of stories, facts, history, herstories, self-gazing, family drama, some Sharia, and a touch of irony—which may have constituted more than the "simple guide" you bargained for.

Well, surprise: Israel's a complicated place! Here's the real quick and dirty:

- The piece of land Israel is located on was a sovereign Jewish state over three thousand years ago. This can be cross-referenced in the Old Testament, the New Testament, and the Quran, and corroborated by many carbon-dated archaeological findings and other nonreligious writings of the era.
- This land was occupied by many empires throughout history, most recently by the Ottomans (or the Turks) and the Brits.
- None of these empires was ever home to a Palestinian state.
- Palestine was a geographic region, never a state. The name was applied to Judea by the Romans after they squashed a Jewish revolt in AD 135, and referred to the nonindigenous Philistines

in a cynical attempt to deliberately erase the Jews connection to their ancestral homeland.

- The Palestinians are not the biblical Philistines, nor are they the Canaanites.
- Even after the Romans exiled the Jews, there were still Jews living in the land of Israel, and Jewish people around the world maintained a strong cultural and practical connection to Jerusalem and to Israel, hoping to have self-determination again.
- The modern Zionist movement started developing in Europe in the late nineteenth century as a result of antisemitism, oppression, discrimination, and persecution of Jews. Zionism was a merger of cultural and national Jewishness and liberal values.
- Zionism was created as a movement for Jewish liberation, it is about the Jewish people having self-determination and self-governance in their ancestral land in a Jewish, *but not an exclusively* Jewish, state.
- Jewish pioneers came from all over the world, bought land legally from absent landowners, the Turks, the Christians, and the Arabs, and started developing it with agriculture, industry, and education systems—an infrastructure for a state.
- The UN granted the Jews the right to a state on November 29, 1947, after the Holocaust (Resolution 181).
- The UN also granted the local Arabs (who were not called Palestinians yet) an independent state as part of that same resolution.
- The Jews said yes; the Arabs said no.
- The day after the declaration of Israel's independence (May 14, 1948), Israel's Arab neighbors invaded and attacked it in order to destroy it.
- Israel won the war, and more land. The Arabs signed a truce (not a peace agreement) and the Green Line was created.
- Before and during the 1948 war, Arab leaders told the Arab res-

idents to leave. In the war some Arab residents got pushed out, some left, some stayed.

- There were 700,000 to 750,000 Arab refugees after 1948. Most Arab countries did not integrate these refugees or give them rights. Instead they put them into refugee camps.
- With the help of UNRWA, a UN organization devoted entirely to Palestinian displaced peoples, there are now 5.6 million registered Palestinian refugees. The refugee status is passed down through the generations.
- Meanwhile, Arab countries in the Middle East have expelled (or "encouraged to leave") approximately 856,000 Jews, many of whom have migrated to Israel.
- Around May 1967, Arab countries planned on destroying Israel yet again. This led to the Six Day War. While defending itself, Israel took the Golan Heights from Syria, the West Bank from Jordan, and the Sinai Peninsula and Gaza from Egypt.
- Five months after the Six Day War, Israel accepted UN Resolution 242, which established the doctrine of "land for peace," signaling it would give back land in exchange for recognition and a lasting peace (which Israel did in exchange for peace with Egypt).
- Israel was eight to eleven miles from side to side (or from the sea to an enemy state) at its narrowest, and so it started building settlements in the West Bank for security reasons at first. There were 900,000 Palestinian-Jordanians living in the West Bank, and they were rightfully not happy about the settlements. There are about 463,901 Jewish settlers and 2.9 milliion Palestinians living in the West Bank today.
- Israel kept the West Bank under military control, waiting to sign a peace agreement and hand them over to a new Palestine. This limbo creates an oppressive way of life for the Palestinians living in those areas.
- On October 6, 1973, Israel was attacked again. This attack was led

by Egypt and Syria with the help of many other Arab countries. The Yom Kippur War was a close call. Israel just barely won.

- On March 26, 1979, Israel and Egypt signed a peace agreement. Egypt acknowledged Israel; Israel dismantled its settlements and returned the Sinai Peninsula, and a cold yet strong peace agreement has held firm since.
- In 1993, peace talks started between the Israelis and the Palestinians, which led to the Oslo Accords signing ceremony on August 20 and the establishment of the Palestinian Authority (PA), which then started to get sovereignty over territories in the West Bank and Gaza for a future Palestinian state.
- The leader of the PA was Yasser Arafat. He refused to sign a final peace deal in the year 2000, and the peace talks fell apart, sending the region into a cycle of bloodshed.
- On October 26, 1994, Israel signed a peace agreement with Jordan, which did not ask for the West Bank back. Another cold yet solid peace continues.
- In September 2005, Israel finished pulling out of Gaza and dismantled all the settlements, intending to hand Gaza over to the PA for the Palestinian state-to-be.
- On the 25th of January 2006, Hamas (an offshoot of the Muslim Brotherhood) won the elections to the Palestinian parliament and a year later took over Gaza by force, murdering opposing members of the Palestinian Authority. Hamas is a terrorist organization that wants to enact Sharia law and wipe Israel off the map.
- Hamas has been controlling Gaza ever since, firing thousands of rockets and mortar shells into Israel. They have built a sophisticated and well-funded network of underground attack tunnels in order to execute terrorist attacks on civilians inside Israel's borders.
- Israel consistently retaliates against Hamas rockets and terror

attacks. The media often refers to these retaliations as "disproportionate responses," and sometimes they are.

- Hamas receives hundreds of millions of dollars mainly from Iran, yet living conditions for Palestinians in Gaza are abhorrent.
- To prevent ammunition from reaching Hamas, *both Israel and Egypt* enacted a blockade on Gaza to examine and control all goods going in.
- The decades-long conflict in the region is not an Israeli-Palestinian conflict; it is an Israeli–Arab world conflict, and it has been going on for almost a century, since long before the State of Israel was created. The race to exterminate Israel has been headed by different countries through the years and is now mainly executed by non-state actors such as Hamas in Gaza and Hezbollah in Lebanon, both sponsored and supported by Iran.
- Iran perceives Israel as Little Satan to the US's Great Satan and has been actively working to attain nuclear power and nuclear weapons. This conflict is not based on any territorial dispute; it is a clash of cultures and values.
- BDS is not a movement about peace or justice, nor is it about the West Bank settlements. The leaders of BDS do not want Israel to exist, and among the movement's financial sponsors are supporters of terrorism.
- Israel is a multicultural, noisy, and democratic melting pot. Racism and inequality exist, but all people have the same legal rights, whether Jews, Muslims, or Christians.
- Arabs living in Israel have more rights and freedoms than they have in almost all other Arab countries.
- Debating or critiquing Israel's government policies is healthy and good; debating or critiquing Israel's right to exist is anti-Zionist.
- Anti-Zionism may not be overtly antisemitic, but the two are in-

extricably linked. So if you are an anti-Zionist and only against one nation's state, you should get that checked.

- The Middle East is messy.
- Israel wants peace.
- Israel.
- Wants.
- PEACE.

GLOSSARY

Agal—A rope accessory worn usually by Arab men, to tie a scarf called a kafiya onto the head.

Aliyah—From the Hebrew word for "to go up," used to describe Jewish migration to Israel.

Annexation—International legal term used to describe when a state applies sovereignty to a territory outside its borders. Today it is often used in the Israeli context when discussing the West Bank.

Arab Spring—A series of anti-government protests, uprisings, and armed rebellions that spread across much of the Arab world in the early 2010s.

BDS—A movement which is promoting Boycott Divestment and Sanctions on Israel.

Benjamin Netanyahu—Israel's long-lasting prime minister from 1996 to 1999, and 2009–?.

Chachtzchhim—A derogatory slang word used to describe a person acting in a reckless and uneducated behavior.

Charedim—Jewish ultra-Orthodox group.

David Ben-Gurion—Israel's first prime minister and minister of defense.

Dawah—In Arabic means "issuing a summons" or "making an invitation," and is used to describe the charitable side of Islam.

Etzel—Also called "the Irgun," a hard-line paramilitary organization active in Palestine before the establishment of the State of Israel, it adhered to a doctrine of active Jewish retaliation against Arab and British targets.

Fatwa—A nonbinding ruling on a point of Islamic law given usually by a mufti, an Islamic juror, in response to a question posed by a private individual, judge, or government.

Golda Meir—Israel's fourth prime minister (1969–74).

Haganah—The main paramilitary organization of the Jewish Yishuv in Mandatory Palestine before the establishment of the State of Israel.

Haman—An evil dude, the main antagonist in the biblical book of Esther.

Hamula—A word to describe an extended family unit.

Hilltop Youth—A hard-line, extremist religious-nationalist group of mostly young men, which often sets up illegal outposts in the West Bank.

IDF—Israeli Defense Force, the Israeli military.

Jihad—An Arabic word meaning "struggling" or "striving," it can be interpreted as an inner struggle to become a better Muslim; however, it is usually meant to describe an Islamic Holy War.

Kibbutz—A Jewish collective community traditionally based on agriculture, originally created as a utopian way of living, combining elements from socialism and Zionist ideology.

Knesset—The legislative body (parliament) of the Israeli government. The Knesset passes laws, elects the prime minister and president, and supervises the work of the Israeli government.

Lehi—The paramilitary organization that sought to use force and violence to push the British out of Mandatory Palestine; also known as the "Stern Gang."

Likud—Also known by its full name, the National Liberal Party. The Likud is a center-right to right-leaning party founded in 1973. It won the election in 1977 and has been the dominant political party in Israel ever since.

Ma'abarot—Refugee absorption camps established to provide accommodation for the influx of refugees arriving in Israel at the early days of the state.

Mahmoud Abbas—Also known as Abu Mazen, the president of the State of Palestine and the Palestinian Authority since 2005.

Mapai—The Workers Party of Israel, a democratic socialist party that was essential in the establishment of the State of Israel from 1930 to 1968. Mapai and its successor parties led every Israeli government from 1948 until 1977.

Menachem Begin—Founder of the Likud Party, former leader of the Etzel, and Israel's prime minister from 1977 to 1983.

Moshava (plural: moshavot)—An agriculture community or a group of people living together on privately owned land, working the land, and adhering to a charter outlining communal principles.

Occupatio Bellica (Belligerent occupation)—A temporary occupation and administration of a land held under military law which is not annexed. Sadly, not so temporary in the West Bank anymore.

Safta—Hebrew for "grandmother."

Settlements—Used in reference to Jewish towns and villages in the West Bank.

Shaheed—An Islamic martyr who died on behalf of a cause, or a jihad.

Two-State Solution—The most commonly agreed-upon way to solve the Israeli-Palestinian conflict: two states for two nations.

West Bank—A 2,183-square-mile piece of land west of the Jordan River, located between Israel and Jordan.

Yishuv—A name given to the network of Jewish towns, villages, communal organizations, and kibbutzim in Mandatory Palestine before the establishment of the State of Israel.

Zionism—A movement to reestablish a Jewish state in Israel.

Zionist Revisionist movement—The ideology to "revise" the "practical Zionism" advocated by Israel's founders, such as David Ben-Gurion, who accepted the UN Partition Plan. By contrast, revisionists, such as Menachem Begin, pushed for the maximalist agenda of a Jewish state in all of the League of Nations lands, including Transjordan.

ACKNOWLEDGMENTS

This book is not just a labor of love, it is a full-on community project. I want to thank these human angels who helped me throughout the way.

First I want to thank all the people who made me look like I know what I'm talking about. I know it wasn't always easy. Dr. Rob Geist Pinfold for fact-checking every single word, and then doing it again, just in case. Einat Wilf and Adi Schwartz for all UNRWA knowledge, information, and cleanups. To Dr. Leah Kinberg for making sure I quote the Quran properly and don't get a Fatwa in the process. To Yael Abadi Nofar from the Degania Alef archives, for providing me with the priceless diaries and writings of my beloved grandmother safta Fania, and to Professor Lynn Schler for the priceless materials from my grandfather Hanan. To Lior Khayat for research assistance in all hours of the night. To ambassador Gilad Erdan, Sarah Weiss Ma'udi, Dina Rovner, and Hillel Neuer for making sure I got every single United Nations fact right. David Sable for his "brand of Israel" information, Ido Daniel and Tzahi Gabrieli for BDS information, and Naomi Firestone Teeter for supporting me and this book from day one. To Dr. Jonathan Schanzer and Julia Schulman for all the hardcore details about BDS; Julia, our nightly chats became such a source of joy. To

David May for yet another, last-minute final round of fact-checking. And last but certainly not least, to my angel, Dr. Ehud Eiran, for hours upon hours of conversations about history, philosophy, and the meaning of life. I would not have been able to do any of this without you. Thank you for your time and for literally *always* being available for me to chew your ears off. You are the definition of a mensch.

To my second readers, who also happen to be some of the best artists in the world, I am so grateful for your time and care. I was terrified for you to read this, relieved when you didn't shred it to pieces, and honored by your generous feedback. Rodrigo Garcia, you were my first test-subject, and your comments gave me the tailwind I needed. Gideon Raff, you and Udi Peleg are my family, and, as always, you provided the soundest creative and all-around life advice. Gahl Sasson for great notes and years of deep friendship and advice on anything and everything in this world and beyond. Sarah Treem, you are my inspiration on every level, and I thank you for your sisterly support throughout the years. Emmanuelle Chriqui, you are my family for life, and I would be lost without your inspiring and loving insights. And Cal Fussman, you gave me the greatest of notes, which took this book to a whole other level.

To my spirit animal, Becky Sweren, the most passionate, focused, smart, and sassy agent a human can have. Becky, your speed in turning around notes on any written material puts the entire entertainment industry to shame. You got me and you got my voice quicker and better than I did, and you did so with such fun, grace, and ease. I am so lucky to have you in my corner.

To my sister in esoteric fascination—a match made in heaven—my Basheret editor Natasha Simons. We didn't even realize just how much we have in common until the deal was signed, but it's clear now that this was beyond meant to be. It was such a delight to talk both work and life with you. You are both powerhouse women. I love you and appreciate you so much.

Thank you to the entire Simon & Schuster team: assistant editor Maggie Loughran for your awesome second-read notes and for being my personal IT gal, PR wiz Kirstin Berndt, Jackie Seow, Kimberly Goldstein, Beth Maglione, Stephen Bedford, and Richard Rhorer. To director of publicity Julia Prosser for our cheeky and awesome first meeting; I hope I delivered on what you said you were looking for. A special thanks to Jonathan Karp for having the vision to acquire this book, and to Dana Canedy for having the guts to publish it.

To my book PR team at Javelin—Keith Urbahn, Frank Schembari, and Megan Stencel—thank you for great work at our launch. To Melissa Blum and Emma Marshall from MT Deco for social media wrangling. To my new team at UTA—Jacob Fenton, Geoff Suddleson, Nancy Gates, Marc Paskin, Ryan Hayden, Stephanie Smith, and everyone else—you swept me off my feet just at the right time, and I am excited about our future together. To my amazing assistant, Jordan Strom, thank you for being there for me with literally everything. You have been my life savior many times over.

And to my public speaking super agent, Jamie Black, you are a unicorn and whoever is lucky enough to work with you knows exactly why.

To Jeff and Lesley Wolman—I would need to write another book just to begin expressing how much you've done for me throughout the years. You are my adopted family in the US, and there is no chance I would have survived here without your continued support. I love you. A huge thank you to my lawyer for this book, Jeremy Weitz; to my lawyer of many years, who has helped me survive any number of trials and tribulations, Douglas Stone; and to my new legal team member, Jonathan Missner, for endless hours of delicate advice.

To Max Neuberger, who accidentally lit a fire underneath me and caused me to write this book at warp speed. To Sara Hurwitz, for being my first proposal reader and my first cheerleader and for your continued love and support. To Mosab Hassan Yousef, who endlessly inspires and teaches me; the world is a better place because of you. To Zohar Yakobson, my manager, sister, sounding board, and life support, for everything, always. To Michael Kives; being your friend has so many perks, my lord. You are one of a kind, and I am forever grateful. To Galit Wertheim, Or Ohana, Reuven Cohen, and Alon Shafransky for years of creativity and a great author photo. To Yoav Gati for the perfect cover design after hours of conversations and a million drafts, all while you were having a second baby. Thank you, Lior, for being patient with him.

To my friends throughout the years, you each have a part in who I am and in this book. To Yaeli Avnery; Keren Amishay (for friendships *and* maps!); Nurit Rimon; Yaron Kafkafi and Ofer Shovavi Regirer; Moti Vavi Reif and Simor Baa'looli Louzon; Sharon Rechter; Guy Oranim; Noa, Netta Dan, and Ron Oranim; Chani Shvimmer; Alona Tal; Marcus Ferez; Elliott Bisnow; Nicole Davis; Ofer Hava; Freddy Wexler; Olivia Wexler; Jonathan Bronitsky; Gala Asher; Ron Prosor; Ram Bergman; Yuli Tamir; Andi Cohen; Alon Shalom; Guy Sagy, Ivana Milicevic; Esther Perel; Benny Radom; Eric and Pia Weinstein; David Wolpe; Adam IN-Q Schmalholz; Alex Banayan; Stephanie Jordan; Mali Damari; Ronen Bergman; Maajid Nawaz; Lynn Schusterman; and Gidi and Betty Grinstein. Each one of you knows exactly what you've done for me, and if you don't—I'll let you know!

Thank you to all the people who helped me after the book came out: Kfir Gavrieli, Joe Sanberg, Nathan Miller, Mark Friedman, Maryam Lieberman, Laura Stein, Shirin Yadager, Adeena Fitterman, Meghan McCain, Eve Barlow, Daniella Greenbaum, Alan Meltzer, Alan Franco, David Victor, Gary Gilbert, Adam and Gila Milstein, Seth Oster, Eden Cohen, and Lorraine Schwartz. To Gidi Cohen for enlightening me in so many ways. To Naty and Debbie Saidoff for your continued love and support both professionally and personally.

To my angel, Danielle Ames Spivak, I am forever grateful for how you showed up for me, and I'm excited about our and our kids' friendship.

Thank you to my seventh- through ninth-grade literature teacher,

Tova Eisenthal, who would always let me write about whatever I want. And to Yair Lapid, who told me twenty-three years ago that I am, in fact, an author. It took me this long, but you were right.

To my family: Nir, Guy, Omer, and Maayan Padan; Eran, Maya, Ella and Adam Krystal; Jonathan and Lanuel Tishby-Tiran; Sean Mautner; Anna and Olie Tishby-Mautner; Daniella Or-El; Margalit Tishby; Guy Harlap; Roni, Rakefet, Yonat, and Shira Efrat and their families; Oded, Hani, Riki Schorr and their families; Noam, Emilia, and Hilli Yavor; and Rafi, Yaron, and Galia Tishby, and to the Hinkle family. To Ross Hinkle for your much-needed pedantic notes and for providing me with the foundation to write this book.

And mostly to my sisters: Mira Artzi-Padan, Iris Tishby, Michal Artzi-Krystal, and Tomoosh Tishby: I am not me without you; you guys are my lifeline and my sanity. I love you more than I can express. To my dad, Daniel, who did not get to see this book in his lifetime. I feel you; I know you're helping us, and I know you would have loved this book. And to my mom, the once in a lifetime safta Yael, for showing us all what it's like to live a passionate, unwavering, and unapologetic life. Your love of knowledge and fights for justice have paved the way for us all. You taught us so much, and we love you for it.

And lastly, to Ari. I told you I'm writing you a book, and here it is. You are the most important thing that ever happened to me, and I'm eternally grateful that you choose me to be your mom. Thank you for hours of Kirbooli, endless laughs, and deep and meaningful conversations. I'm sorry for spoon-feeding you, literally, not figuratively, until way too late, and I'm sorry for practicing the age-old Jewish mom custom: "I'm cold, you should wear a sweater." Oh, and thanks for turning me into a grandmother!

Too soon?*

I love you more than words can ever even begin to describe.

---

* When this book came out, Ari was five and a half. So yeah, probably too soon.

NOTES

Chapter One: A Brief History of Me

1 This is according to the United Nations Report of the Secretary-General's Panel of Inquiry on the 31 May 2010 Flotilla Incident, September 2011, https://www.un.org/unispal/document/auto-insert-205969/.

2 Nine men died on that day; another man passed a few years later.

Chapter Two: A Brief History of the Land of Israel

1 For the number of members in the Arab League, https://arab.org/directory/league-of-arab-states/.

2 https://quran.com/17.

3 https://quran.com/10/93.

4 https://quran.com/7/137.

5 Biblical Archaeology Society, "Does the Merneptah Stele Contain the First Mention of Israel?" January 17, 2012, https://www.biblicalarchaeology.org/daily/ancient-cultures/ancient-israel/does-the-merneptah-stele-contain-the-first-mention-of-israel/.

6 United Nations Resolution 181, https://unispal.un.org/unispal.nsf/0/7F0AF2BD897689B785256C330061D253.

Chapter Three: A Brief History of the Middle East in the Last Century

1 Just a side note to acknowledge that Burning Man started out as an authentic celebration of humanity's ingenuity, but sadly it kinda morphed into somewhat of a Libertarian mishmash of capitalism and self-indulgence . . . I really hope it goes back to its original essence.

2 These images later inspired the amazing Academy Award–winning movie *Lawrence of Arabia*, which I highly recommend, but for more on this great man's life you should really read Michael Korda's *Hero: The Life and Legend of Lawrence of Arabia* (New York: HarperCollins, 2010).

3 David Garnett, ed., *The Letters of T. E. Lawrence* (New York: Doubleday, Doran, 1938), p. 71.

4 Letter from Faisal to the U.S. Zionist Felix Frankfurter, March 1, 1919.

5 Yale Law School, The Avalon Project, The Palestine Mandate, The Council of the League of Nations, Article 2, https://avalon.law.yale.edu/20th_century/palmanda.asp.

6 Korda, *Hero*, p. 418.

7 Lowell Thomas, *With Lawrence in Arabia* (Charles River Editors, 2018), p. 15.

8 Ibid.

9 Joel Hodson, Lowell Thomas, "T. E. Lawrence and the Creation of a Legend," History Net, https://www.historynet.com/lowell-thomas-t-e-lawrence-and-the-creation-of-a-legend.htm.

10 Korda, *Hero*, p. 560.

11 T. E. Lawrence, "The Changing East," *Round Table*, September 1920, http://www.telstudies.org/writings/works/articles_essays/1920_changing_east.shtml.

Chapter Four: A Brief History of Zionism

1 My grandmother writes in her diaries that at the time she thought that they were the ones who came up with the "Young Pioneer" groups concept, but she later learned that similar groups had already existed in other places like Latvia and Poland.

2 Jonathan Freedland, "Antisemitism Matters: Jews Are the Canary in the Coalmine," *Guardian*, March 30, 2018, https://www.theguardian.com/commentisfree/2018/mar/30/antisemitism-jews-canary-coalmine-fake-news.

3 The "Department for Protecting the Public Security and Order"—the Okhrana, a gnarly group.

4 For Ford's antisemitism, see PBS, https://www.pbs.org/wgbh/americanexperience/features/henryford-antisemitism/.

5 Ruth Harris, *Dreyfus* (New York: Henry Holt and Co., 2010), p. 18.

6 Theodor Herzl, *The Jewish State* (New Orleans, LA: Quid Pro Books, 2014), pp. 36, 53, and 60.

7 *The Diaries of Theodor Herzl* by Theodor Herzl and Marvin Lowenthal reviewed by Franz Kobler, *Jewish Social Studies* 19, no. 3/4 (1957): 141–45, www.jstor.org/stable/4465553, accessed September 23, 2020.

8 Theodor Herzl, *Altneuland: The Old-New-Land* (Rockville, MD: Wild Side Press LLC., 2018), p. 261.

Chapter Five: Chasing That Dream

1 The law passed in 2011, but women got to actually vote for the first time in Saudi Arabia in 2015.

2 Full disclosure: Gal is a friend, and I am an uber-fan of hers. She got the role not *because* she's Israeli but because she's an incredible actress. Knowing how Israeli women are, who Wonder Woman is, and who Gal is, I just thought the correlation was interesting.

3 This unit was a part of Gdud Haavoda, the Workers Corps, a unionized labor entity that was traveling through the country and supplying workers in small "units" to build roads and infrastructure wherever they were needed.

4 A British census from October 23, 1922, registers 13,413 Arabs, 14,699 Christians, and 33,971 Jews living in Jerusalem, https://archive.org/details/PalestineCensus1922/page/n3/mode/2up.

5 Eyal Barouch, Ayelet Levi-Riper, Avraham Faust, "Advancement in the Research of Jerusalem," Bar Ilan University, Israel, studies faculty, Ramat Gan, 2010, https://www.ariel.ac.il/wp/oded-shay/wp-content/uploads/sites/194/2019/04/אבלס-חידושים-חקר-ירושלים.pdf.

6 Aqaba was held under the British mandate of Transjordan, populated by 322 Muslim and 8 Christian residents according to a 1922 British census, https://archive.org/details/PalestineCensus1922/page/n3/mode/2up.

7 Roberto Bachi, *The Population of Israel* (CICRED, 1974), http://www.cicred.org/Eng/Publications/pdf/c-c26.pdf; David Wollenberg, "The Myth of Jewish 'Colonialism': Demographics and Development in Palestine," *Harvard Israel Review*, http://www.hcs.harvard.edu/~hireview/content.php?type=article&issue=spring01/&name=myth.

8 US Census, https://openstax.org/books/us-history/pages/f-united-states-population-chart.

9 Countries such as the US, UK, etc., had huge population growth because of the Industrial Revolution, whereas in Palestine there was very little industrialization or growth at the time.

10 Mark Twain, *The Innocents Abroad, or The New Pilgrims' Progress* (New York: American Publishing Company, Harper and Brothers Publishers, 1869), p. 606.

11 Wollenberg, "The Myth of Jewish 'Colonialism.'"

13 Gershon Gera, ed., *Kineret Yard and Her People: The Story of the First National Farm, 1922–2002* (1996). חצר כנרת ואנשיה: סיפורה של החווה העברית הראשונה: דברים בשם אומרם ליקט וערך גרשון גרא 1922–2002.

13 *Establishment of a National Home in Palestine*, Hearings Before the Committee on Foreign Affairs, House of Representatives, Sixty-Seventh Congress, second session, Washington, DC, April 18–21, 1922, https://bit.ly/3jQxaj5.

Chapter Six: A State Is Born

1 According to Yad Vashem: The World Holocaust Remembrance Center, https://www.yadvashem.org/articles/general/displaced-persons-camps.html.

2 Elad Ben-Dror, *Ralph Bunche and the Arab-Israeli Conflict: Mediation and the UN, 1947–1949* (Abingdon-on-Thames, UK: Taylor & Francis Ltd., 2015), pp. 53–43.

3 Yoram Shahar, "The Early Drafts of the Declaration on Independence," *Aionei Mishpat*, November 2002, http://ihi.org.il/media/1168/http://ihi.org.il/media/1168/פרופ-יורם-שחר-מאמר-מגילה-הטיוטות-המוקדמות.pdf.

4 For the full declaration in Hebrew see: https://main.knesset.gov.il/About/Occasion/Pages/IndDeclaration.aspx.

5 Benny Morris, *The Birth of the Palestinian Refugee Problem Revisited* (Cambridge, UK: Cambridge University Press, 2012), p. 53.

6 David Ben-Gurion, *My Talks with Arab Leaders* (Jerusalem: Keter Books, 1972), Chapter 5.

7 Elad Ben-Dror, *Ralph Bunche and the Arab-Israeli Conflict: Mediation and the UN, 1947–1949* (Abingdon-on-Thames, UK: Taylor & Francis Ltd., 2015), pp. 43–53

8 Benny Morris, "Gideon Levy Is Wrong About the Past, the Present, and I Believe the Future as Well," *Haaretz*, January 21, 2019, https://www.haaretz.com/opinion/.premium-eventually-there-will-be-one-state-between-the-mediterranean-and-the-jordan-1.6856140.

9 Benny Morris, "For the Record," *Guardian*, January 13, 2004, https://www.theguardian.com/world/2004/jan/14/Israel.

10 Excluding Jordan, which did grant them citizenship while they are still holding refugee status with the UN.

11 "Jewish Refugees from Arab and Muslim Countries," Israel Ministry of Foreign Affairs, April 3, 2012, https://mfa.gov.il/mfa/foreignpolicy/peace/guide/pages/jewish_refugees_from_arab_and_muslim_countries-apr_2012.aspx.

12 Constantine Zureiq, "The Meaning of the Disaster (Ma'na al-Nakba)," August 5, 1948.

13 Dr. Rafael G. Bouchnik-Chen, "The False Nakba Narrative," Begin-Sadat (BESA) Center for Strategic Studies Perspectives Paper No. 1,143, April 16, 2019, https://besacenter.org/wp-content/uploads/2019/04/1143-The-False-Nakba-Narrative-Bouchnik-Chen-final-1.pdf.

14 Another agency, UNKRA, was created for the Korean War refugees. It operated from 1950 to 1953, and when it had done its job, it closed down—unlike UNRWA, which has not done its job, and has not closed down.

15 See UN Resolution 302, December 8, 1949, https://www.unrwa.org/content/general-assembly-resolution-302.

16 A little less so nowadays, since the US defunded them in 2018.

17 Adi Schwartz and Einat Wilf, *The War of Return: How Western Indulgence of the Palestinian Dream Has Obstructed the Path for Peace* (New York: St. Martin's Publishing Group, 2020), p. 107.

18 Ibid.

19 Ibid.

20 Chloé Benoist, "Sixty-Eight Years of Temporary Aid—The Curious Case of UNRWA," *Equal Times*, March 19, 2018, https://www.equaltimes.org/sixty-eight-years-of-temporary-aid#.X0auoS-z2jQ.

21 Ibid.

22 The New Palestinian School Curriculum, grades 1–12—2016–2019, April 2019, http://www.impact-se.org/wp-content/uploads/PA-Reports_-Combined-Selected-Examples.pdf.

23 Neville Teller "UNRWA in Trouble," *Jerusalem Post*, October 14, 2019, https://www.jpost.com/opinion/unrwa-in-trouble-604632.

Chapter Seven: A Tug of War and Peace

1 Jordan officially renounced its claims to the West Bank in 1988, during and because of the First Intifada.

2 Yael Hadar, "A Historic Overview: Israeli Public Opinion on Peace Between Israel and Egypt," Israel Democracy Institute, March 25, 2009, https://www.idi.org.il/articles/8609.

3 "1979: Israel and Egypt Shake Hands on Peace Deal," BBC, http://news.bbc.co.uk/onthisday/hi/dates/stories/march/26/newsid_2806000/2806245.stm.

4 Around the time the book was going to print, talks of normalization with Morocco, Sudan, Oman, and Saudi Arabia have been brewing and I hope they become a reality by the time the book comes out.

Chapter Eight: Settlements

1 And which was taken by Jordan in 1948, which had been under Brit rule since 1917, and under the Ottomans since 1516, etc. See chapter two for a refresher.

2 Jordan did annex the West Bank after 1948, but the international community largely did not recognize the legitimacy of this annexation.

3 Though not on the Jordanian side. King Hussein of Jordan did not want to officially open another war front on his border and only assisted, after Arab pressure, by sending Jordanian divisions to Syria to fight Israel from the north

4 Eshkol had a dry and highly un-PC sense of humor. He was clearly making a bad joke, but the message is clear: Israel knew the nine hundred thousand people living in the West Bank were not going to be happy with this changed reality.

5 There is so much out there on this topic, but for now you can see: Tricia McDermott, "Arafat's Billions: One Man's Quest to Track Down Unaccounted-for Public Funds," CBS *60 Minutes*, November 7, 2003, https://www.cbsnews.com/news/arafats-billions/; David Samuels, "In a Ruined Country: How Yasir Arafat destroyed Palestine," *Atlantic*, September 2005, https://www.theatlantic.com/magazine/archive/2005/09/in-a-ruined-country/304167/.

6 Noor Dahri, "Yasser Arafat, a Fake Hero, a Lord of Corruption," *Times of Israel, Jewish News* (blog), April 2, 2017, https://blogs.timesofisrael.com/yasser-arafat-a-fake-hero-a-lord-of-corruption/.

7 This is no one's quote. I am just paraphrasing what I am (pretty safely) assuming the general vibe of the Israeli public would be should a real deal actually be available.

8 Yair Atinger, "Let Me Speak to Hamas," *Haaretz*, June 26, 2006, https://www.haaretz.co.il/misc/1.1115402.

9 Here is a link to the verse; just saving you some Google time here: https://quran.com/17/104?translations=48,27,41,40,101,85,84,21,20,17,22,19,95,18.

Chapter Nine: Arabs

1 Michal Feldman, Daniel M. Master, Raffaela A. Bianco, Marta Burri, Philipp W. Stockhammer, Alissa Mittnik, Adam J. Aja, Choongwon Jeong, Johannes Krause,"Ancient DNA Sheds Light on the Genetic Origins of Early Iron Age Philistines," *Science Advances* 5, no. 7 (July 3, 2019), eaax0061, DOI: 10.1126/sciadv.aax0061, https://advances.sciencemag.org/content/5/7/eaax0061.

2 The name Palestine was used in various writings as early as the fifth century BC to describe the geographical location, but the Romans were the first to officially designate the place by that name.

3 Tradition dates the beginning of Islam to approximately AD 610.

4 "Golda Meir Prime Minister Interview," *Thames TV This Week*, 1970, https://www.youtube.com/watch?v=w3FGvAMvYpc.

5 Thomas Friedman, "This Is Just the Start," *New York Times*, March 1, 2011, https://www.nytimes.com/2011/03/02/opinion/02friedman.html?referringSource=articleShare.

6 Israeli Central Bureau of Statistics, Jerusalem, September 16, 2020, https://www.cbs.gov.il/he/mediarelease/DocLib/2020/296/11_20_296b.pdf.

7 Ahia Rabed, Ynet, March 7, 2018, https://www.ynet.co.il/articles/0,7340,L-5148666,00.html.

8 Quran, chapter 4, verse 34, https://quran.com/4/34.

9 Ronen Bergman, *Rise and Kill First: The Secret History of Israel's Targeted Assassinations* (New York: Penguin Random House, 2018), p. 616.

10 *Real Time with Bill Maher*, HBO, October 6, 2014, https://www.youtube.com/watch?v=vln9D81eO60.

11 Here it is: Hamas Charter, Yale Law School, the Avalon Project, August 18, 1988, https://avalon.law.yale.edu/20th_century/hamas.asp.

12 Ronen Bergman, *Rise and Kill First*, p. 626.

13 Ian Black and Mark Tran, "Hamas Takes Control of Gaza," *Guardian*, June 15, 2007, https://www.theguardian.com/world/2007/jun/15/israel4.

14 Benny Morris, *The Birth of the Palestinian Refugee Problem Revisited* (Cambridge, UK: Cambridge University Press, 2012), p. 95.

Chapter Ten: BDS

1 This quote is from BDS founder Omar Barghouti, and you can read it here: BDS, "In Their Own Words," CUFI.ORG, https://www.cufi.org/bds-in-their-own-words/ and watch the video here: May 26, 2014, https://www.youtube.com/watch?v=vYvpsGd8K4Y&feature=youtu.be.

2 Benny Morris, *The Birth of the Palestinian Refugee Problem Revisited* (Cambridge, UK: Cambridge University Press, 2012), p. 94.

3 David M. Halbfinger, Michael Winers, and Steven Erlanger, "Is BDS Antisemitic? A Closer Look at the Boycott Israel Campaign," *New York Times*, July 27, 2019, https://www.nytimes.com/2019/07/27/world/middleeast/bds-israel-boycott-antisemitic.html.

4 BDS, "In Their Own Words."

5 "Defeating Denormalization: Shared Palestinian and Israeli Perspectives on a New Path to Peace," in Khaled Abu Toameh, *The Palestinian Authority's Policy of Denormalization*, Jerusalem Center for Public Affairs, November 2017.

6 Keren Zuriel-Harari, "Producing Peace, and on the Way—Soda," *Calcalist*, December 24, 2018, https://www.calcalist.co.il/local/articles/0,7340,L-3752290,00.html.

7 Nabil Bashrat, "BDS Causes the Most Damage to Palestinians," *Mida*, June 18, 2018, https://mida.org.il/2018/06/18/תנועת-ה-bds-גורמת-נזק-בעיקר-לעובדים-הפלסט/?fbclid=IwAR0pYJ1yI9_l6fJBEJU1ko1-UvQzyCkKA4vkkSpdi7IztmNr3DLKcJzfYoE2018.

8 RAND International, "Calculating the Costs of the Israeli-Palestinian Conflict," https://www.rand.org/international/cmepp/costs-of-conflict/calculator.html.

9 "BDS Co-Founder Omar Barghouti Warns the First Bank of Abu Dhabi and the Other UAE Companies Against Doing Business with Israel: We Will Call for Boycott of Any Such Company or Bank," MEMRI, September 17, 2020, https://www.memri.org/tv/bds-co-founder-omar-barghouthi-warns-abu-dhabi-uae-banks-companies-business-israel.

10 *Israel Imperiled: Threats to the Jewish State*, Joint Hearing Before the House Foreign Affairs Committee, Subcommittee on Terrorism, Nonproliferation, and Trade and the Subcommittee on the Middle East and North Africa, Washington, DC, April 19,

2016, https://docs.house.gov/meetings/FA/FA18/20160419/104817/HHRG-114-FA18-Wstate-SchanzerJ-20160419.pdf.

11 Despite BDS/AMP claims to be working on a dime—and I have looked through their Form 990—what they do seems way more expensive to produce than the amount of cash they show in their bank account, which is what leads experts to demand a proper financial review.

12 NGO Monitor, March 23, 2020, https://www.ngo-monitor.org/ngos/american-muslims-for-palestine-amp/, http://www.ngo-monitor.org/nm/wp-content/uploads/2016/05/AMP-nonprofit-1.jpg. [Au: Two URLs OK?]

13 *Israel Imperiled: Threats to the Jewish State.*

14 Ibid.

15 Ofir Hovav, "Despite Pressure from BDS This Successful Jordanian Artist Was Not Afraid to Perform in Israel," *Haaretz*, January 15, 2020, https://www.haaretz.co.il/gallery/music/.premium-1.8403895.

16 *Israel Imperiled: Threats to the Jewish State*.

Chapter Eleven: May the Melting Pot Not Melt Us All

1 Israeli Central Bureau of Statistics, Jerusalem, December 31, 2019, https://www.cbs.gov.il/he/mediarelease/DocLib/2020/296/11_20_296b.pdf.

2 Israeli Central Bureau of Statistics, June 27th, 2018, https://www.cbs.gov.il/he/mediarelease/pages/2018/אוכלוסיית-ישראל-לפי-דת-והגדרה-עצמית-של-מידת-דתיות-נתונים-נבחרים-מתוך-דוח-פני-החברה-מס-10.aspx.

3 PEW Research Center, "Religious Divide in Israeli Society," p. 21, https://www.pewresearch.org/wp-content/uploads/sites/7/2016/03/israel_survey_overview.hebrew_final.pdf.

4 Here to help: https://18e9cae9-a-62cb3a1a-s-sites.googlegroups.com/site/debiprueba/home/research/Picture2.jpg?attachauth=ANoY7cqrO9jdXiDx29b8gw1yoTcbXXmt2wfZXe_VPvcuaaKSy1m5iuaDtEuNdFbUXgPmEL8qCGlyEfU15_upc1yvJvMvPhBW_2dlEiF6jLidz4-mFdJJnzVtOvLvT3gl8mTu6wFzKjL0lRn9UnnxKytg0Tzb6ufcdCySd726Pk3lNFUZzWEd_LQ9JvZ1JTaw8gmPbJHgReFuIBFndxrbXVolkUX-fDvFqFO-Tq7MBkPUCUNbmKcpdlM%3D&attredirects=0.

5 If you speak Hebrew, you can enjoy Begin's speech here: https://www.youtube.com/watch?v=Tx4vdUqOW2o.

6 The origin of this is from the book of Isaiah, used to describe people who "tremble before God." והיעשי וס, ה "שְׁמְעוּ דְּבַר 'ה הַחֲרֵדִים אֶל דְּבָרוֹ".

7 Israel Democracy Institute, 2018, p. 3, https://www.idi.org.il/media/11852/haredim-2018-summary.pdf.

8 "Religious Divide in Israeli Society," PEW Research Center, p. 23, https://www.pewresearch.org/wp-content/uploads/sites/7/2016/03/israel_survey_overview.hebrew_final.pdf.

9 Josephus Flavius, *The Jewish War 4*, (AD 75), pp. 241–43.

10 Josephus Flavius, *The Jewish War 5*, (AD75), pp. 363–74.

11 I took the name for this section from Desmond Seward's incredible book by the same name.

Chapter Twelve: Up Up Nation

1 Ronny Linder, "How an Israeli Hospital Took in Syrians and Became the World Leader in Treating War Wounds," *Haaretz*, April 24, 2018, https://www.haaretz.com/middle-east-news/syria/.premium-israeli-hospital-takes-in-syrians-leads-world-in-treating-war-wounds-1.5467873.

2 Ibid.

3 Dror Feuer, "Israeli Hospitals Provide Care to Thousands of Syrians," *Globes*, March 26, 2018, https://en.globes.co.il/en/article-israel-becomes-health-center-for-syrian-children-1001229351.

4 Israeli Humanitarian Relief: MASHAV—Israel's Agency for International Development Cooperation, http://www.israel.org/MFA/ForeignPolicy/Aid/Pages/Israeli%20Humanitarian%20Relief-%20MASHAV%20 %20the%20Israel%20F.aspx.

5 "Haiti: First Baby Born in IDF Field Hospital," January 17, 2010, https://www.makorrishon.co.il/nrg/online/1/ART2/041/392.html.

6 For more on this, check out: https://www.israaid.org/about.

7 "Could Israeli Expertise Save Flood Survivors in Japan?," *MAKO*, July 10, 2018, https://www.mako.co.il/good-news-news/Article-500b8c7d3a38461006.htm.

8 Ido Efrati, "The Recovery of Traumatized Yazidi Women Goes Through Israel," *Haaretz*, July 4, 2019, https://www.haaretz.co.il/news/education/.premium-1.7449804.

9 Liad Osmo, "With the Syrian Refugees in Lesbos: Israel Is No Longer the Enemy," Ynet, March 3, 2019, https://www.ynet.co.il/articles/0,7340,L-5472523,00.html.

10 Dan Senor and Saul Singer, *Start-Up Nation: The Story of Israel's Economic Miracle* (New York: Hachette Book Group, 2009).

11 Mike Hale, "The 30 Best International Shows of the Decade," *New York Times*, December 20, 2019, https://www.nytimes.com/2019/12/20/arts/television/best-international-tv-shows.html.

12 Israeli Ministry of Economic and Industry Innovation Authority, https://innovation israel.org.il/sites/default/files/books/Innovation_Authority_BOOK_PRESS.pdf.

13 "Best Inventions 2019," *Time*, https://time.com/collection/best-inventions-2019/.

14 You can enjoy some of these stylish cuties here: https://www.nununuworld.com/nununu_press/.

15 Israeli Ministry of Economic and Industry Innovation Authority, https://innovation israel.org.il/sites/default/files/books/Innovation_Authority_BOOK_PRESS.pdf.

Chapter Thirteen: What's with the Obsession, World?

1 https://www.vmlyr.com/sites/www/files/2020-11/Brand%20Israel%202019%20Deck%2011%2013%2019.pdf.

2 NGO UN Watch, https://unwatch.org/database/.

3 Theodor Herzl, *Altneuland: The Old-New-Land* (Rockville, MD: Wild Side Press LLC., 2018), p. 191. The awful term "Negro problem" was still acceptable in 1902.

4 Resolution Adopted on the Reports of Special Political Committee, https://www.un.org/ga/search/view_doc.asp?symbol=A/RES/1192(XII).

5 UN General Assembly Resolutions Singling Out Israel, UN Watch, September 24, 2020, https://unwatch.org/2019-un-general-assembly-resolutions-singling-out-israel-texts-votes-analysis/.

6 Ibid.

7 "UN Resolutions Disproportionately Condemn Israel," UN Watch, https://unwatch.org/database/.

8 See UN DGACM Synopsis of the General Debate (2018).

9 These statistics refer only to thematic resolutions and not to resolutions pertaining to technical assistance.

10 For a full list of these commissions of inquiries and fact-finding missions, see: ohchr.org/EN/HRBodies/HRC/Pages/ListHRCMandat.aspx.

11 While the WHO also reports on other countries and regions, it does so in reports that cover global or regional trends and phenomena; no other country besides Israel has a report that focuses solely on that state.

12 The tenth Emergency Session—which was also established to address alleged "Illegal Israeli actions . . ."—has never been formally concluded, which is why, in essence, it remains pending. See https://www.un.org/en/ga/sessions/emergency.shtml.

13 Secretary-General's briefing to the Security Council on the Situation in the Middle East, including the Palestinian question [as delivered], https://www.un.org/sg/en/content/sg/statement/2016-12-16/secretary-generals-briefing-security-council-situation-middle-east.

14 You can find all the articles archived at the National Library of Israel, Tel Aviv University, https://web.nli.org.il/sites/JPress/English/Pages/default.aspx.

15 Ibid.

16 Ibid.

17 Ibid.

18 For the complete resolution: https://unispal.un.org/UNISPAL.NSF/0/761C1063530766A7052566A2005B74D1.

19 UN revoking 3379: https://www.un.org/unispal/document/auto-insert-180327/.

20 "Antisemitic Incidents Hit All-Time High in 2019," New York, ADL, May 12, 2020,

https://www.adl.org/news/press-releases/antisemitic-incidents-hit-all-time-high-in-2019.

21 Maajid Nawaz, "We Muslims Are Totally Self-Unaware Cry-Bullies in the School Playground," *Times of Israel*, August 23, 2017, https://blogs.timesofisrael.com/we-muslims-are-totally-self-unaware-cry-bullies-in-the-school-playground/.

22 Watch my two spirit animals having a profound conversation here: *Real Time with Bill Maher*, HBO, November 2, 2018, https://www.youtube.com/watch?v=U-9ry71e0fU.

INDEX